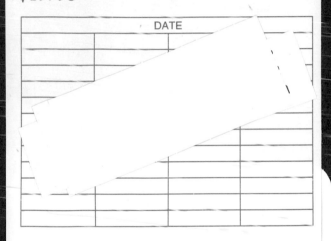

# DICTIONARY of
# THE EARTH

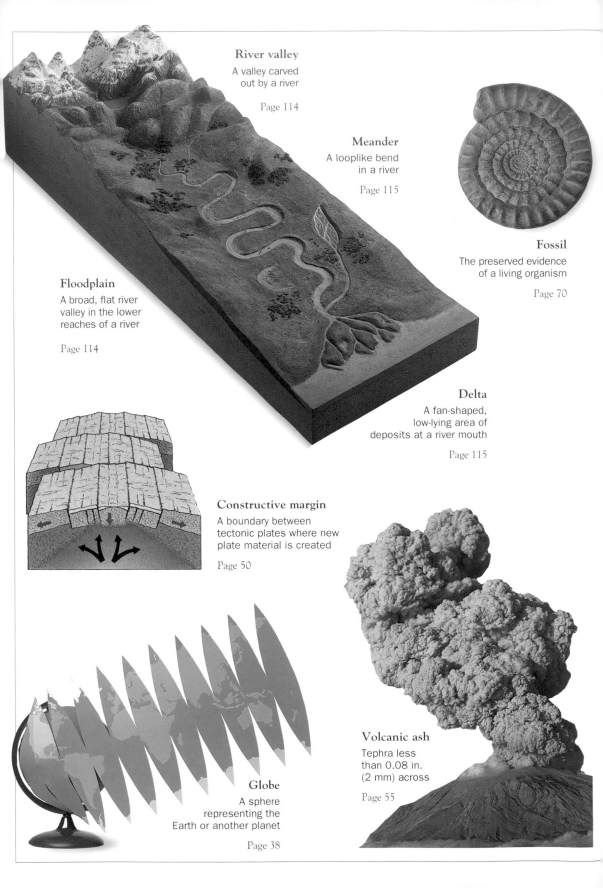

### River valley
A valley carved
out by a river

Page 114

### Meander
A looplike bend
in a river

Page 115

### Fossil
The preserved evidence
of a living organism

Page 70

### Floodplain
A broad, flat river
valley in the lower
reaches of a river

Page 114

### Delta
A fan-shaped,
low-lying area of
deposits at a river mouth

Page 115

### Constructive margin
A boundary between
tectonic plates where new
plate material is created

Page 50

### Globe
A sphere
representing the
Earth or another planet

Page 38

### Volcanic ash
Tephra less
than 0.08 in.
(2 mm) across

Page 55

# DICTIONARY *of* THE EARTH

Written by John Farndon

**DORLING KINDERSLEY**

London • New York • Stuttgart

A DORLING KINDERSLEY BOOK

**Project Editor** Stephen Setford

**Project Art Editor** Christopher Howson

**Editor** Gillian Cooling

**Art Editors** Karen Fielding, Carole Oliver

**Designers** Nicola Webb, Jessica Cawes

**Production** Louise Barratt

**Managing Editor** Helen Parker

**Managing Art Editor** Peter Bailey

**Special Photography** Michael Dunning

**Picture Research** Sharon Southren

**US Editor** Jill Hamilton


**Educational Consultants** Frances Halpin,
The Royal Russell School, Croydon, Surrey
Jefferey Kaufmann, Ph.D., Irvine Valley College, California
**Editorial Consultant** Dr. John Nudds, Keeper of Geology,
The Manchester Museum


First American Edition 1994
2 4 6 8 10 9 7 5 3

Published in the United States by
Dorling Kindersley Publishing, Inc.,
95 Madison Avenue, New York, New York 10016

ISBN 1-56458-709-8

Reproduced by Colourscan, Singapore

Printed and bound in Great Britain by Butler and Tanner

## Safe collecting

There is no doubt that first-hand observation is the key to finding out about the Earth, but a methodical approach and attention to safety is vital. Rivers, mountains, waves, and many other geographical features can be dangerous if not treated with due respect. Moreover, careless sample collecting can destroy valuable scientific evidence.

## Geographical terms

Although many geographical terms are universal, some countries have their own names for certain geographical features. For example, ice-eroded hollows (page 122) are called "cirques" in France, "cwms" in Wales, "corries" in Scotland, and different names in other countries. Limited space makes it impossible to list all the alternatives, so the term given in this book is usually the most widely used, or the most scientifically accurate. Similarly, the geological timescale and the names of geological periods vary considerably from country to country. Again, the timescale and period names given are the most widely used. But when studying a particular area, it is important to find out if a different local timescale and nomenclature should be used.

## A note on numbers

Two alternative systems of measurement are used. In each case, the figure is the value expressed in imperial or USCS units. The second figure, which always appears in parentheses ( ), is the same value expressed in metric or SI units, rounded up or down.

**Geodimeter (page 16)**
*Taking accurate measurements is crucial to map making. Surveyors use geodimeters and theodolites to measure distance. More about the work of Earth scientists on pages 12–27.*

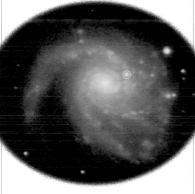

**Spiral galaxy (page 31)**
*Scattered throughout space are millions of galaxies, each containing billions of stars like our own Sun. More about galaxies, stars, and the Solar System on pages 30–36.*

**The Earth's chemistry (pages 42–43)**
*When the Earth was young, dense elements such as iron sank deep into its interior to form a core of molten metal. More about the chemistry and structure of the Earth on pages 40–65.*

# Contents

# THE AGE OF THE EARTH 66–79

*How geologists use rocks, fossils, and other dating techniques to calculate the Earth's age and chronicle its development*

# ROCKS & MINERALS 80–97

*The minerals that make up the rocks of the Earth's crust, the different types of rock, and how rocks are continually being broken down and reformed*

# THE CHANGING LANDSCAPE 98–129

*How landscapes are created and altered by the action of wind, rain, ice, heat, rivers, and waves on the rocks of the Earth's surface*

# SOIL 130–133

*The composition of soil, its properties, how it forms and develops, and systems of soil classification*

# SEAS & OCEANS 134–137

*How the currents and tides of the Earth's great oceans are caused, and the "landscape" features of the ocean bottom*

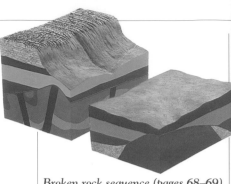

**Broken rock sequence (pages 68–69)**
*Geologists often look for sudden breaks or unconformities in the sequence of rock layers. These breaks indicate that a dramatic change occurred after the rocks were formed. More about how the Earth's history is revealed by rocks and fossils on pages 66–79.*

**Crystal group (page 83)**
*Rocks are made up of minerals, often in the form of crystals. This crystal group contains feldspar, quartz, and mica – the main minerals in granite. More about rocks, minerals, and crystals on pages 80–97.*

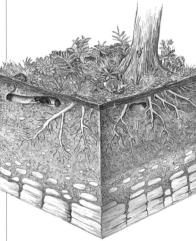

**Soil profile (pages 130–131)**
*Soil is a mixture of fragments of weathered rock and rotting plants and animals. But the rich variety of organisms living within it turn it into a dynamic, ever-changing system. More about soil on pages 130–133.*

*The atmosphere (pages 138–139)*

*The Earth is surrounded by a thin "blanket" of gases called the atmosphere. It is divided into a number of distinct layers, from the thick, cloudy troposphere in which we live, up to the rarefied heights of the exosphere far above the ground. More about the Earth's atmosphere on pages 138–157.*

# ATMOSPHERE, WEATHER, & CLIMATE 138–157

*The structure of the atmosphere, the influence of the Sun's energy, the different aspects of weather, and how they may be predicted*

|---|---|
| The atmosphere | 138 |
| Solar energy | 140 |
| Air pressure & wind | 142 |
| Wind circulation | 144 |
| Moisture in the air | 146 |
| Rain & snow | 149 |
| Air masses | 150 |
| Storms | 152 |
| Climate | 154 |
| Weather forecasting | 156 |

# THE LIVING WORLD 158–165

*How the living and nonliving parts of the Earth interact, and how agriculture affects natural communities of plants and animals*

|---|---|
| Living things | 158 |
| World biomes | 162 |
| Agricultural ecosystems | 164 |

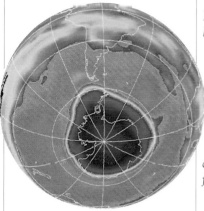

*The ozone hole (page 175)*

*The layer of ozone gas in the atmosphere shields us from the Sun's harmful rays – but it is getting dangerously thin. More about the ozone hole and the other human impacts on the environment on pages 166–179.*

# THE HUMAN IMPACT 166–179

*How the human race makes use of the Earth's natural resources and changes the landscape, the resulting environmental effects, and the need for a more sustainable way of life*

|---|---|
| Gems & metals | 166 |
| Fossil fuels | 168 |
| Bulk materials | 169 |
| Locating resources | 170 |
| Water resources | 172 |
| Pollution | 174 |
| Changing the land | 176 |
| Earth management | 178 |

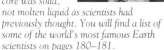

*Inge Lehmann (page 181)*

*Danish geophysicist Inge Lehmann monitored earthquakes to show that the Earth's inner core was solid, not molten liquid as scientists had previously thought. You will find a list of some of the world's most famous Earth scientists on pages 180–181.*

# EARTH SCIENCE PIONEERS 180–181

*More than 70 of the most influential figures in the development of Earth science*

# INDEX 182–192

*More than 2,000 key words, terms, and concepts used in Earth science today*

# ACKNOWLEDGMENTS 192

# How to use this book

This dictionary explains the most important words and concepts in Earth science, and illustrates how they are used. It is a thematic dictionary, which means that the words are arranged into subject areas, such as "Soil" or "Oceans," instead of being arranged alphabetically. This enables you to find out about a whole subject, as well as about individual words. The Contents on pages 5–7 lists the different sections and subjects covered in this book. To look up a word, turn to the index at the back of the book.

### Entry headings
This entry is Global seismology.

### Definitions
This definition is a short, precise description. This one tells you that global seismology is the study of the Earth's structure.

### Explanations
The explanation tells you more about the entry. It can also help you understand the definition. This explanation describes how scientists learn about the Earth's interior by studying the vibrations from earthquakes.

### Annotation and captions
A headed caption explains what you can see in a picture. This caption explains that scientists monitor the passage of certain types of earthquake vibrations through the body of the Earth. Details in a picture, such as the focus of the earthquake, are pointed out by annotation.

### Using the index
The index lists all the entries in alphabetical order and gives their page numbers. If you look up the term "continental crust" in the index, for example, you will find that the entry is on page 40. The word or term you want may be a main entry, or it may be a subentry, which is to be found in bold type within an entry. It may also be an entry in a table.

### Main headings and introductions
A main heading introduces the subject. All the entries in this subject are concerned with the Earth's internal structure. Each subject begins with an introduction that gives you a brief outline of what follows.

---

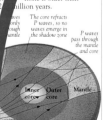

40 • The Structure of the Earth

## Inside the Earth

People once thought that the Earth was completely solid, but scientific interpretation of vibrations from earthquakes has revealed a more complex structure. We now know that the Earth has a soft interior beneath its rigid shell, and a core of solid metal.

*Atmosphere*
*Crust*
*Mantle*
*Outer core*

### Global seismology
The study of the Earth's structure using vibrations from earthquakes and explosions

Seismic waves ■ are vibrations that radiate from an earthquake ■. These waves shudder through the body of the Earth as well as along its surface. Body waves ■ are known as primary (P) waves ■ and secondary (S) waves ■. Like light rays passing through a lens, the waves are refracted, or bent, as they pass through the different layers inside the Earth. The way in which the body waves bend helps scientists to understand the Earth's true structure. **Seismic tomography** uses computers to build up three-dimensional images of variations in the density and temperature of the mantle from crisscrossing body waves. **Seismic reflection profiles** are cross-sections of the Earth's interior made by studying the reflection of sound vibrations set off by a long line of large explosions. A **shadow zone** is an area through which no waves from a distant earthquake pass.

**Seismic waves**
*The movement of S waves and P waves through the Earth tells scientists about the Earth's interior.*

*P wave*
*S wave*
*Focus of earthquake*

### Crust
The Earth's hard outer shell

The Earth is made up of three layers, or concentric shells. The innermost shell is the core, the middle shell is the mantle, the outermost is the crust. E... shell has a different c... composition ■. Th... the thin topmost lay... ts upon the softer, den... ntle.

### Oceanic crust
The part of ... Earth's crust under the ocea...

The c... s thinnest under the ocea... rying from 4–7 miles (6–... m) thick. The rocks of th... anic crust are relatively yo... – none is older than 2... illion years.

*...ves ...nly ...ough ...antle*
*The core refracts P waves, so no waves emerge in the shadow zone*
*P waves pass through the mantle and core*

*Inner core*
*Outer core*
*Mantle*
*Shadow zone*
*Crust*

### Continental crust
... art of the Earth's crust under ...ontinents

Th... crust is thickest under the continents, averaging 19–25 miles (30–40 km) but extending as far as 43 miles (70 km) beneath the biggest mountain ranges. It is older than oceanic crust – some rocks date back 3.8 billion years. It floats on the mantle in a st... or bala... calle... isostasy ■.

### Basement
The bulk ... ncient rock that makes ... a continent

The contine... rust is mostly ancient c... alline rock. This "baseme... rock is divided into two lay... The upper half consists main... granitelike ■ rocks, schists ■, gneisses ■, while the lower half ... made up of basalt ■ and diorite ■.

### Discontinuity
A boundary between the layers of the Earth's interior

The **Mohorovicic discontinuity**, or **Moho**, is the boundary between the crust and the mantle, while the **Gutenberg discontinuity** separates the core and the mantle.

---

### Subentries
A subentry is printed in **bold type**. It gives the meaning of a word or term that is related to a main entry. This subentry explains the meaning of the term "Gutenberg discontinuity," which is the boundary between the Earth's core and mantle.

## Main illustrations
*A large photograph or artwork usually illustrates several related entries. It helps to explain the entries, or show how they are linked. This cutaway artwork demonstrates the different layers inside the Earth.*

## Diagrams and other illustrations
*Diagrams are used to show the structure of the Earth's physical features, or to explain the principles of Earth science. This diagram enlarges a portion of the main illustration to show the composition of the Earth's upper layers.*

## Running heads
*For quick reference, the running head shows you which section you are in. This section is The Structure of the Earth.*

## Tables and boxed features
*The dictionary contains a number of tables that give extra information not found in the main entries. The table of minerals on page 85, for example, lists 30 of the most common minerals and their properties. Boxed features, such as this one comparing the grain size of different granitic rocks, present information in a more visual form.*

---

The Structure of the Earth • 41

### Mantle
The soft interior of the Earth that lies above the core

Just under the crust is the mantle. It is about 1,800 miles (2,900 km) thick and makes up nearly 80 percent of the Earth's total volume. It is made largely of a rock called peridotite ▪, which is sometimes thrown up onto the surface by volcanic eruptions. The mantle rock is so hot that it is often partially molten.

**Earth cutaway**
*Here, sections of the Earth have been removed to show its internal structure.*

Oceanic crust · Continental crust · Lithosphere · Upper mantle · Asthenosphere (part of mantle)

Mantle continues down to outer core

Outer core of molten metal

Solid metal inner core

### Lithosphere
The rigid upper layer of the Earth

The lithosphere consists of the crust and the rigid upper layers of the mantle. The average thickness is about 62 miles (100 km) but it varies from just a few miles under the oceans to 186 miles (300 km) under the continents.

### Asthenosphere
The soft layer of the Earth under the lithosphere

The temperature of the Earth's interior increases with depth. About 62 miles (100 km) down, the temperature reaches 2,600°F (1,400°C). This is enough to melt some of the material in the mantle rock. As a result, the rock is able to flow slowly, creating a soft layer about 124 miles (200 km) thick called the asthenosphere, on which the rigid lithosphere floats like ice on a pond.

### Mesosphere
The layer of the mantle under the asthenosphere

Little is known of the mesosphere, but it is thought to flow less easily than the asthenosphere.

### Borehole
A hole drilled into the Earth to gain information about the rocks below

Because no drill has ever gone deeper than 9 miles (15 km) boreholes can only tell us about the rocks in the Earth's crust.

### Core
The metallic center of the Earth

The core of the Earth is a dense ▪ the elements ▪ iron and nickel. ▪ **outer core** is so hot that the m▪ ▪ always molten, but in the **inner** ▪ are so great that it cannot even though temperatures there reach 6,700°F (3,700°C).

### Rheology
The study of how rocks and other materials flow

The crust and the upper mantle are chemically different, but they behave in similar ways. Geologists studying plate tectonics ▪ prefer to identify the Earth's layers not by their chemical makeup, but according to how easily they ▪ ▪. They call these la▪ ▪ and the mesosphere.

#### See also
Basalt 89 • Body wave 59
Bulk composition 42 • Diorite 91
Earthquake 58 • Element 42
Gneiss ▪ Granite 90 • Isostasy 65
▪otite 91 • Plate tectonics 46
▪ 59 • Schist 97
Seismic wave 5▪

---

Rocks & Minerals • 91

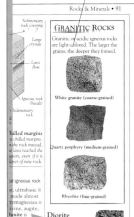

Sedimentary rock covering · Large crystals · Lava flow · Igneous rock (basalt) · Sedimentary

#### GRANITIC ROCKS
Granitic or acidic igneous rocks are light-colored. The larger the grains, the deeper they formed.

White granite (coarse-grained)

Quartz porphyry (medium-grained)

Rhyolite (fine-grained)

**Chilled margins**
▪e chilled margins.
▪e the rock instead.
▪e lava reached the
▪sion, even if it is
▪ layer of new rock.

▪d igneous rock
▪e, ultrabasic ▪
▪ made almost
▪romagnesian ▪
▪ivine, augite,
▪unite is
▪e, but it

▪ of these
▪own. They
▪ the base of
▪r in areas of
▪. They may
▪f the Earth's

### Diorite
A light-colored, coarse-grained igneous rock

Diorite

Diorite is the coarse-grained, plutonic equivalent of andesite ▪, and forms when granitic magma is contaminated with impurities. It often forms in offshoots of large granite intrusions.

## Biographies
*On page 65, you will find a biography of Grove Karl Gilbert, a key figure in the study of mountain building. The dictionary contains short biographies of some of the most famous Earth scientists, linked to the subjects that they investigated. There is an alphabetical list of famous Earth scientists on pages 180–181.*

---

The Structure of the Earth • 65

*Eiger and Mönch, Swiss Alps
These fold mountains have been easily weathered into dramatic peaks because the rock was so fractured by the folding.*

### Lystric fault
A huge, curved slippage of rock in a region of mountain building

When continents collide, the old crystalline basement ▪ of one plate is subducted ▪ below the other, while the younger rocks on top crumple up to form fold mountains. The crumpled younger rocks can become detached from the basement. The boundary between them is called the **décollement horizon**. Occasionally the strain may snap the younger rocks altogether, creating a huge, curved fault ▪ right down to the décollement horizon. This is a lystric fault.

### Block mountain
A mountain created by a massive uplift

Not all mountains are built by folding. When horst blocks ▪ are raised high up between two faults or when the land surrounding the fault sinks, tall, flat-topped, block mountains are often formed. Mountains can also ▪ ▪ ▪ ▪▪

### Massif
A very large mountain or rock structure

Huge single mountains, or areas of mountains with similar characteristics, are sometimes described by the French term *massif*. The old crystalline basement of rock in a mountain system are also called massifs.

### Isostasy
The balance between the height of mountains and the depth of their "roots"

The Earth's rigid continental crust it floats on the mantle is like a ship on the sea. Just as a boat floats lower in the water if it is heavily laden, so the crust floats lower in the mantle if it is heavy above. High mountain areas sink farther, and so have deeper "roots" to balance their height. When mountains are worn down, they float upward to compensate for the change in weight and maintain the balance, or **isostatic equilibrium**. Similarly, the crust may sink under the weight of an ice sheet ▪ and bounce slowly back up again once the ice sheet melts.

*With little soil on top of it, the polystyrene does not sink far into the water*

### Grove Karl Gilbert
American geologist (1843–1918)

Gilbert, one of the great figures of geology around the turn of the century, was one of the first people to distinguish between fold and block mountains. He coined the word "orogeny" to describe the process of mountain building.

### Orogeny
The process of building mountains

Orogeny, or mountain building, is limited to a few specific areas in the world, called **orogenic belts**, usually along the edges of colliding tectonic plates. Two examples of these belts are the Andes and the Himalayas. Although most of the world's mountain ranges are continually getting higher as the tectonic plates collide, mountain building is believed to have been most active during certain episodes in the Earth's history, called **orogenic phases**. Each of these extended over many millions of years. Different phases are recognized in different places, such as the Caledonian, Hercynian, and Alpine phases in Europe, and the Huronian, Nevadan, and Pasadenian phases in North America.

*More sand is piled on the polystyrene* · *The roots now extend deeper into the water*

*Height and depth
In this experiment, sand represents the ▪ ▪ ▪*

#### See also
Basement 40 • Collision zone 48
Crust 40 • Fault 60
Fold 62 • Horst block 61
Ice sheet 120 • Mantle 41
Sediment 92 • Sedimentary rock 92

---

## Cross references
*A small gray square (▪) after a word shows that the word is either an entry or a subentry elsewhere in the dictionary. The "See also" box gives the page number of the entry.*

## "See also" boxes
*You will find a "See also" box with each subject. This directs you to other entries or subentries that can help you understand the subject better. This "See also" box points to the principle of isostasy and the rock diorite, which forms part of the continental crust.*

# Studying the Earth

Striding across a windy hilltop, you notice a huge, black boulder, perched like a weird statue on a stony pedestal. Looking closer, you see that the rock glistens in the sunlight, unlike the dull brown rock beneath. Altogether, it looks quite out of place. How did it get there? Where did it come from? What is it made of? Why is it so different from the other rock? These are the kinds of questions Earth scientists try to answer when they look at the world around them. They examine the Earth's different physical features, trying to discover how they came to be and how they are being shaped and changed all the time. In this way, they gradually build up a detailed picture of our home, the planet Earth, and how it works.

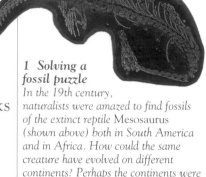

**1 Solving a fossil puzzle**
In the 19th century, naturalists were amazed to find fossils of the extinct reptile Mesosaurus (shown above) both in South America and in Africa. How could the same creature have evolved on different continents? Perhaps the continents were once joined by a land bridge, now buried beneath the ocean.

**2 A possible solution**
In the 1920s, Alfred Wegener argued that all the continents were once joined together, like the pieces of a jigsaw, but then slowly drifted apart. The map above is Wegener's drawing of the ancient "supercontinent" Pangaea.

## Down to Earth

The Earth is a minute dot in a vast universe of stars, galaxies, and empty space. Satellites can circle right around it in just a few hours. Yet it is still large enough for our understanding of it to be fairly elementary. Earth science is a comparatively young science. Less than 200 years ago, most people thought that the Earth was just a few thousand years old and that it had changed very little since its creation,

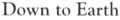

**Searching for oil**
Geologists will examine these rock cores, drilled from the bottom of the North Sea, to test for the presence of oil.

so there was little interest in studying it. But early in the 19th century, scientists discovered that the age of the Earth was immense – now estimated at more than four and a half billion years – and that it has undergone huge changes during its history. The science of geology was born with the realization that this fascinating history is recorded in the rocks of the Earth's crust.

**3 Looking for clues**
In the 1960s, deep-sea research submarines such as Alvin allowed scientists to explore the ocean bed for the first time. Alvin picked up rock samples that showed how underwater volcanic eruptions were constantly adding new material to the ocean floor along a vast ridge in the middle of the Atlantic.

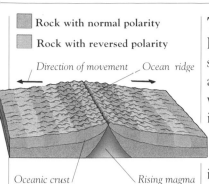

■ Rock with normal polarity

▨ Rock with reversed polarity

*Direction of movement* — *Ocean ridge*

*Oceanic crust* — *Rising magma*

### 4 Further evidence
*In 1962, magnetic patterns or "stripes" were found on the ocean floor. Every few million years, the Earth's magnetic poles are reversed. New rocks added to an ocean ridge become magnetized with the polarity of the Earth's magnetic field at that time. The changing magnetism recorded in the rocks suggests that the oceans are growing steadily wider.*

### 5 Convincing proof
*Rocks drilled from the ocean bed by the research ship Glomar Challenger showed that rocks are older farther away from the Mid-Atlantic Ridge. This convinced scientists that the ocean floor is spreading, and that the continents are slowly moving apart all the time.*

### 6 Cause and effect
*Earth scientists now know that the Earth's crust is broken into moving pieces called plates. Continental drift, seafloor spreading, and earthquakes are all caused by this plate movement.*

## The plate revolution
Every now and then, each science is revolutionized by an important discovery, which not only greatly increases our understanding, but also reveals new areas to study. This has happened in the last 25 years in Earth science, with the discovery that the Earth's surface – far from being solid and immobile – is broken into sections that are constantly shifting this way and that, jostling and crashing into each other. This discovery, studied in the new branch of Earth science known as plate tectonics, helps to explain how continents and oceans have changed through the ages, why earthquakes occur, where volcanoes might erupt, how mountain ranges are thrown up, why climates changed in the past, and much more. Many cherished theories have had to be abandoned, and many new avenues for investigation have been opened up. The possibility that we might be able to learn how to predict earthquakes and volcanic eruptions – and so save lives – adds extra urgency to these investigations.

***History in ice***
*By examining ice cores drilled from the ice sheets of the polar regions, Earth scientists find evidence of past climate changes, and current trends in atmospheric pollution are revealed.*

## Why study the Earth?
The knowledge of Earth scientists already plays a crucial role in all our lives. Geologists, for example, help locate valuable mineral and energy reserves. Hydrologists help us to prepare against floods and locate water resources, and meteorologists give us advance warning of hurricanes and storms. Earth scientists are also making us increasingly aware of the very real dangers our activities may pose to the well-being of the planet, whether through polluting industries and agricultural systems or the wasteful use of precious and limited resources. It is now becoming clear that knowledge of the Earth and how it works may not simply be interesting, but also vital to our survival. Without a better understanding of our planet, the Earth, we may eventually destroy the basis of life upon it.

# What is Earth science?

The field of study for the Earth scientist is vast – essentially the entire planet and all its physical characteristics. While biologists study life on Earth, Earth scientists study virtually everything else – from the motion of the atmosphere to the formation of rocks or the eruption of a volcano.

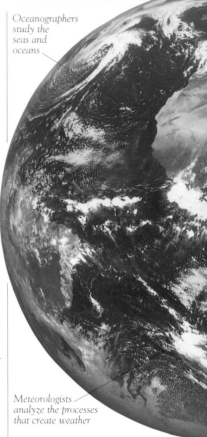

*Oceanographers study the seas and oceans*

*Meteorologists analyze the processes that create weather*

### A world of knowledge
*Earth scientists study every aspect of the Earth and how it works.*

## Geology

The study of the Earth's history, structure, and composition

Geology embraces virtually every field of Earth science except for meteorology. It focuses primarily on the study of rocks ■ and the makeup of the Earth's crust ■.

## Historical geology

The study of the evolution of the Earth

Historical geology investigates the Earth's complex and varied history, from its beginnings about 4.6 billion years ago to the present day. It includes the science of stratigraphy ■, as well as **palaeogeography**, which tries to discover how land masses and oceans have changed shape through time.

## Petrology

The study of rocks

Petrology is the branch of geology that involves detailed study of the origin, structure, and composition of rocks. **Mineralogy** is the branch of geology that studies the minerals ■ from which rocks are made.

## Geophysics

The study of the physical processes that occur in and around the Earth

Although geophysics includes such subjects as meteorology, it concentrates on plate tectonics ■ and what goes on in the Earth's interior. **Geochemistry** studies the Earth's chemical composition, as well as that of the Moon and the planets of the Solar System.

## Volcanology

The study of volcanoes

Volcanology or **vulcanology** investigates volcanoes ■ and related phenomena such as geysers ■. Earthquakes ■ and vibrations within the Earth are studied in global seismology ■.

### History in rocks
*The science of stratigraphy has shown that a layer of sedimentary rock is always older than the layer above it, unless faulting or folding has overturned the layers.*

### Volcanic eruption
*Lava gushes out of Yasur volcano, on Tanna Island in the South Pacific.*

*Geographers study the Earth's surface*

*Geomorphologists investigate how the landscape is shaped*

*Geologists study the makeup of the Earth's hard outer crust*

# Geography

The study of the Earth's surface

Geography investigates how the Earth's surface varies from place to place and from time to time. It is often called a "spatial science" because it studies how things relate to each other spatially – that is, on the Earth's surface. **Human geography** studies the patterns of human activity around the world, such as the distribution of population, agriculture, industry, and transportation. **Physical geography** examines the Earth's physical environment, which includes everything from weather to landforms.

# Geomorphology

The study of landforms

Geomorphology analyses the landscape and the processes that shape it. It includes the study of hills and valleys, mountains and plains, rivers and glaciers, the effect of waves upon the land, and the weathering ▦ of rocks. **Hydrology** is the study of how water is distributed around the Earth and how it behaves. It focuses particularly on inland and underground water resources.

# Paleontology

The study of fossil remains

The study of fossils ▦ helps not only to provide a picture of the history of life on Earth, but also enables Earth scientists to work out the age of rocks by biostratigraphy ▦.

**Preserved in rock**
*Rocks can be dated by the presence of fossilized creatures, such as this trilobite.*

**Shaping the land**
*The Grand Canyon in Arizona was carved out by the Colorado River.*

## See also

Atmosphere 138 • Biostratigraphy 72
Climate 154 • Crust 40 • Earthquake 58
Ecosystem 158 • Fossil 70 • Geyser 53
Global seismology 40 • Mineral 82
Ocean 134 • Plate tectonics 46
Rock 80 • Stratigraphy 68 • Volcano 52
Weather 139 • Weathering 98

# Oceanography

The study of the oceans

Oceanography investigates the chemistry of the oceans ▦, ocean currents, the ocean bed, and marine life. **Hydrography** is the surveying and mapping of large bodies of water. **Hydrographic charts** are vital navigational aids, showing coastlines, currents, tides, and the terrain of the sea floor.

# Ecology

The study of relationships between living things and their environment

Ecologists study ecosystems ▦, which are interacting collections of living organisms and their surroundings.

# Meteorology

The study of the atmosphere

Meteorology focuses on the processes in the atmosphere ▦ that generate weather ▦. **Climatology** is the study of world climates ▦ – that is, patterns of typical weather around the world.

**Storm warning**
*Meteorological observations enable bad weather to be forecast in advance.*

# Earth scientists at work

Unlike chemists and physicists, Earth scientists can rarely test out their ideas with controlled experiments in a laboratory; glaciers, mountains, hurricanes, and tectonic plates are far too vast for such an approach. Instead, they must collect data and test out their theories in the real world, even if this means braving an erupting volcano or bitter arctic winds.

**Collecting data in the field**
*This photograph shows a geologist using a laser measuring device to monitor a slowly growing bulge on the northwest flank of Mount St. Helens volcano, Washington. The bulge later exploded on May 18, 1980, destroying the observation site.*

## Field work

The collection of data out in the open

Collecting data in the open or "in the field" is a vital part of Earth science. It may involve anything from measuring stream flow ■ or rainfall, to examining rock strata ■. Each field work project must be carefully designed to ensure that the right data is collected.

### See also

Depression 142 • Ecosystem 158
Flow 112 • Meteorology 13
Strata 68 • Wave 127

## Sampling

Collecting a representative selection of measurements

It is impossible to count every grain of sand on a beach or every rain drop, so scientists take small measurements called **samples**. But the spread of the samples must be great enough to show variations. There are various ways to ensure that the sample is representative. **Systematic sampling** is collecting data at regular intervals – for example, by dividing the study into units and taking a sample from the same point in each unit. **Random sampling** is selecting data collection points at random. **Stratified random sampling** is collecting data from any point in each unit. **Nested sampling** is collecting data only from certain points within chosen areas.

**Systematic sampling**

**Random sampling**

**Stratified random sampling**

**Nested sampling**

## Deduction

An explanation found by theoretical argument

Many early theories about the Earth were arrived at deductively – that is, by logical argument alone. A geologist might deduce a theory of landscape evolution, for example, and use it to explain the shape of a hill. Most modern theories are **inductive**. This means collecting data first, then analyzing it to make connections.

## Hypothesis

A suggested explanation that can be tested against reality

When starting an investigation, scientists often have an idea or hypothesis to test. To avoid their results being biased, they try to disprove their idea by testing a **null hypothesis**. This is a direct contradiction of the hypothesis. If the hypothesis is that the size of sediment varies across a river, the null hypothesis will be that the size of sediment does not vary. If the null hypothesis is rejected because a strong variation is discovered, then the original hypothesis may later be proven correct after further tests.

## Model

A theoretical representation of the real world

Earth scientists use theoretical versions of the real world to make predictions, control events, or simply explain things. Meteorologists ■, for example, use a theoretical model of a depression ■ to forecast weather. **Scale models** are versions of the real world scaled up or down for easier study. **Conceptual models** are entirely theoretical, and may be presented as a diagram. **Mathematical models** use only mathematical expressions to describe real events.

# System

An interrelated set of objects and events

A system can be anything from a drop of water to the entire Universe. Examples are weather systems, ecosystems ■, and river systems. In all systems, there is a flowthrough of energy (an **energy system**) or materials (a **materials system**). **Systems analysts** try to account for all the energy and materials passing through a system by discovering all the pathways that they take.

# Open system

A system in which energy is always entering and leaving

In open systems, energy or matter constantly enters in some places and leaves in others. In a river, for example, energy enters the system as rain, and leaves as the stream flows into the sea. Energy or matter entering an open system are **inputs**, and those leaving are **outputs**. In a **closed system**, there are no significant inputs or outputs; energy and matter flow through the system but do not enter or leave.

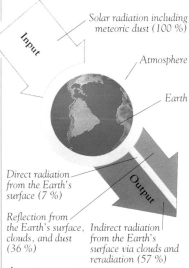

*Solar radiation including meteoric dust (100 %)*

*Atmosphere*

*Earth*

*Direct radiation from the Earth's surface (7 %)*

*Reflection from the Earth's surface, clouds, and dust (36 %)*

*Indirect radiation from the Earth's surface via clouds and reradiation (57 %)*

**An open system**
*The Earth is an open system with energy and matter entering and leaving.*

## *Negative feedback*
*This river system is an example of a negative feedback system. Heavy rainfall increases stream velocity, which causes other changes, ultimately resulting in decreased stream velocity.*

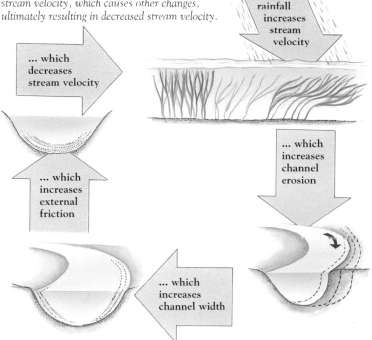

Heavy rainfall increases stream velocity

... which increases channel erosion

... which increases channel width

... which increases external friction

... which decreases stream velocity

# Dynamic equilibrium

A balance between input and output

If the balance between the amount of energy or material entering a system is equal to that leaving, the system is said to be in a state of dynamic equilibrium. If the system is not in equilibrium, energy or matter either builds up in the system or drains away. For example, if water from the taps runs into a bath at the same rate as it drains away, the bath is in a state of dynamic equilibrium. If the taps are turned down or off, the water will drain away; if the drain is plugged, the bath fills up. Many natural systems are in a state of dynamic equilibrium, such as ecosystems and river channels. In a section of river channel, there is not only a balance between the flow of water entering and leaving the section, but also between the flow of water and the shape of the channel.

# Feedback

A way in which a system regulates itself to maintain an equilibrium

Equilibrium in a system is maintained by feedback. Feedback occurs when a change in one part of the system creates changes in other parts of the system. These changes feed back in turn to influence the initial change, thereby regulating it. If waves ■ crashing on a beach get bigger, sand is washed away and the beach gets shallower. Shallow beaches make waves bigger. So as the beach gets shallower, this change feeds back to the waves, which get bigger still, making the beach even shallower. This is called **positive feedback**. Positive feedback is when the changes feed back to reinforce the initial change. **Negative feedback**, which is more common, is when the changes feed back to reduce the effect of the initial change.

# Field techniques

Earth scientists practice three kinds of field work: collecting samples such as stream sediment or rain, measuring movements such as continental drift or a stream's flow, and mapping features such as hillslopes and the ocean bed to discover how they change and to reveal relationships. Some tasks need special instruments; some can be done with simple homemade equipment.

*Searching for fossils*
*A geologist uses a geological hammer to search for fossils in Carboniferous limestone in Yorkshire, England.*

## Specimen hunting

Searching for items to catalogue or analyze in the laboratory

In the past, specimen hunting played an important role in geology ■. Many early geologists built up huge collections of rocks and fossils ■, either found loose or chipped out of rock beds with a geological hammer. Unfortunately, many valuable sites were damaged by over-enthusiastic collectors. Today, specimen hunting is kept to a minimum.

## Area survey

The mapping of a particular area

The ground can be surveyed in many ways. Aerial photography ■ provides a quick but costly way of mapping large areas. Small areas are better mapped in detail on the ground, either by a chain survey or by triangulation.

## Chain survey

A survey technique involving measuring distances

Small areas can be surveyed by measuring the distance between points. A chain with links of known length may be used or, more commonly nowadays, a metal or linen measuring-tape.

*Calculating distances*
*This geodimeter is being used to survey a region of the Libyan desert.*

## Triangulation

A survey technique based on a system of triangles

Triangulation is used in mapping. A surveyor measures a **baseline**, which forms one side of a triangle. Lines from the ends of the baseline to a distant point complete the triangle. A **theodolite** – a device that measures angles – is aimed at the distant point from each end of the baseline. The angle between the baseline and the two unknown sides of the triangle is measured. Once these angles are known, the exact location of the distant point can be calculated using simple geometry. The lines to the distant point are then used as baselines for further triangles to extend the survey. Distances are also measured with a **geodimeter**, which sends out a beam of infrared light. The time the light takes to travel to a reflector and back indicates the distance.

*Theodolite*

*B*

*Baseline*

*A*

*Angle being measured*

*Triangulation*
*The tree's location is calculated by using a theodolite to measure angles A and B between the baseline and the other two sides of the triangle.*

# Morphological mapping

Mapping the exact shape of slopes and other landscape features

To understand why the landscape is a particular shape, and the processes operating on it, geomorphologists ▪ must make accurate maps. Morphological maps use symbols to show important landscape features such as a sharp break in slope, woodland, flat land, and so on. Mapping a slope profile ▪ involves working out the angle of the slope at different points. This can be done with a homemade device, or with a clinometer or Abney level.

**Measuring slope angle**
*The girl is looking down the sighting tube of a simple clinometer to measure the angle of a slope.*

# Clinometer

An instrument for measuring the slope or dip angle

Clinometers are more expensive than Abney levels but are easier to use and just as accurate. A **Watts clinometer** has a pendulum that swings across a graduated arc. An **Indian clinometer** has a sighting tube with a spirit level, and an adjustable degree marker. A **surveyor's level** is the most sophisticated and accurate way of measuring slope angle, but it is expensive and bulky.

**Abney level**
*This simple instrument allows quick calculation of slope angles.*

# Abney level

A simple survey instrument for measuring the angle of a slope

An Abney level consists of a hand-held sighting tube linked to a spirit level. The bubble in the spirit level is reflected in the eyepiece. To measure a slope's angle, the surveyor erects two poles of known height at the top and bottom of the slope, and then sights the upper pole from the lower pole through the Abney level. The angle of the sighting tube is then adjusted until the bubble in the spirit level coincides with the upper pole. The tube angle then corresponds to the slope angle.

# Young pit

A method of measuring soil creep down a hillslope

A Young pit is a simple way of measuring soil creep ▪ on a slope. A deep pit is dug into a slope. A heavy stake is driven into the bedrock against the back wall of the pit to act as a marker. A series of rods is then driven into the ground in a vertical line, next to the stake, using a plumb-line as a guide. The back wall is covered with polythene and photographed before being filled in and left for a few months or a year. As soil moves down the slope the line of rods bends downhill due to the movement of the soil. The pit is then carefully dug out and the back wall exposed. The new position of the rods relative to the marker stake shows the amount of soil creep down the slope.

# Sediment trap

A box for measuring sheetwash on a hillslope

A sediment trap is a simple way of measuring sheetwash ▪. It is a plastic container inserted into a hole dug in a slope. A narrow opening like that of a mail box faces up the slope to catch all the water and sediment ▪ washed down the slope.

# Throughflow collector

A system for measuring throughflow on a slope

Hydrologists ▪ measure throughflow ▪ by first digging a pit in a slope. A series of plastic gutters are then placed inside the pit running across the slope at different heights. These carry water flowing through the soil to collectors where it is measured.

**Measuring throughflow**
*Throughflow is being measured at different depths with a special collector.*

## See also

*Continued on next page* ➤

# Flow meter

A device for measuring a stream's velocity

A stream's velocity can be measured simply with a flow ■ meter. This is usually a propeller mounted on a pole that sits on the stream bed. The propeller is attached by a cable to a counter that records the number of times the propeller turns in a given time. To accurately assess stream velocity, the meter must be carefully positioned. The meter is typically held at 0.6 of the depth of the stream for 20 readings, taken at even intervals across the stream. Multiplying the cross-sectional area of the stream by the velocity gives the discharge ■.

*Measuring stream velocity*
*A flow meter is being held upright in the water to determine the stream's velocity.*

# Dilution gauging

A method for measuring stream discharge electrically

A **conductivity meter** allows stream discharge to be measured directly, so there is no need to measure either the stream's cross-sectional area or its velocity. A **tracer** such as salt is added to the water to measure how fast it spreads through the water. The concentration of salt affects the water's electrical conductivity, so the meter shows the changing salt concentration by measuring the water's changing conductivity.

# Gauging station

A place where river flow is measured

Flume

Flow meters and dilution gauging are only really suitable for small rivers. For large rivers, gauging stations are often constructed. Here, the river is fed over a weir of a certain shape – typically a 90° **V-notch weir** – or funneled through a narrow channel called a **flume**. The area of the channel in the notch or flume is known, and basic hydrodynamic laws are used to calculate the river's velocity. **Hydrodynamics** is the science of the pressure of water flowing through channels and pipes, and over weirs. The discharge can be measured simply with a **stageboard**, which shows the depth of the water.

# Bedload trap

A trench in a stream bed for measuring bedload

In shallow streams, bedload ■ can be measured by cutting a trench right across the stream bed. The stream washes its bedload into the trench. The material can then be extracted and measured after a certain time – or the fieldworker can work out how long it takes to fill to a certain level. Where a bedload trap is impractical, a **quadrat** can be used. This is simply a square net laid directly on the stream bed.

# Evaporation pan

An open tray of water for gauging evaporation

An evaporation pan is a tray of water, typically 19 sq. ft. (1.8 m²) in area. It is left out in the open, but in a sheltered place. The fluctuating levels of water in the pan provide an indication of potential evaporation rates in the area, once the input from rain has been accounted for.

# Potometer

A device for measuring transpiration from plants

The amount of water a plant takes up through its roots is proportional to the amount lost through its leaves by transpiration ■. Potometers measure water uptake through a plant's roots, making it possible to calculate the amount lost through transpiration.

# Lysimeter

A device for measuring evapotranspiration

Evapotranspiration ■ is the combined effects of transpiration and evaporation. A column of soil and vegetation is put in a container and replaced in the ground from where it came. Water input is measured by rain gauges, and output is measured as drainage from the container. The soil is weighed to estimate the change in soil moisture content.

*Desert lysimeters*
*These large round lysimeters measure water input, output, and storage.*

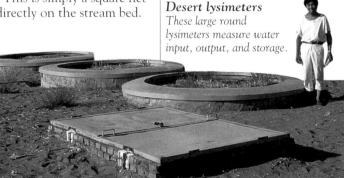

◄ Continued from previous page

# Rain gauge

An instrument for measuring rainfall

Rainfall is measured by the depth of water collected in a rain gauge. A rain gauge has a collecting funnel with a rim 5 or 8 in. (125 or 200 mm) in diameter, and is mounted 12 in. (30 cm) above the ground. Rainwater runs from the funnel into a narrow collecting tube, which is emptied regularly into a measuring flask to check rainfall.

*Outer container*  *Measuring flask*

*Collecting tube*  *Collecting funnel*

***Rain gauge and measuring flask***
*This simple measuring device is used to collect and then measure rainfall.*

# Hygrometer

An instrument for measuring humidity

There are many different kinds of hygrometer. An **absorption hygrometer** consists of a pair of scales and an absorbent substance such as paper, which gets heavier as it absorbs water in moist air. An **expansion hygrometer** relies on the fact that some substances such as wood expand as they absorb water. **Hair hygrometers** are expansion hygrometers that use a length of human hair. As the air gets moister, the hair gets longer. **Weather houses** are simple hair hygrometers that use the hair to let a "fair weather maid" or a "foul weather man" emerge from the house according to humidity ▨.

*Weather cock*

# Weather vane

A pointer that shows wind direction

Weather vanes have a big fin on the end of a pivoting arm. Air pressure ▨ on the fin swings the arm round to point into the wind, indicating the wind direction. A **weather cock** is a weather vane in the shape of a rooster; the cock's head points into the wind.

# Wet-and-dry bulb thermometer

A device for measuring relative humidity

A **psychrometer** is a hygrometer that shows relative humidity. A wet-and-dry bulb thermometer is a type of psychrometer. It has two thermometers: an ordinary one (the dry bulb) and another with its bulb wrapped in moist muslin (the wet bulb). Evaporation of moisture from the muslin lowers the wet bulb temperature – this is the **wet bulb depression**. Just how much cooler the wet bulb gets depends on how fast the water evaporates, which in turn depends on the relative humidity. The wet bulb depression (the difference in temperature between the wet and dry bulbs) therefore provides a direct measure of relative humidity.

*Wet-and-dry bulb thermometer*

# Anemometer

A device for measuring wind speed

Anemometers come in many different forms. The most widely used is a **cup anemometer**, which has three or four cups that spin on a spindle. As the cups rotate they generate an electric current, the strength of which indicates the wind speed. A **pressure-plate anemometer** has a swinging metal plate that swings up to higher angles as the wind speed increases. A **pressure-tube anemometer** measures the difference in air pressure between two tubes, one facing into the wind and one away from the wind. A **sonic anemometer** works in the same way but relies on pulses of high-frequency sound rather than air pressure.

***Setting up a weather station***
*These climatologists are setting up some cup anemometers and other apparatus, in order to measure wind speed, temperature, and humidity on Ellesmere Island, Canada.*

## See also

Atmospheric pressure 142
Bedload 112 • Discharge 109
Evapotranspiration 108 • Flow 112
Humidity 146 • Transpiration 108

# Data handling

Earth science is based largely on observation of the real world, rather than experiment. So observational data is the Earth scientist's raw material. This is why proper presentation and analysis of data and statistics is so important.

**Gathering raw data**
*Measuring variations in the discharge of a river provides a set of numerical observations. To be useful, this raw data must first be sorted and analyzed.*

## Statistics

Numerical observations and data

Statistics may be sorted into **rank order**, which simply means placing the numbers in order of size. The **range** is the difference between the smallest and largest. The **mean** is the average, which is calculated by adding all the figures and dividing the total by the number of figures involved. The **median** is the middle figure when they are placed in rank order. The **mode** is the figure that occurs most frequently.

## Graph

A visual display of the relationship between two sets of data

Graphs show how two sets of figures or **variables** change in relation to one other. The **independent variable** is fixed in value; the **dependent variable** is the value that changes. In a graph of monthly rainfall ■, for example, the months are the independent variable and the rainfall is the dependent variable.

## Line graph

A graph that uses a line to link a set of changing values

A line graph usually shows a set of points, or **coordinates**, plotted on a grid between two perpendicular axes. A line graph is appropriate for related values that vary continuously, such as average monthly temperatures. A **bar graph** or **bar chart** is better for unconnected or cumulative values, such as monthly rainfall. It shows the dependent variable as a series of vertical bars of the appropriate height. A **pie graph** or **pie chart** shows proportions well, since each value appears as a part of a circle (pie graphs appear on pages 42 and 138).

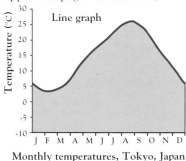

**Monthly temperatures, Tokyo, Japan**

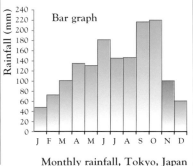

**Monthly rainfall, Tokyo, Japan**

## Rose diagram

A spoked diagram showing size and direction

On a rose diagram, the length of a spoke indicates a value in a particular direction. On a **wind rose**, for example, the spokes may represent points on the compass. The length of each spoke may vary according to the average strength of the wind ■ from that direction, or the number of days on which wind blew from that direction.

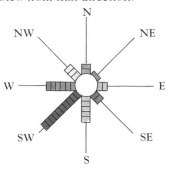

**Simple wind rose**
*Each colored section on the spokes of this wind rose represents a day when the wind blew from a particular direction.*

## Flow diagram

A diagram that shows how one thing leads to another in a complex sequence of movements or actions

A flow diagram can be used to show, for example, how overland flow ■ and groundwater ■ combine to give the discharge ■ of a river. The width of the arrows may be proportional to the size of the movement.

**River discharge**
*This flow diagram shows the discharge in different branches of a river system. The width of the arrows is proportional to the size of the discharge.*

*The resulting width may equal the combined width of the merging streams*

# Proportional circle

A circle whose area represents a particular value at a specific place on a map

Proportional circles are a useful way of showing variations of a particular measurement from place to place on a map ▪. The circles are drawn on the map in proportion to the value for each place. So an area with high rainfall, for example, will have a large circle, and an area with low rainfall will have a small circle. Proportional circles are often used on maps to show the comparative populations of towns and cities.

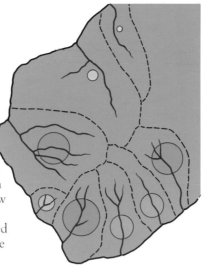

## See also

Catchment area 109 • Climograph 154
Discharge 109 • Groundwater 108
Map 22 • Overland flow 108
Rain 149 • Wind 142

**Key to river discharge in cusecs (cubic meters per second):**

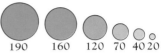

190   160   120   70   40  20

*Proportional discharge*
*This diagram shows the flow of rivers in different catchment areas. The dotted lines indicate the boundaries of the catchment areas.*

---

# MEASUREMENTS & CONVERSIONS

## Metric units to imperial / USCS units

**Length**

| | |
|---|---|
| 1 kilometer (km) | = 0.621 mile |
| 1 meter (m) | – 1.094 yards |
| 1 meter (m) | = 3.281 feet |
| 1 centimeter (cm) | = 0.394 inch |
| 1 millimeter (mm) | = 0.039 inch |

**Area**

| | |
|---|---|
| 1 square kilometer (km²) | = 0.386 square mile |
| 1 hectare (ha) | = 2.471 acres |
| *1 hectare = 10,000 square meters* | |
| 1 square meter (m²) | = 10.764 square feet |
| 1 square centimeter (cm²) | = 0.155 square inch |

**Volume**

| | |
|---|---|
| 1 cubic meter (m³) | = 35.315 cubic feet |
| 1 liter (l) | = 0.22 gallon |
| 1 liter (l) | = 1.76 pints |
| *1 liter = 1,000 cubic centimeters* | |
| 1 cubic centimeter (cm³) | – 0.061 cubic inch |

**Mass**

| | |
|---|---|
| 1 tonne (t) | = 0.984 ton |
| *1 tonne = 1,000 kilograms* | |
| 1 kilogram (kg) | = 2.205 pounds |
| 1 gram (g) | = 0.035 ounce |

**US Measures**

| | |
|---|---|
| 1 liter (l) | = 0.264 gallon |
| 1 liter (l) | = 2.113 pints |
| 1 tonne (t) | = 1.102 tons |

## Imperial / USCS units to metric units

| | |
|---|---|
| 1 mile (mi.) | = 1.609 kilometers |
| 1 yard (yd.) | = 0.914 meter |
| 1 foot (ft.) | – 0.305 meter |
| 1 foot (ft.) | = 30.48 centimeters |
| 1 inch (in.) | = 25.4 millimeters |

| | |
|---|---|
| 1 square mile (sq. mi.) | = 2.589 square kilometers |
| 1 acre | = 0.405 hectare |
| *1 acre = 4,840 square yards* | |
| 1 square foot (sq. ft.) | = 0.093 square meter |
| 1 square inch (sq. in.) | = 6.452 square centimeters |

| | |
|---|---|
| 1 cubic foot (cu. ft.) | = 0.028 cubic meter |
| 1 gallon (gal.) | = 4.546 liters |
| 1 pint (pt.) | = 0.568 liter |
| *1 pint = 34.68 cubic inches* | |
| 1 cubic inch (cu. in.) | = 16.387 cubic centimeters |

| | |
|---|---|
| 1 ton | = 1.016 tonnes |
| *1 ton = 2,240 pounds* | |
| 1 pound (lb.) | = 0.454 kilogram |
| 1 ounce (oz.) | = 28.35 grams |

| | |
|---|---|
| 1 gallon | = 3.785 liters |
| 1 pint (28.88 cu. in.) | = 0.473 litre |
| 1 ton (2,000 lb.) | = 0.907 tonne |

Example: to find out what 16.5 inches equals in millimeters, simply multiply 16.5 by 25.4, to give 419.1 mm or 41.91 cm

---

**Temperature**
To convert °Celsius or Centigrade to °Fahrenheit multiply by 9, divide by 5, and add 32
To convert °Fahrenheit to °Celsius or Centigrade subtract 32, multiply by 5, and divide by 9

# Maps & mapping

Maps are one of the Earth scientist's most valuable tools. They are an effective way of displaying data such as the distribution of rainfall or the location of volcanoes. They also provide a means of studying large areas of the landscape, and reveal a great deal about an area's geography.

## Legend

The meaning of the symbols on a map

Detailed maps need to use a wide variety of symbols to show all the different features. Many symbols have an obvious meaning, but a legend helps the user understand those symbols whose meaning is not so clear.

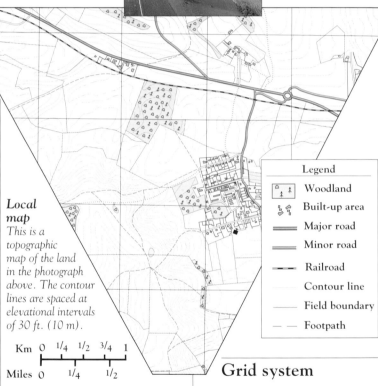

## Map

A flat, visual representation of part of the Earth's surface

The form of a map ■ depends on what it is intended to show. Most maps show features the same relative distance and direction from one another as they are in reality. But this is not always true. Many transportation maps show the order of stops on a particular route, but with only a suggestion of direction and distance.

## Scale

The ratio of distances on a map to distances in reality

On a map that is drawn to scale, a certain distance in reality (such as 1 mile or 1 km) is shown as a standard distance on the map (such as 1 in. or 1 cm). The Earth's spherical shape means that some features on a map are distorted more than others, so scales are never totally accurate. When a map shows just a city or a small region, this distortion is insignificant. **Small-scale maps** show large areas in little detail; **large-scale maps** show small areas in great detail.

### See also

Isobar 142 • Isotherm 141 • Latitude 37
Longitude 37 • Magnetic north pole 44
Map projection 38 • True north 44

*Local map*

*This is a topographic map of the land in the photograph above. The contour lines are spaced at elevational intervals of 30 ft. (10 m).*

Km  0   1/4  1/2  3/4  1

Miles  0      1/4      1/2

**Legend**

| | |
|---|---|
| ▵ ↟ | Woodland |
| ↟ ⚘ | Built-up area |
| ▬▬ | Major road |
| ── | Minor road |
| ▬·▬ | Railroad |
| —— | Contour line |
| ── | Field boundary |
| – – | Footpath |

## Scale statement

A map scale expressed in words

If 1 mile in reality is shown as 1 inch on a map, the scale statement reads "1 inch to 1 mile." A **representative fraction** or **RF** is the scale of the map shown as a ratio or fraction. The RF of a map with a scale of 1 inch to 1 mile is 1:10,000 or 1/10,000. The RF is the same for all measurement units. A **linear scale** is a graduated line with distances marked in proportion to distances in reality.

## Grid system

A pattern of columns and rows on a map to help pinpoint locations

Some maps use lines of latitude ■ and longitude ■ for the grid. On an **alphanumeric grid**, the rows may be lettered and the columns numbered, so the location of a place within a grid square can be given by a number-letter pairing. In many countries, the maps have their own **national grid**. Places are located by **grid references**, given in **eastings** (the number of squares eastward) and **northings** (the number of squares northward).

# Township and Range System

The grid system used in the US

The US is divided into squares or **townships** using north-south lines called **principal meridians** and east-west lines called **base lines**. A township is located by its **township number** (the number of squares north or south of a base line) and its **range number** (the number of squares east or west of a principal meridian).

# Topographic map

A detailed map of the landscape

Topographic maps show a wide range of features, including hills, valleys, rivers, and woodlands.

# Choropleth map

A map that uses shading to show variations in a measurement

Different densities of shading on a choropleth map show how a particular measurement, such as rainfall, varies from area to area.

# Dot map

A map that represents data with dots

Dot maps show distribution and density. Data, such as the location of woodlands, is shown as dots in the appropriate places.

# Land-use map

A map that shows how land is used

Land-use maps may use different shades or colors to indicate the ways in which land is used.

# Azimuth

A direction in relation to true north or magnetic north

A direction or **bearing** may be given as an azimuth – that is, the angle between it and true north or magnetic north. So a course due east has an azimuth of 90°.

*Isarithmic relief*
*This model was made by plotting the contour lines of Kilimanjaro in Tanzania. Each stage shows all the points at a particular height.*

# Isarithm

A line on a map that links all points with the same value

**Isoline maps** use isarithms to link points that have the same value. Isotherms are lines that link places of equal temperature, while **isobar maps** use isobars to link points of equal pressure. **Isohyets** link areas with equal annual rainfall, and **isobaths** link areas with equal depths of water.

# Relief map

A map showing hills and valleys

The most accurate and useful way of showing relief is by using **contour lines**. These are isarithms that link points of equal height. The **contour interval** is the difference in height between one contour and the next. It varies according to the scale of the map and the density of the relief. On small-scale maps, the contour interval may be colored to make high areas instantly obvious. **Hill-shading** uses realistic shadows to show the relief on a map, almost as if it were a model. Often such maps have **spot heights**, which are actual heights at particular places. **Hachuring** uses short shading lines to indicate relief.

## TYPES OF MAP

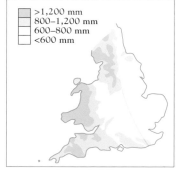

>1,500
1,000–1,500
500–1,000
<500

Choropleth population map

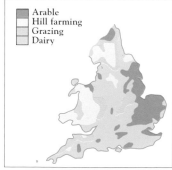

· 500–600      200–300
· 400–500      · 100–200
· 300–400      · <100

Dot population map

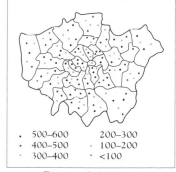

>1,200 mm
800–1,200 mm
600–800 mm
<600 mm

Isohyet rainfall map

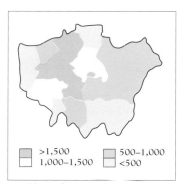

Arable
Hill farming
Grazing
Dairy

Agricultural land-use map

# Geological maps

Geological maps are valuable aids to the work of geologists. They show the types of rock that occur in a particular place. From this, a geologist can work out the three-dimensional structure of rock formations, their interrelationship, and even the history of how the formations evolved and how the landscape was shaped through the ages.

## Geological map

A map showing the distribution of different rocks in a particular area

Some geological maps, called **drift maps**, show just loose surface sediment ■, such as the sediment deposited by glaciers ■. Most, however, show the solid rocks beneath. These are **solid maps**.

## Key

An explanation of symbols on a map

A geological map usually uses patches of different color to represent the different rocks in a region. Igneous rocks ■, for example, are usually shown in shades of purple or magenta, depending on whether they are intrusive or extrusive. Metamorphic rocks ■ are usually shades of pink and gray-green. Sedimentary rocks ■ are usually shades of brown, yellow, and green – except for limestones ■, which are typically blue-gray. Uncolored maps use different types of shading or patterns called **ornament**.

Key to rocks:  ▨ Clay
▨ Upper chalk  ☐ Lower chalk

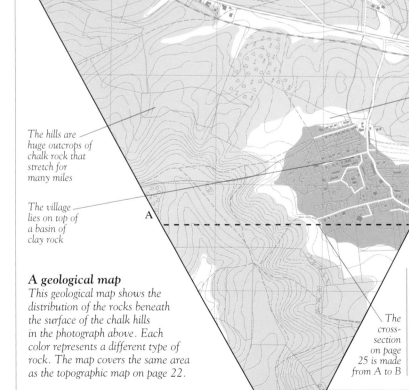

The bands of lower chalk run along the length of the valley, and surround the clay beneath the village

The hills are huge outcrops of chalk rock that stretch for many miles

The village lies on top of a basin of clay rock

A ----------- B

## Outcrop

A place where a particular rock appears at the surface

Where a solid rock formation reaches the surface, it is said to be an outcrop, even though it may be hidden beneath a thin sheet of deposits. Outcrops that are not covered with deposits are called **exposures**. The pattern of the outcrops on a geological map helps to indicate the three-dimensional structure of the rocks. A series of parallel bands of rocks, for example, is usually a formation of uniformly dipping rock strata ■.

*A geological map*
*This geological map shows the distribution of the rocks beneath the surface of the chalk hills in the photograph above. Each color represents a different type of rock. The map covers the same area as the topographic map on page 22.*

The cross-section on page 25 is made from A to B

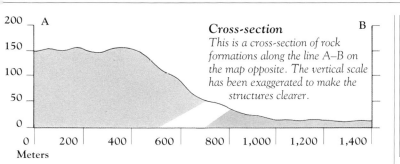

*Cross-section*
*This is a cross-section of rock formations along the line A–B on the map opposite. The vertical scale has been exaggerated to make the structures clearer.*

## Cross-section

A diagram that shows the vertical distribution of rocks along a line

A cross-section is a representation of a vertical slice through the rock formations, showing how they are arranged beneath the surface. Experienced geologists can often construct a cross-section simply with the aid of a geological map. Cross-sections can also be made using results from boreholes ▪ and from seismic surveys ▪. Most cross-sections are drawn at right angles to the strike ▪ of the rocks to show the structure clearly.

## Vertical exaggeration

The exaggeration in a cross-section of depth in relation to length

Some geological structures are hundreds of miles across. In order to show them clearly, the cross-section has to be vertically exaggerated – that is, the vertical scale must be greater than the horizontal scale. This also distorts the structures a little, so that they appear thicker, and dip ▪ more sharply than they do in reality.

## Datum plane

The baseline of a cross-section

The horizontal line along the bottom of a cross-section is called the datum plane, and each rock formation is usually shown in relation to this. Typically, sea level is used as the datum plane, but on large-scale maps, a local datum plane might be used.

## Stratigraphic section

A cross-section that shows rock formations as they were laid down

Geologists construct stratigraphic sections to show rock formations as they once were – before they were faulted ▪ or folded ▪, for example. A stratigraphic section can be made by treating one particular rock formation as the datum plane. This formation is drawn as a straight line, and all the others are shown by their height above or below this formation. Such sections are widely used by oil ▪ prospectors. A cross-section that shows rock structures as they are today is called a **structure section**.

## Fence diagram

A three-dimensional diagram or model of a rock structure, made from interlocking cross-sections

One of the simplest ways to show three-dimensional arrangements of rocks is to construct a series of cross-sections at right-angles to each other. The sections are cut out from cardboard as **panels** and then stood upright so that they interlock at the right places, like a series of fences. Fence diagrams are often made as drawings, rather than as actual cardboard models.

## Block diagram

A drawing that show a three-dimensional block of the landscape

A block diagram can be made by showing two cross-sections meeting at right-angles to form the nearest corner of the block, with the surface map for the area overlaid on top. In **isometric block diagrams**, the vertical scale is exactly the same as on the cross-sections, so all the edges of the block are parallel. In **perspective block diagrams**, the vertical and horizontal scales decrease toward the far edges. This gives a more realistic effect, but introduces some distortion.

*Fence and block diagrams*
*The fence diagram below is constructed from four cross-sections from the map opposite, including the one representing A–B. The block diagram above has the surface details overlaid in between the cross-sections.*

# Pictures from above

Photographs taken from above the Earth, whether from airplanes or satellites in space, are now among the Earth scientist's most valuable tools. They provide an accurate and rapid overview of huge areas, often revealing structures and patterns that might not be seen any other way.

*False-colored city*
*This false-color image shows Tokyo, Japan, from the air. Vegetation is shown in red and buildings in blue. The black area represents the sea.*

## Remote sensing

The recording of information at a distance

The best known and most widely used remote sensing device, or **remote sensor**, is a camera, which records pictures of distant scenes using visible light. Photography of the landscape from aircraft is called **aerial photography**. Other remote sensing sysems include thermal infrared, radar, and sonar.

*Flight path*

*Points at which photographs are taken*

A

B

*Area shown in photograph A*

A

B

A

B

## Stereoscopy

The use of overlapping pairs of photographs to give a three-dimensional view of the ground

Stereoscopy involves taking two photographs at once using cameras mounted at either end of an aircraft. Each camera gives a slightly different view, like each of our eyes. The two photographs are then viewed together through a device called a **stereoscope**, which consists of two lenses mounted on a stand. This gives a three-dimensional image and enables cartographers to work out the heights of different objects.

*Aircraft*

*Overlapping area shown in both photographs*

*Area shown in photograph B*

*Stereoscopy*
*Aerial photographs enable vast areas to be mapped very quickly. A simple aerial photograph gives only a flat, two-dimensional picture of the ground. So cartographers prefer to use stereoscopy, which gives a three-dimensional image.*

## False-color image

A photograph that records light which our eyes cannot see

**Infrared films** record not only visible light, but also light beyond the red end of the spectrum, called infrared light. Photographs taken on infrared film show unusual false colors, so they are called false-color images. They are particularly useful for agricultural and forestry surveys. Healthy broad-leaved plants, for example, appear red, while conifers are brown to purple, but diseased plants show up as dark red to blue. Infrared films are also good for photographing through mist.

## Thermal infrared

A sensor for recording heat radiation

A hot object emits infrared light; the hotter the object, the more intense the infrared light it emits. By recording variations in the intensity of infrared light, thermal infrared scanners or **radiometers** show natural variations in the temperatures of clouds, water, land, oceans, and buildings. This is very useful for tracking clouds, ocean currents, forest fires, thermal pollution, and heat loss from manufactured objects. Thermal infrared is not the same as infrared photography.

# Radar

A remote sensing system that uses radio waves

Radar is short for "radio detection and ranging." Radar works by sending out a beam of radio waves, which is reflected back by any object in its path. A scanner picks up the reflections of the beam. The time it takes for the signal to return indicates the distance of an object from the scanner. Radar can be used to detect ships and aircraft, and to track rainfall, thunderstorms, and hurricanes. The satellite **Seasat 1**, which operated for 99 days in 1978, used radar scanning to provide a wealth of information on the seas and oceans.

# Sonar

A remote sensing system that uses sound echoes

Sonar is short for "sound navigation ranging." It works by sending out a high-frequency pulse of sound. The time it takes for the sound pulse to echo or bounce back from unseen objects indicates how far away they are. Oceanographers use sonar to map the ocean floor and determine the thickness and nature of seabed deposits.

**Sonar survey**
*The sonar system GLORIA can scan an area of ocean floor up to 37 miles (60 km) wide. The sonar "towfish" makes two scans that enable submarine features to be viewed from both sides, giving a clearer picture of the ocean floor.*

Parent ship

GLORIA sonar "towfish"

Two diverging sonar beams scan either side of the ship's course

Ocean floor

# Multispectral scanning

Remote sensing using various kinds of radiation

Multiple spectral scanning requires special radiometers called **multispectral scanners (MSS)**. MSS react only to selected wavelengths of radiation. Each MSS image records all of these wavelengths simultaneously.

# Satellite imaging

Remote sensing by satellites orbiting in space

Satellites orbiting the Earth can provide instant pictures of large areas of the Earth's surface. **Geostationary satellites** orbit at an altitude of 22,300 miles (35,900 km) above the equator. In this position, the satellite stays directly above the same point on the ground all the time. Geostationary orbits are ideal for recording meteorological information and relaying telecommunications. **Polar-orbiting satellites** circle the Earth from pole to pole less than 620 miles (1,000 km) above the ground, providing a more detailed picture of a smaller area.

# Weather satellite

A satellite that monitors the weather

There are dozens of weather satellites operated by the US, the European Space Agency, Japan, and Russia. They include the American **NOAA (National Oceanic and Atmospheric Administration) satellites**, which scan the atmosphere twice daily from a polar orbit 530 miles (854 km) above the Earth. Their MSS show cloud patterns clearly.

**The heat of the Earth at night**
*A weather satellite recorded this thermal infrared picture. The blue (coldest) areas are the cloud formations; the red (warmest) areas are generally oceans.*

# Landsat

A satellite that monitors the Earth's resources

The American Landsats orbit at an altitude of about 560 miles (900 km). They circle the Earth 14 times each day and pass over every part of the Earth's surface once every 18 days. Their MSS and false-color sensors record details of mineral and water resources, land use, and pollution. **SPOT (Satellite Probatoire pour l'Observation de la Terre)** is a similar French satellite.

## See also

# World map

Arctic Ice

ARCTIC

Eurasian Plate

Ob'

Yenisey

Lena

Lake Baikal

Amur

Baltic Sea

Volga

A S I A

EUROPE

Giant's Causeway

Jura Mountains

Puy-de-Dôme

Rhine

Danube

Alps

Pyrenees

Tiber

Mt. Vesuvius

Caucasus

Mediterranean Sea

Caspian Sea

Gobi Desert

Yellow River

Mt. Fuji

K2 (Mt. Godwin Austen)

Himalayas

Iranian Plate

Dead Sea

Sinai Desert

Mt. Everest

Ganges

Yangtze

Great Eastern Erg Desert

Qattara Depression

Kharga Depression

Sahara Desert

Sahel

Niger

A F R I C A

African Plate

Red Sea

Arabian Plate

Nile

Mariana Trench

Philippine Plate

Philippine Trench

Ruwenzori Mountains

Great Rift Valley

Lake Victoria

Kilimanjaro

Congo

Mt. Pinatubo

Lake Toba

I N D I A N

O C E A N

Java Island Arc

Victoria Falls

Zambeze

Mt. Tambora

Indo - Australian Plate

AUSTRALIA

Namib Desert

Kalahari Desert

Uluru (Ayers Rock)

Great Victoria Desert

Murray

Gt. Barrier Reef

Mid-Atlantic Ridge

Antarctic Plate

S O U T H E R N     O C E A N

## Key

| | |
|---|---|
| —— Subduction zone | ➜ Movement of plate |
| —— Mid-ocean ridge and faults | ▲ Volcano |
| —— Collision zone | ❋ Earthquake zone |
| - - - Uncertain plate boundary | |

*e t*

*AN*

Yukon

Mt. Denali

N O R T H

A M E R I C A

Rocky Mountains

Devil's
Tower

Missouri

Great Lakes

North American
Plate

Mt. St. Helens
**Juan de
Fuca Plate**

Mendocino
Fracture Zone

Sierra Nevada

San Andreas
Fault

Grand
Canyon

Monument
Valley

Mississippi

Niagara
Falls

Mid-Atlantic Ridge

Emperor
Sea Mounts

Hawaiian
Island Chain

Sonoran Desert

Baja California

Rio Grande

A T L A N T I C

O C E A N

**Caribbean
Plate**

**P a c i f i c    P l a t e**

P A C I F I C

**Cocos
Plate**

Angel Falls

O C E A N

Amazon

S O U T H
A M E R I C A

Andes

Tonga
Trench

East Pacific Rise

Lake Titicaca

Atacama
Desert

**South American
Plate**

**Nazca
Plate**

Aconcagua

Mt. Cook

*Sutherland Falls*

Scotia Plate

A N T A R C T I C A

# The universe

Our world is a tiny speck in the vastness of space. We live on a planet called the Earth, which is one of the nine planets that travel around the Sun and make up the Solar System. The Sun is just one of roughly 200 billion stars in a galaxy called the Milky Way. In total there are about 100 billion galaxies in the universe.

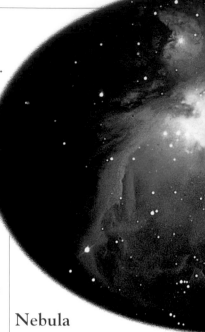

## Universe

All the countless planets, stars, and galaxies – everything that exists, including ourselves

The universe stretches away from us in all directions. We do not know how big it is, but bright galaxies have been detected as far away as 82,023 billion billion miles (132,000 billion billion km).

*Big Bang – origin of the universe*
*Small atoms formed within minutes of the Big Bang. But it was not until over a billion years later that material came together to form galaxies. The explosion was so huge that material is still hurtling away in all directions at amazing speeds.*

## Big Bang

The idea that the universe began in a huge explosion

Most astronomers now think the universe burst into existence about 15 billion years ago, in a gigantic explosion called the Big Bang. One moment there was just an incredibly hot ball of matter, smaller than an atom ■; the next moment it exploded, starting off the process that created the universe. The **Milky Way galaxy** formed after 5 billion years, and the Sun ■ after 10 billion years. The Earth and other planets evolved from the Sun's debris. The first lifeforms appeared on Earth about 12 billion years after the Big Bang.

## Nebula

A vast cloud of dust and gas in space

A nebula may be the birthplace of stars. Stars may begin to form as clumps of dust and gas in a nebula ■ are drawn together by their own gravity. As the clumps are pulled tighter together into dark blobs, or **dark nebulae**, the increasing pressure heats gases at the center to very high temperatures. Once the core reaches 18 million °F (10 million °C), nuclear reactions occur and new stars begin to shine.

## Expanding universe

The idea that the universe is getting bigger and bigger

The astronomer **Edwin Hubble** (1889–1953) discovered that the galaxies of the universe are moving farther and farther apart. Most astronomers believe this means the universe is getting continually bigger. Some believe it will continue to expand forever. This is called the **open universe theory**. Most believe it will expand only so far. Once the energy from the Big Bang is exhausted, the universe will collapse inward to a **Big Crunch**.

6 *Clouds of stars cluster to form galaxies*

5 *The gases form into nebulae*

4 *Strands of gases form strands*

3 *Hydrogen and helium molecules form*

2 *Atoms form*

1 *The Big Bang explosion*

| Event | | | | | | |
|---|---|---|---|---|---|---|
| **Time** | 0 *seconds* | 3 *minutes* | 10,000 *years* | 700,000 *years* | 1 billion *years* | 1.5 billion *years* |

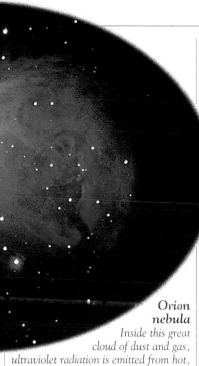

*Orion nebula*
*Inside this great cloud of dust and gas, ultraviolet radiation is emitted from hot, recently born stars. The radiation causes hydrogen in the nebula to glow red.*

## Star

A huge glowing ball of hot gas in space

The stars you see in the night sky are a fraction of the 20,000 billion billion scattered throughout the universe. Most stars are about the same size. But some **supergiant stars**, such as Antares, are hundreds of times larger than the Sun, while some **dwarf stars** are no bigger than the Earth. **Neutron stars** may be only 9 miles (15 km) across, but they are very dense. Stars vary in color according to their temperature, from the cooler red stars, warmer yellow stars like our Sun, to the hottest bluish-white stars. Stars shine because they are fueled by **nuclear fusion reactions**. Deep inside each star, hydrogen atoms fuse together to form helium atoms, creating so much energy that the temperature reaches millions of degrees and the star glows brightly. It glows until the hydrogen is burned up, when the star dies.

## Gravity

The force that holds the universe together

Gravity is the invisible force that makes things fall to the ground, keeps the Earth moving around the Sun, and holds stars and galaxies together. It remains a mystery quite how it works, but everything, no matter how small, has gravity, which is the power to pull things toward it. The strength of this force depends on how heavy an object is, so only massive objects such as planets and stars have a really strong pull. It is the pull of the Earth's gravity that holds you on the ground. It is the pull of the Sun's gravity that keeps the Earth circling, or orbiting, around it.

## Black hole

A region in space where gravity is so strong that light is sucked in

Supergiant stars "die" in a massive explosion called a **supernova**. The core of material left at the center may be so dense that it collapses under its own gravity, with such force that nothing can stop it. The more it shrinks, the stronger its gravity becomes. When it is just a few miles across, its gravity is so strong that even light is sucked in and cannot escape, creating a black hole.

*Giant supernova*
*The supernova 1987a is situated near the Tarantula nebula. It is the large, bright star near the bottom right.*

## Galaxy

A vast cluster of stars, dust, and gas

The biggest galaxies are almost as old as the universe; smaller ones may still be being born. Spinning clouds of gas condensed to form stars, and gravity pulled these stars together into galaxies. The largest galaxies are sphere-shaped **giant elliptical galaxies** with over 1,000 billion stars. Our Sun is one of the 200 billion stars that make up the Milky Way galaxy, which is a **spiral galaxy**, like a giant Catherine wheel. A third type is the **irregular galaxy**, with no definite shape.

*Spiral galaxy*
*This is M99, a spiral galaxy that is part of the Virgo cluster of galaxies. Also visible is a supernova, encircled in yellow.*

## Light-year

The distance light travels in a year

Distances in space are so vast that astronomers use a unit called the light-year to measure them. This is $5.875 \times 10^{12}$ miles ($9.465 \times 10^{12}$ km), the distance light travels in a year. The most distant galaxy yet detected is 13 billion light-years away, so we see it not as it is today but as it was 13 billion years ago, soon after the universe was born.

### See also

Atom 42

Nebular hypothesis 32

Planetary orbit 32 • Sun 32

# The Solar System

The Earth is one of nine huge spheres called planets circling continually in space around the Sun. Comets, asteroids, and other space debris also hurtle around the Sun, while moons and rings of gas and dust circle the planets. Together, all these things make up the Solar System.

## Solar System

The Sun, the nine planets, and all the other matter circling the Sun

The Sun makes up 99.8 percent of the Solar System's mass. Most of the rest lies in the planets and the comets. A **planet** is a large sphere of gas or rock, like the Earth, that spins around a star.

## Sun

A vast, fiery ball of gas and dust that provides the Earth with energy

The Sun is a star ■ like billions of others in the universe ■. It is an average-sized star, but it has a diameter 1,000 times larger than the Earth. It is made mainly of hydrogen and helium gases. The surface temperature is about 9,900°F (5,500°C), but its atmosphere soars to nearly 1.8 million °F (1 million °C). At the center, huge pressures fuse hydrogen atoms together, raising temperatures to more than 27 million °F (15 million °C). This intense heat erupts on the surface in patches called **granules**. There are also dark, cooler patches called **sunspots**.

## Planetary orbit

The path of a planet around the Sun

In space, gravity often pulls stars, planets, and other objects into circular paths or **orbits** around one another. The material of the Solar System, including the planets, orbits the Sun because of the Sun's huge gravitational pull. The planet's orbits are not quite perfect circles, but ellipses. All except Pluto orbit in the same plane and the same direction. Pluto's orbit cuts across at an angle and at times swings nearer to the Sun than Neptune. The farther a planet is from the Sun, the longer it takes to orbit.

Jupiter

*Orbits*

**The Solar System**
*The nine planets circle in their own orbits around the Sun.*

Sun

Venus

Mercury

Earth

Mars

Asteroid belt

Saturn

## Terrestrial planet

One of the four rocky planets nearest the Sun

The four rocky planets are Mercury, Venus, Earth, and Mars. Each has a core of hot iron and a rocky crust. **Mercury** is so close to the Sun that during the day temperatures can soar to 800°F (425°C), but because it has almost no atmosphere to hold in the heat, nights can plummet to −290°F (−180°C). **Venus** is the nearest planet to the Earth. It is also the brightest object in the night sky apart from the Moon, because it is shrouded in dense white clouds that reflect the Sun. These clouds seal in the Sun's heat, creating a perpetual greenhouse effect ■, boosting surface temperatures to over 880°F (470°C). The **Earth** is the only planet with an atmosphere ■ capable of sustaining life. **Mars** is known as the red planet because of the reddish iron oxide dust spread across its surface of craters, chasms, and giant volcanoes. Like the Earth, Mars has polar ice caps of frozen water, and may also have frozen water underground.

## Nebular hypothesis

The idea that the Solar System formed from clouds of gas and dust

About five billion years ago, the Solar System was probably just a nebula ■ – a spinning cloud of dust and gas. Gradually, however, the center of the cloud condensed and shrank to form the Sun. The gas planets (Jupiter, Saturn, Uranus, and Neptune) formed in the same way as they clumped together. The terrestrial planets (Mercury, Venus, Earth, and Mars) may also have formed like this, or they may be debris flung off by the new-born Sun that condensed into rocky lumps called **planetesimals**.

## Gas planet

One of the four outer planets made mainly of gas

Each of the four big outer planets of the system – Jupiter, Saturn, Uranus, and Neptune – are made largely of hydrogen, with just small, rocky cores. **Jupiter** is the biggest, with a diameter over 11 times bigger than that of the Earth, but it takes just 10 hours to rotate on its axis. Its surface is swathed in belts of gas, in which there is a huge swirl called the **Great Red Spot**, just below the planet's equator ▪. **Saturn's** beautiful rings of tiny ice-coated fragments are clearly visible through a telescope. Saturn has such a low density that it would actually float if you could find an ocean big enough to put it in. **Uranus** is blue-green because of the methane gas, mixed in with hydrogen and helium, in its outer layers. Its axis ▪ is tilted over at 98° – compared with 23.5° for the Earth. **Neptune** is similar to Uranus, but because there is less methane in its outer layers it appears pale blue. It has a **Great Dark Spot** similar to Jupiter's Great Red Spot.

Uranus

## Pluto

The outermost of all the planets in the Solar System

Pluto is so far from the Sun's heat that it is incredibly cold. It is made mostly of ice and frozen gases, and temperatures on the surface can plunge below –380°F (–230°C). Pluto is also the smallest of the planets, with a diameter less than one fifth of that of the Earth and smaller than the Moon. It has a moon called Charon, which is over half the size of Pluto itself.

Pluto

Neptune

## Comet

An icy, rocky lump orbiting the Sun

Comets are thought to have come from a vast cloud of material known as **Oort's Cloud.** This cloud surrounds the outer fringes of the Solar System beyond Pluto. Every so often, lumps from the cloud travel toward the Sun. These can sometimes be seen shooting through the night sky with a long tail trailing out behind. The heart of a comet is like a dirty snowball less than 0.62 mile (1 km) across, surrounded by a halo, or **coma**, of gas and dust. The tail is also a trail of gas and dust.

## Nicolas Copernicus

Polish astronomer (1473–1543)

Copernicus was a priest at Frauenberg Cathedral in Germany. He also spent many years studying the night sky. Copernicus showed that the planets, including the Earth, circle around the Sun – not around the Earth, as had previously been thought.

## Asteroid

A small rocky planet orbiting the Sun

Most asteroids orbit the Sun in the **asteroid belt** between Mars and Jupiter. The largest of them, Ceres, is 570 miles (920 km) in diameter, but most are smaller than this. Billions of tiny lumps called **meteoroids** also hurtle through the Solar System. When they enter the Earth's atmosphere they are called **meteors**. Many burn up as they hit the Earth's atmosphere, but a few larger ones reach the ground as **meteorites**. The surface of the Moon is pitted with craters made by meteor impacts because there is no protective atmosphere.

## Moon

A natural satellite of a planet

Most planets have another body orbiting around them. These bodies are smaller than the planet itself. The Earth's Moon, for example, has a diameter 27 percent the size of the diameter of the Earth.

### See also

### PLANETARY STATISTICS

| Planet | Diameter | Average distance from Sun | Time taken to orbit Sun | Number of moons |
| --- | --- | --- | --- | --- |
| Mercury | 3031 miles | 36,000,000 miles | 88 days | 0 |
| Venus | 7,520 miles | 67,200,000 miles | 225 days | 0 |
| Earth | 7,926 miles | 93,000,000 miles | 365 days | 1 |
| Mars | 4,217 miles | 141,600,000 miles | 687 days | 2 |
| Jupiter | 88,846 miles | 483,600,000 miles | 12 years | 16 |
| Saturn | 74,898 miles | 887,000,000 miles | 29 years | 18 |
| Uranus | 31,763 miles | 1,784,000,000 miles | 84 years | 15 |
| Neptune | 30,775 miles | 2,794,000,000 miles | 165 years | 8 |
| Pluto | 1,419 miles | 3,675,000,000 miles | 249 years | 1 |

*Background picture:* the Moon's surface        **NB** 1 mile = 1.609 kilometers

# Earth, Sun, & Moon

The Earth may seem still beneath your feet, but it is really spinning like a top and hurtling around the Sun. Orbited by its companion, the Moon, the Earth travels at more than 65,000 mph (105,000 kph), covering millions of miles each year as it journeys through space.

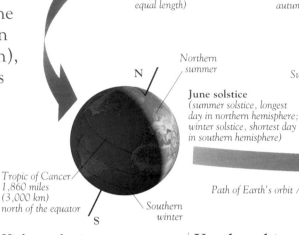

*Equator*

**March equinox** *(day and night are equal length)*

S

*Northern spring*

*Southern autumn*

N

*Northern summer*

*Sun*

**June solstice** *(summer solstice, longest day in northern hemisphere; winter solstice, shortest day in southern hemisphere)*

N

*Tropic of Cancer 1,860 miles (3,000 km) north of the equator*

*Southern winter*

S

*Path of Earth's orbit*

## Earth's rotation

The daily turning of the Earth

The Earth spins around once every 24 hours. It turns first toward the Sun ■, giving us daylight, and then away from the Sun, giving us night. The **Earth's axis** is the line around which the planet turns. It runs through the Earth from north to south; the northern end is the **North Pole** and the southern end is the **South Pole**. The Earth's axis is not quite at right angles to the Sun, but tilts over at an angle of 23.5° – this is the **angle of inclination**. Although the Earth is tilted over, it still orbits the Sun in a constant plane, known as the **plane of the ecliptic**. The equator ■ cuts across this plane at an angle of 23.5°.

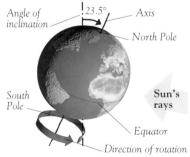

*Angle of inclination*

!23.5°

*Axis*

*North Pole*

*South Pole*

**Sun's rays**

*Equator*

*Direction of rotation*

### The rotating Earth
*Because the Earth rotates in a west-east direction, we see the Sun rising every day in the east and sinking in the west.*

### High-speed spin
*Different places on the Earth's surface move at different speeds. Places near the Poles barely move at all, while those on the equator zoom around at more than more than 1,000 mph (1,600 kph).*

## Calendar year

The time it takes for the same date to come around again

Because the Earth takes just over 365 days to go once around the Sun, the Western calendar year is 365 days long. This means the Sun is always at the same place in the sky on the same date each year. This is not true of the Muslim year, which has 354 or 355 days, or the Jewish year, which varies between 353 and 385 days. But even with the 365-day year, the Sun is not quite in step with the calendar because the Earth actually takes 365.242 days to complete its annual journey. To compensate for this, the Western calendar adds an extra day to every fourth year, called a **leap year**, but misses out a leap year three centuries out of four.

## Yearly orbit

The Earth's path around the Sun

The Earth travels 584,018,150 miles (939,886,400 km) in a single orbit. As the orbit is not a perfect circle but an ellipse (an oval), the Earth is closer to the Sun at some times and farther away at others. Its closest point, the **perihelion**, is 91,402,300 miles (147,097,800 km), and occurs on January 3. Its farthest point, the **aphelion**, is 94,509,400 miles (152,098,200 km), and occurs on July 4.

## Solar day

The time between two successive noons

A solar day lasts 24 hours. A **sidereal day** is measured by how long it takes the star pattern to return to the same position in the sky – 23 hours, 56 minutes, and 4.09 seconds. A solar day is longer, as the Earth travels a little way around the Sun each day. This means that the Earth must rotate an extra 1° before the Sun returns to the same place in the sky.

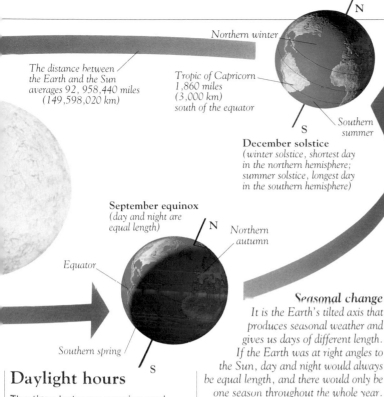

The distance between the Earth and the Sun averages 92, 958, 440 miles (149,598,020 km)

*Northern winter*

*Tropic of Capricorn 1,860 miles (3,000 km) south of the equator*

*Southern summer*

*S*

**December solstice**
*(winter solstice, shortest day in the northern hemisphere; summer solstice, longest day in the southern hemisphere)*

**September equinox**
*(day and night are equal length)*

*N*

*Northern autumn*

*Equator*

*Southern spring*

*S*

## Season

One of the four weather periods of each year

As the Earth travels around the Sun, the tilt of the Earth's axis means that each place leans gradually nearer to the Sun, and then farther away from it. This gives four distinct phases of weather.

**Summer** is when your part of the world leans toward the Sun. The Sun climbs high in the sky, making the days long and the weather warm. In **autumn**, the Earth begins to tilt you away from the Sun, bringing cooler weather. In **winter**, you are tilted farthest away from the Sun. The Sun is low in the sky, and days are short and sometimes very cold. In **spring**, the Earth begins to tilt you back toward the Sun again.

*Seasonal change*
*It is the Earth's tilted axis that produces seasonal weather and gives us days of different length. If the Earth was at right angles to the Sun, day and night would always be equal length, and there would only be one season throughout the whole year.*

***Northern summer***
*As the northern hemisphere tilts toward the Sun, it brings warm summer days.*

## Daylight hours

The time between sunrise and sunset

The tilt of the Earth's axis means that daylight varies throughout the year. It varies most at the Poles, where it is never completely dark in summer and never completely light in winter. It varies least at the equator, where there are always about 12 hours of daylight.

## Tropics

The area either side of the equator in which the midday Sun is directly overhead

The Sun is overhead at midday at the equator about March 21. For the next three months, the zone in which the midday Sun is overhead moves north. By about June 22 it has reached a line of latitude ▦ called the **Tropic of Cancer**. For the next six months, the overhead Sun moves south. It reaches a line of latitude equally far south of the equator, called the **Tropic of Capricorn**, around December 22. It then begins to move north again.

## Solstice

The time when the midday Sun is directly overhead at one of the tropics

There are two solstices each year, called the **summer solstice** and the **winter solstice**, depending on the season during which they occur. The first is around June 22, when the Sun is overhead at the Tropic of Cancer (23°30' N), giving the longest day in the northern hemisphere and the shortest in the southern hemisphere. The second occurs around December 22, when the Sun is overhead at the Tropic of Capricorn (23°30' S), giving the shortest day in the northern hemisphere and the longest day in the southern hemisphere. Midway between the solstices are the **equinoxes**, around March 21 and September 22, when the overhead Sun crosses the equator. At the equinoxes, day and night are equally long (12 hours) throughout the world.

***Northern winter***
*As the Earth orbits the Sun, the northern hemisphere gradually tilts away from the Sun's heat, bringing cooler winter days.*

### See also

Equator 37 • Latitude 37
Longitude 37 • Sun 32

*Continued on next page ➤*

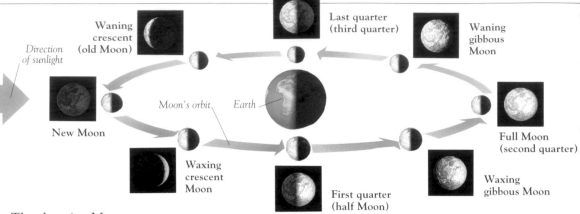

*Direction of sunlight*

Waning crescent (old Moon)

Last quarter (third quarter)

Waning gibbous Moon

New Moon

*Moon's orbit*  *Earth*

Full Moon (second quarter)

Waxing crescent Moon

First quarter (half Moon)

Waxing gibbous Moon

### The changing Moon

*The Moon has a bright side lit by the Sun, and a dark side not visible from Earth. As the Moon circles the Earth, we see varying amounts of its bright side.*

## Time zone

An area of the world where clocks record the same time

As the Earth rotates ■, the Sun is always rising in one place and setting in another, so the time of day varies around the world. When it is dawn in the US, for example, it may be noon in Europe, and sunset in Australia. To make it easier to set clocks, the world is divided into 24 time zones, one for each hour of the day. As you go east around the world, you put clocks forward by one hour for each time zone you pass through – until you reach a line running through the Pacific Ocean called the **International Date Line**. When you cross the Date Line, you continue to put the clock forward, but put the date on the calendar back by one day. The width of each time zone is about 15° of longitude ■. The time at 0° longitude is called **Greenwich Mean Time**. The Date Line roughly follows the 180° meridian ■.

### See also

Earth's rotation 34 • Longitude 37
Meridian 37 • Moon 33

## Phases of the Moon

Changes in the Moon's visible shape

A **New Moon** ■ is when the Moon is completely dark; a **Full Moon** is when we see all of its bright side. The Moon is said to be **waxing** as it grows from a New to a Full Moon over two weeks, and **waning** as it shrinks back to a New Moon over the next two weeks. A waxing or waning Moon seems to bulge on the side nearest the Sun, so it is often called **gibbous**.

## Lunar month

The time it takes for the Moon to go through all its phases

It takes the Moon 27.3 days to circle the Earth, but it takes 29.53 days to go from one Full Moon to the next, because the Earth moves as well as the Moon. A cycle of 29.53 days is a lunar month.

## Solar eclipse

When the Moon passes directly between the Sun and Earth

The New Moon occasionally passes directly between the Sun and the Earth. In some parts of the world this causes a **total eclipse**, during which the Sun completely disappears behind the Moon. Over a much wider area, however, the eclipse is **partial**, which means that the Moon obscures only part of the Sun's disk. A **lunar eclipse** occurs when the Moon passes into the Earth's shadow and appears very dark, or dark red in color.

### Eclipses of the Sun and Moon

*During a solar eclipse, people in the area where the Moon's inner shadow falls see a total eclipse; those under the outer shadow see a partial eclipse. At a lunar eclipse, the Moon is still faintly lit by light rays bent by the Earth's atmosphere.*

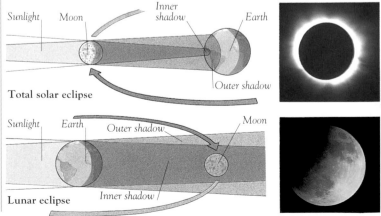

*Sunlight*  *Moon*  Inner shadow  *Earth*

Total solar eclipse

Outer shadow

*Sunlight*  *Earth*  Outer shadow  *Moon*

Lunar eclipse  Inner shadow

◀ *Continued from previous page*

# The shape of the Earth

Recent pictures taken from space have finally shown what people worked out long ago yet could never see for themselves – that the Earth is round.

## Geoid

**An Earth-shaped object**

The Earth is not a perfect sphere. It spins faster at the equator than at the Poles, so it is flung out more at the equator. As a result, it has an equatorial bulge and flattened Poles. The Earth was once described as an **oblate spheroid**, or flattened sphere. It is now simply called a geoid, because satellite measurements have revealed many irregularities.

## Earth's circumference

**The distance around the equator**

Modern measurements show that the distance around the Earth is 24,870 miles (40,024 km) at the equator. Its diameter at the equator is 7,927 miles (12,758 km). This is very slightly larger, by 26.7 miles (43 km), than the vertical diameter at the Poles. The equatorial bulge is 26 ft. (8 m) bigger at some places south of the equator than north of it.

### See also

Earth's rotation 34 • Globe 38
Great circle 38 • Map projection 38

*North Pole*

90°
75°
60°
45°
30°
15°

*Equator (0° parallel)*

**Southern Hemisphere**

60° 45° 30° 15° 0°

*45° W meridian*   *South Pole*   *Prime meridian (0°)*

### Dividing up the world
*Mapping and navigation are made easier by dividing the globe with meridians (lines of longitude) and parallels (lines of latitude). Both are measured in degrees, as if taken as an angle from the center of the Earth. Any point on the Earth can be described using these lines. On the globe above, the point X is at 45° N, 30° E.*

## Latitude

**A north-south division of the Earth**

Lines of latitude are imaginary circles, or **parallels**, drawn around the Earth parallel to the equator. Positions of latitude are given in degrees north or south of the equator. The equator itself has a latitude of 0°, the North Pole a latitude of 90° N, and the South Pole a latitude of 90° S.

## Equator

**A line midway between the Poles**

The equator divides the world precisely into two halves. The half to the north is the **Northern Hemisphere**, and the half to the south is called the **Southern Hemisphere**. The equator is at 90° to the Earth's axis.

*45° N parallel*

*30° N parallel*

**Northern Hemisphere**

## Longitude

**An east-west division of the Earth**

It is possible to pinpoint just how far east or west any place is in terms of longitude. Lines of longitude are imaginary lines or **meridians** drawn around the world from the North Pole to the South Pole. These divide the world into 360 **degrees** (°), like the segments of an orange. The **prime meridian**, 0°, runs through Greenwich in England. Positions in terms of longitude are given in degrees east or west of this line.

***Illuminated meridian***
*Since 1851, the prime meridian (0°) has been defined by a north-south line passing through the Royal Observatory at Greenwich, England.*

*Continued on next page* ➤

# Globe

A sphere representing the Earth or another planet

A globe is by far the best way to represent the world, because the Earth is round. All flat maps involve some distortion, but on a well-made globe the continents and oceans appear in their correct shapes and proportions. This makes it easy to plot the shortest route over vast distances. Most globes are made by printing the surface details on 12 or more flat, shield-shaped paper segments called **gores**. The printed gores are then stuck carefully onto a plain sphere to complete the globe. **Relief globes**, which show height differences on the Earth's surface, are usually made in a mold.

*Gores*

*Unpeeling a globe*
*This model shows the construction of a globe. Surface details are usually printed on a number of flat paper gores, which are then wrapped around a sphere.*

## See also

Equator 37 • Grid system 22
Hemisphere 37 • Latitude 37
Longitude 37 • Map 22
Parallel 37 • Summer solstice 35

# Map projection

A way of showing the Earth's curved surface on a flat map

Map projections are made as if light is shone through a globe to project the grid ■ of latitude ■ and longitude ■ lines onto paper. **Cartographers** make maps ■ mathematically, rather than by projecting light, but the principle remains the same. The grid provides the basis for the accurate placing of geographical features. There are many different projections, but all are a compromise, showing some features accurately while allowing others to be distorted.

# Great circle

A line corresponding with the circumference of the Earth

The equator ■ is the best known great circle, but a line drawn around the globe in any direction is a great circle as long as it is drawn at the globe's widest point. The shortest route between two points on a globe is along a great circle that runs through both points. Only one map projection – a type of planar projection called a **gnomonic projection** – shows great circles as straight lines. This means that navigators usually have to plot a curved course if they want to take the shortest route.

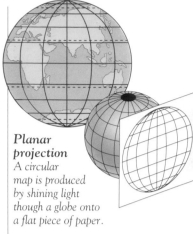

*Planar projection*
*A circular map is produced by shining light though a globe onto a flat piece of paper.*

# Planar projection

A map projection onto a flat surface

Planar projections are also called **azimuthal** or **zenithal projections**. They are made as if a light is shone through half a globe onto a flat piece of paper. They are essentially circular maps, although they can be cut to form rectangles. This means that they can show only half the Earth at once. Most planar maps are centered on one of the Poles, so that they show either the northern or southern hemisphere ■. But the center, or **azimuth**, can be placed anywhere. Planar projections show the true direction between two points.

# Conformal map

A map that shows shapes accurately

No map can show the shape of large areas such as continents with absolute accuracy, but conformal maps show smaller shapes such as islands well. To do this, the lines of latitude and longitude on the map must cross at right angles, just as they do on a globe. Similarly, no map can show a constant scale for large distances, but **equidistant maps** give accurate distances in a certain direction or radiating from a certain point. **Equal-area maps** give the true area of every place shown, but distort shape.

◄ Continued from previous page

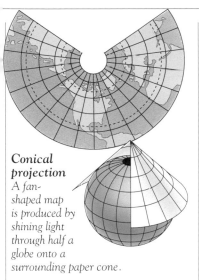

*Conical projection*
*A fan-shaped map is produced by shining light through half a globe onto a surrounding paper cone.*

## Conical projection

A map projection onto a cone

Conical projections are made as if light is shone through half a globe onto a paper cone wrapped around the globe. When the cone is unrolled, it gives a flat map that is a compromise between planar and cylindrical maps. These maps show shapes almost as accurately as cylindrical maps, but do not grossly distort countries at high latitudes. They are very accurate near the **standard parallel** ▪, which is the line of latitude where the cone touches the globe.

## Rhumb line

A straight course indicated by a compass

Direction is particularly difficult to show accurately on maps, yet it is crucial for steering aircraft and ships. A map may correctly show the location of an aircraft's destination but not the **compass heading** – that is, the direction that the pilot needs to follow. This is because the Earth's surface is curved, so a compass heading that is straight in reality (a rhumb line) appears as a curve on a map. Only with a Mercator projection is a straight line on the map a rhumb line in reality.

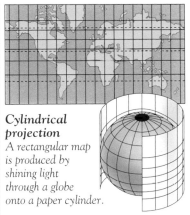

*Cylindrical projection*
*A rectangular map is produced by shining light through a globe onto a paper cylinder.*

## Cylindrical projection

A map projection onto a cylinder

Cylindrical projections are made as if light is shone from the center of a globe onto a surrounding cylinder of paper. The cylinder is then rolled out flat to make the map. This projection has the advantage that it can show the entire Earth on a single map. Most cylindrical projections are conformal, and show shapes accurately. But countries near the Poles, such as Greenland, are exaggerated in size, and tropical countries such as India appear shrunken.

## Mercator projection

A cylindrical map projection widely used for navigation

A Mercator projection is made mathematically, by plotting the lines of latitude so that the distance between them increases as the lines move farther away from the equator. It was devised by the Dutch mapmaker **Gerardus Mercator** (1512–1594).

*Navigational aid*
*Mercator maps are widely used for navigation because straight courses can be plotted simply by drawing a straight line and the shapes of continents are accurate.*

# Inside the Earth

People once thought that the Earth was completely solid, but scientific interpretation of vibrations from earthquakes has revealed a more complex structure. We now know that the Earth has a soft interior beneath its rigid shell, and a core of solid metal.

Atmosphere

Crust

Mantle

Outer core

## Global seismology

The study of the Earth's structure using vibrations from earthquakes and explosions

Seismic waves ■ are vibrations that radiate from an earthquake ■. These waves shudder through the body of the Earth as well as along its surface. Body waves ■ are known as primary (P) waves ■ and secondary (S) waves ■. Like light rays passing through a lens, the waves are refracted, or bent, as they pass through the different layers inside the Earth. The way in which the body waves bend helps scientists to understand the Earth's true structure. **Seismic tomography** uses computers to build up three-dimensional images of variations in the density and temperature of the mantle from crisscrossing body waves. **Seismic reflection profiles** are cross-sections of the Earth's interior made by studying the reflection of sound vibrations set off by a long line of large explosions. A **shadow zone** is an area through which no waves from a distant earthquake pass.

*Seismic waves*
*The movement of S waves and P waves through the Earth tells scientists about the Earth's interior.*

P wave

S wave

Focus of earthquake

## Crust

The Earth's hard outer shell

The Earth is made up of three layers, or concentric shells. The innermost shell is the core, the middle shell is the mantle, and outermost is the crust. Each shell has a different chemical composition ■. The crust, the thin topmost layer, floats upon the softer, denser mantle.

## Oceanic crust

The part of the Earth's crust under the oceans

The crust is thinnest under the oceans, varying from 4–7 miles (6–11 km) thick. The rocks of the oceanic crust are relatively young – none is older than 200 million years.

S waves pass only through the mantle

The core refracts P waves, so no waves emerge in the shadow zone

P waves pass through the mantle and core

Inner core

Outer core

Mantle

Shadow zone

Crust

## Continental crust

The part of the Earth's crust under the continents

The crust is thickest under the continents, averaging 19–25 miles (30–40 km) but extending as far as 43 miles (70 km) beneath the biggest mountain ranges. It is older than oceanic crust – some rocks date back 3.8 billion years. It floats on the mantle in a state of balance called isostasy ■.

## Basement

The bulk of ancient rock that makes up a continent

The continental crust is mostly ancient crystalline rock. This "basement" rock is divided into two layers. The upper half consists mainly of granitelike ■ rocks, schists ■, and gneisses ■, while the lower half is made up of basalt ■ and diorite ■.

## Discontinuity

A boundary between the layers of the Earth's interior

The **Mohorovicic discontinuity**, or **Moho**, is the boundary between the crust and the mantle, while the **Gutenberg discontinuity** separates the core and the mantle.

## Mantle

The soft interior of the Earth that lies above the core

Just under the crust is the mantle. It is about 1,800 miles (2,900 km) thick and makes up nearly 80 percent of the Earth's total volume. It is made largely of a rock called peridotite ▦, which is sometimes thrown up onto the surface by volcanic eruptions. The mantle rock is so hot that it is often partially molten.

**Earth cutaway**
*Here sections of the Earth have been removed to show its internal structure.*

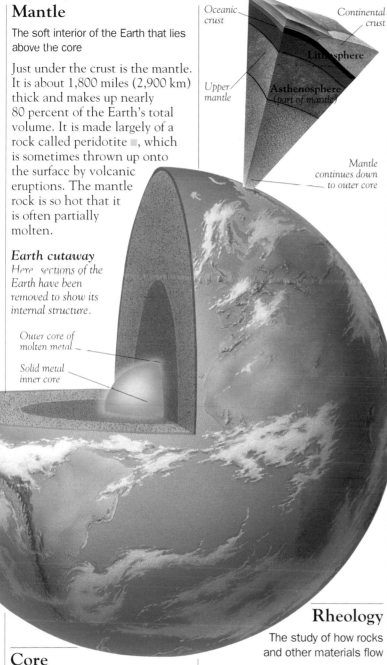

Oceanic crust

Continental crust

Lithosphere

Upper mantle

Asthenosphere (part of mantle)

Mantle continues down to outer core

Outer core of molten metal

Solid metal inner core

## Lithosphere

The rigid upper layer of the Earth

The lithosphere consists of the crust and the rigid upper layers of the mantle. The average thickness is about 62 miles (100 km) but it varies from just a few miles under the oceans to 186 miles (300 km) under the continents.

## Asthenosphere

The soft layer of the Earth under the lithosphere

The temperature of the Earth's interior increases with depth. About 62 miles (100 km) down, the temperature reaches 2,600°F (1,400°C). This is enough to melt some of the material in the mantle rock. As a result, the rock is able to flow slowly, creating a soft layer about 124 miles (200 km) thick called the asthenosphere, on which the rigid lithosphere floats like ice on a pond.

## Mesosphere

The layer of the mantle under the asthenosphere

Little is known of the mesosphere, but it is thought to flow less easily than the asthenosphere.

## Borehole

A hole drilled into the Earth to gain information about the rocks below

Because no drill has ever gone deeper than 9 miles (15 km) boreholes can only tell us about the rocks in the Earth's crust.

## Rheology

The study of how rocks and other materials flow

## Core

The metallic center of the Earth

The core of the Earth is a dense ball of the elements ▦ iron and nickel. The **outer core** is so hot that the metal is always molten, but in the **inner core** pressures are so great that it cannot melt, even though temperatures there reach 6,700°F (3,700°C).

The crust and the upper mantle are chemically different, but they behave in similar ways. Geologists studying plate tectonics ▦ prefer to identify the Earth's layers not by their chemical makeup, but according to how easily they flow. They call these layers the lithosphere, the asthenosphere, and the mesosphere.

### See also

# The Earth's chemistry

We cannot be certain what the Earth is made of, since it is impossible to take rock samples from depths greater than about 9 miles (15 kilometers). But we can get a good idea by studying the Sun and other planets, and by analyzing meteorites.

## Element

A basic chemical substance

Everything in the universe is made up of minute particles called **atoms**. An atom itself contains even smaller particles: **protons** and **neutrons** cluster in the atom's center or **nucleus** (plural: **nuclei**), which is orbited by **electrons**. There are about 109 different types of atom. Each has a different number of electrons and protons, and its own particular weight or **atomic mass**. An atom is the smallest part of an element that can exist independently. Just as there are 109 different types of atom, so there are 109 different elements. Every other substance is made from different combinations of these elements, either joined chemically as **compounds** or simply mixed together. A group of two or more atoms linked together is a **molecule**.

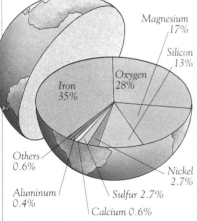

*Magnesium 17%*
*Silicon 13%*
*Oxygen 28%*
*Iron 35%*
*Others 0.6%*
*Nickel 2.7%*
*Aluminum 0.4%*
*Sulfur 2.7%*
*Calcium 0.6%*

**Elemental Earth**
*This model shows the proportions of the elements that make up the Earth.*

## Bulk composition

The chemical make up of the Earth

More than 80 elements occur naturally on the Earth. But the bulk of the Earth is made of iron, oxygen, magnesium, and silicon. The evidence for this comes from geophysical data produced by seismic surveys ■, gravimetric surveys ■, and magnetic surveys ■, as well as knowledge of the composition of stars, meteorites, and the rest of the Solar System.

## Crustal chemicals

The chemicals in the Earth's crust

The dominant crustal elements are oxygen and silicon, followed by aluminum, iron, calcium, magnesium, sodium, potassium, and titanium. The crust ■ also has small quantities of 64 other elements, including manganese and hydrogen.

## Mantle chemicals

The chemicals in the Earth's mantle

The chemicals of the upper mantle ■ are probably silicates ■ of iron and magnesium; the lower mantle is mostly sulfides ■ and oxides ■ of silicon and magnesium.

## Core chemicals

The elements in the Earth's core

The core ■ is mostly iron, plus a little nickel and tiny quantities of some lighter elements – possibly sulfur, carbon, oxygen, silicon, and potassium.

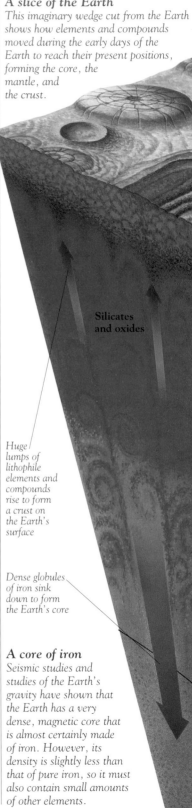

**A slice of the Earth**
*This imaginary wedge cut from the Earth shows how elements and compounds moved during the early days of the Earth to reach their present positions, forming the core, the mantle, and the crust.*

**Silicates and oxides**

*Huge lumps of lithophile elements and compounds rise to form a crust on the Earth's surface*

*Dense globules of iron sink down to form the Earth's core*

**A core of iron**
*Seismic studies and studies of the Earth's gravity have shown that the Earth has a very dense, magnetic core that is almost certainly made of iron. However, its density is slightly less than that of pure iron, so it must also contain small amounts of other elements.*

## Crustal composition

*Analysis of rock samples and seismic studies show that the most abundant crustal elements are oxygen and silicon – light elements that drifted to the surface as the molten Earth slowly cooled.*

Crust

Mantle

Sulphides

*Large blobs of chalcophile elements and compounds spread upward and out, like clouds, to form the mantle*

Siderophiles

Outer Core

Inner Core

## Mantle makeup

*Geochemists believe that the upper mantle mainly consists of silicates of iron and magnesium, while in the lower mantle oxides and sulfides of silicon and magnesium are more common.*

# Lithophile

An element that easily forms compounds with oxygen and silicon

As the young Earth slowly cooled, heavy elements such as iron sank toward the Earth's center. Lighter elements such as oxygen and silicon drifted up to the surface to form the crust. Some heavy elements such as uranium and thorium also ended up in the crust, despite their weight. This is because they combine readily with oxygen to make compounds called **oxides**, and with oxygen and silicon to make compounds called **silicates**. **Chalcophile** elements such as zinc and lead, on the other hand, join easily with sulfur to form **sulfide** compounds. Sulfides are found mainly in the mantle. **Siderophile** elements such as nickel and gold combine readily with iron and are probably concentrated in the core.

# Solar composition

The Sun's chemical makeup

Analysis of sunlight shows that the Sun ▪ is mostly hydrogen and helium, with small amounts of other elements. Because the Earth formed from the same cloud of dust and gas as the Sun, it is very likely that the Earth started with the same basic makeup. Most of the helium and hydrogen was probably lost in the early stages of the Earth's life.

Hydrogen 72%

Helium 25%

Other elements 3%

## Solar elements

*Like other stars, the Sun is made up almost entirely of the elements hydrogen and helium.*

## Rocks from space

*The Earth may have formed from the same space debris of which meteorites are made. Most meteorites are either chondrites or achondrites.*

Chondrite

Achondrite

# Chondrite model

The idea that the Earth's composition is like that of meteorites

There are two main types of meteorite: **iron** and **stony**, perhaps reflecting the Earth's iron core and stony mantle. Almost 90 percent of all meteorites falling on the Earth are stony and made largely of silicates. Stony meteorites are divided into chondrites and achondrites. **Chondrites** get their name because they contain **chondrules**, once-molten globules of silicate. **Achondrites** do not contain chondrules. Chondrites appear to have altered little since they were formed in the earliest days of the Solar System. Still locked within a particular kind of chondrite, called a **carbonaceous chondrite**, are bubbles of carbon dioxide gas, which shows that they have hardly changed at all. Some geochemists believe that the Earth's composition may be similar to that of carbonaceous chondrites.

## See also

Core 41 • Crust 40
Gravimetric survey 171 • Mantle 41
Magnetic survey 170 • Oxide 83
Seismic survey 171 • Silicate 82
Sulfide 82 • Sun 32

# Magnetic Earth

Because of its dense core of iron, the Earth is like a giant magnet. Sailors and navigators have used its magnetic properties to find their way for thousands of years. Today, traces of the Earth's magnetic past are helping geologists to find out about the history of our planet.

## Magnetic north pole

The direction in which a magnetic compass points

The magnetism of the Earth's core is so powerful that it affects every magnet on Earth. When a magnet is allowed to swing freely, one end always ends up pointing to the magnetic north pole and the other to the **magnetic south pole**. **Compass needles** are simply tiny magnets that rotate until they point to magnetic north. The position of the magnetic north pole varies all the time. It is now on Prince of Wales Island in northern Canada, while the magnetic south pole is in South Victoria Land, Antarctica.

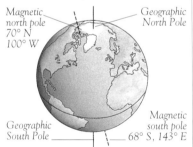

Magnetic north pole 70° N 100° W

Geographic North Pole

Geographic South Pole

Magnetic south pole 68° S, 143° E

***One Earth, four poles***
*The picture above shows the current positions of the magnetic poles in relation to true north and true south.*

### See also

Atmosphere 138 • Atom 42
Continental drift 46 • Core 41
Magnetite 85 • Mineral 82
Molecule 42 • Seafloor spreading 50
Volcanic rock 88

## Geomagnetic field

The region affected by the Earth's magnetism

The Earth's magnetism, or **geomagnetism**, may be caused by the way in which the intense heat at the center of the Earth keeps its fluid outer core moving. The core is rich in magnetic material such as iron, so this circulation generates electricity, similar to a dynamo on a bicycle. The resulting electric currents create the geomagnetic field. The field is constantly varying from place to place and from time to time. Some changes are short term, or **transient**; some are long term, or **secular**.

## Magnetic declination

The angle between true north and magnetic north

Compass needles always point to magnetic north, rather than to the Earth's geographic North Pole, or **true north**. To steer a course by compass, you need to know the magnetic declination and then make adjustments. Maps that show the magnetic declination are called **isogonic maps**. Because declination varies from place to place and from time to time, isogonic maps frequently have to be updated. On an isogonic map, points with the same declination are linked by **isogonic lines**.

## Magnetic mineral

A naturally magnetic substance

Magnetism is induced artificially in compass needles, but some minerals ■ are naturally magnetic. Two strongly magnetic common minerals are **pyrrhotine** and magnetite ■, or **lodestone**. Both are compounds of iron.

***Magnetic rock***
*Magnetite is permanently magnetized. It attracts iron or steel objects such as paper clips and iron filings. It was used in compasses more than 1,500 years ago.*

## Magnetic dip

The tilt of a free-swinging magnet

A free-swinging magnet not only points north, but also tilts down. The angle at which it tilts from the horizontal is called the dip, or **magnetic inclination**. This angle varies from virtually 0° at the equator to almost 90° (straight down) at the magnetic poles.

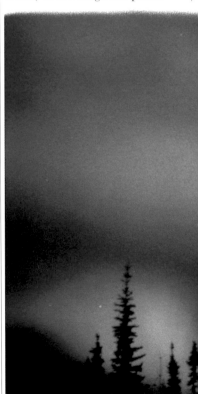

# Paleomagnetism

The study of the Earth's magnetic history

Most volcanic rocks ▦ contain particles of a magnetic substance called iron oxide. When the rock forms, these particles align with the Earth's magnetic field, each acting like a minute compass. This provides a permanent record of the direction of the magnetic field at the time the rock formed. Studying these particles reveals that the magnetic north and south poles are continually alternating. This is called **geomagnetic polarity reversal**, or simply **magnetic reversal**. Plotting these reversals in seafloor rocks – called **magnetic stripes** – has proved the theory of seafloor spreading ▦. Paleomagnetism supports the idea of continental drift ▦, since it can be used to map the paths the continents took as they drifted over the Earth millions of years ago.

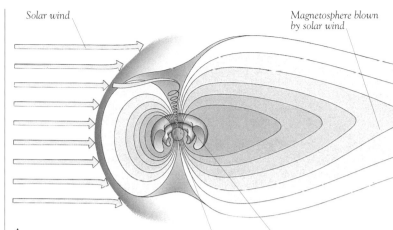

Solar wind

Magnetosphere blown by solar wind

Earth    Van Allen radiation belts

*The Earth's magnetosphere*
*The solar wind is deflected away from Earth by the magnetosphere. But some charged particles are trapped by the Van Allen radiation belts. Others enter the atmosphere through gaps in the magnetosphere over the magnetic poles, causing auroras.*

# Aurora

Spectacular colored lights seen in the night sky above polar regions

The **aurora borealis**, or **Northern Lights**, are seen in or near the Arctic; the **aurora australis**, or **Southern Lights**, are seen in or near the Antarctic. Auroras are thought to be caused by charged particles from the Sun striking atoms ▦ and molecules ▦ in the Earth's upper atmosphere ▦.

# Magnetosphere

The area around the Earth where the geomagnetic field stretches out into space

The influence of the Earth's magnetism is not limited to magnets and other materials on the planet's surface. It also affects electrically charged particles beyond the Earth's atmosphere, reaching more than 37,000 miles (60,000 km) into space. On the side of the Earth facing away from the Sun, it stretches four times this distance. This is because it is blown out of shape by the **solar wind** – the constant stream of electrically charged particles that rushes outward from the Sun. The solar wind probably causes auroras.

*Alaskan aurora*
*This picture shows the night sky over Alaska aglow with the Northern Lights. Auroras occur at high latitudes, and may take the form of rays, arcs, bands, streamers, and even pulsating "curtains" of light, often colored red or green.*

# Plate tectonics

Even as you read this page, continents are splitting apart and crunching together, new oceans are opening up and old ones are being crushed out of existence. This is because the Earth's crust is made up of a number of moving pieces, or plates, that are always colliding or pulling apart.

*Eye socket* *Nostril* **Lystrosaurus skull**

*Tooth*

## Continental drift

The theory that the continents have slowly drifted across the surface of the Earth over millions of years

A look at a world map shows how well the east coast of South America would fit into the west coast of Africa. This is because they were once joined together. About 220 million years ago the world's continents were all part of a giant supercontinent now known as **Pangaea**. This was surrounded by a vast ocean called **Panthalassa**. Pangaea split, and a long arm of ocean called the **Tethys Sea** opened up. The fragment to the south was **Gondwanaland**. It included South America, India, Africa, Sri Lanka, Madagascar, New Zealand, Australia, and Antarctica. To the north was **Laurasia**, which included Asia, Europe, North America, and Greenland. Laurasia and Gondwanaland eventually broke up as the Atlantic Ocean formed.

### See also

Conservative margin 50
Constructive margin 50 • Crust 40
Destructive margin 48 • Earthquake 58
Fossil 70 • Lithosphere 41 • Mantle 41
Mid-ocean ridge 50 • Mountain 64
Sea-floor spreading 50 • Strata 68
Triangulation 16 • Volcano 52

**Pangaean reptile**
*Lystrosaurus was probably a semiaquatic, herbivorous reptile. It had only two teeth in its massive jaws.*

## Lystrosaurus

A reptile of southern Pangaea

*Lystrosaurus* lived in Africa, India, and China 200 million years ago. The discovery in the 1960s of a fossil of *Lystrosaurus* in Antarctica was evidence to support the idea of continental drift. The only plausible explanation was that all these continents were once joined. Similar proof has come from the discovery of fossils of the reptile **Mesosaurus** in Africa and South America, of the fern **Glossopteris** in Australia and India, and of the insect **Diadectid** in Europe and North America. Other evidence is the existence of identical species of turtles, lizards, and snakes on both sides of the Atlantic.

**Fossilized fern**
*These fossilized leaves come from Glossopteris, a tree-sized fern that grew during the Permian Period.*

## Tectonic plate

One of the pieces that make up the Earth's rigid shell

The Earth's shell, or lithosphere ▪, is split into nine large plates and about a dozen smaller ones. The continents are embedded in **continental plates**, while **oceanic plates** make up much of the sea floor. The study of tectonic plates – called **plate tectonics** – helps to explain continental drift, seafloor spreading ▪, why volcanoes ▪ erupt, and how mountains ▪ form.

## Mantle convection

The circulation of mantle rock that causes plate movement

The force that drives the movement of tectonic plates may be the slow churning of the mantle ▪ beneath them. Mantle rock is constantly driven up toward the surface by the enormous temperatures below. It then cools and sinks back down again over millions of years. The tectonic plates may simply be "passengers" carried on huge **convection currents** that extend right down through the mantle. Alternatively, the plates may be active parts of much smaller convection systems that circulate only in the upper mantle.

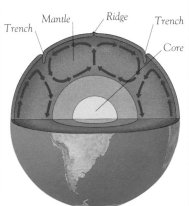

*Trench* *Mantle* *Ridge* *Trench* *Core*

**Convection currents**
*Large convection systems in the mantle may carry along the plates of the lithosphere like a conveyor belt.*

*Pangaea*

*Panthalassa*

### 220 million years ago
*There is only one land mass, Pangaea, in a vast ocean called Panthalassa.*

*Laurasia*

*Tethys Sea*

### 200 million years ago
*The growing Tethys Sea splits Pangaea into Gondwanaland and Laurasia.*

## Slab-pull

The movement of a tectonic plate under the force of its own weight

Just as a tablecloth pulls itself off a table once enough hangs over the side, ocean plates may be dragged along by their own weight as their edges sink into the mantle. This is called slab-pull. Mid-ocean ridges ■, where new crustal ■ material wells up from the mantle, are 1–2 miles (2–3 km) higher than the rims of the ocean plates. It may be that the ocean plates simply slide downhill, away from the ridges. This is called **ridge-push**.

## Plate margin

A boundary between tectonic plates

Mountains, earthquakes ■, and volcanoes occur largely where two tectonic plates meet. At these margins, the plates may be moving apart (constructive margins ■), crunching together (destructive margins ■), or just gently sliding past one another (conservative margins ■). At some margins, a mixture of all three takes place.

## Laser ranging

A way of measuring continental drift

Laser beams are sent between observatories in two different continents by bouncing the beams off reflecting mirrors on space satellites. Triangulation ■ of the reflected beams gives the distance between the observatories. Laser ranging suggests that Europe and America move apart by 0.8 in. (20 mm) each year.

*India*

*Gondwanaland*

*Africa*

## Alfred Lothar Wegener
German meteorologist (1880–1930)

Wegener was the first to propose seriously the idea of continental drift. He cited as evidence not only the matching coastlines of the continents, but also matching rock strata ■ in continents separated by huge oceans. Continental drift, Wegener argued, also explained the existence of fossils ■ of tropical ferns on the Arctic island of Spitsbergen. His ideas were ridiculed at the time, and only gained acceptance in recent years.

*India*

### 135 million years ago
*Gondwanaland splits into Africa and South America as the South Atlantic opens up. India drifts toward Asia.*

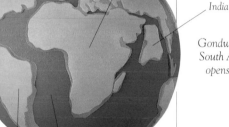

*North Atlantic*

*Europe*

*Asia*

*South America*

*South Atlantic*

*North America*

### 10 million years ago
*Antarctica and Australia drift apart. Laurasia breaks up as the North Atlantic opens up, with North America moving away from Europe. The map of the world looks similar to the one we know today.*

*Antarctica*

*Australia*

# Converging plates

In many places, the huge plates of the Earth's surface are moving together – slowly but with unimaginable force. Sometimes the edge of one plate is gradually destroyed as the force of the collision pushes it down into the Earth's interior. At other times, the impact simply crumples the plates' edges, throwing up great mountain ranges.

***Java – an island arc***
*The peaks of Java's chain of volcanic islands protrude above the clouds. Java is an island arc created by colliding tectonic plates.*

## Subduction zone

A region where one tectonic plate bends beneath another

**Subduction** is the process by which one tectonic plate ▪ is forced beneath another as the two collide. Subduction usually occurs where an oceanic plate ▪ runs into a continental plate ▪, such as along the Pacific coast of South America. The dense oceanic plate dips beneath the lighter continental plate into the asthenosphere ▪. The asthenosphere is so hot that the subducted plate melts. This is why a subduction zone is often called a **destructive margin**. Subduction typically creates a series of parallel features: an ocean trench is followed by an accretionary wedge, then an island arc, and so on. But if the plates converge very slowly, some of the features may not form. There is no trench, for example, where the Juan de Fuca plate converges with the North American plate off the coast of Washington and Oregon.

## Collision zone

A region where continental plates collide

As continental plates collide, one plate splits into two layers: a lower layer of dense mantle ▪ rock and an upper layer of lighter crustal ▪ rock, too buoyant to be subducted. As the mantle layer subducts, the crustal layer peels off, crumpling up against the other plate to form massive mountain ranges ▪ such as the Alps and the Himalayas.

***The Alps – crumpled mountains***
*This aerial view of the Swiss Alps shows clearly how the force of colliding plates has crumpled the crust into mountains.*

## Ocean trench

A long, deep dip in the ocean floor

Most of the world's deepest ocean trenches are in the Pacific, where the Mariana Trench plunges down 35,640 ft. (10,863 m). Ocean trenches are comparatively narrow – rarely more than 62 miles (100 km) across – but they may be thousands of miles long. Most form where an oceanic plate is subducted.

## Island arc

A long chain of volcanic islands

As a subducted oceanic plate sinks into the hot asthenosphere, it begins to melt. Huge globules of hot molten magma ▪ float upward, burning their way through the overlying plate and creating volcanoes ▪ where they erupt on the surface. These volcanoes form a long arc of islands, such as the Philippines, Japan, and Java, along the edge of the plate.

*Continental crust*

*Mohorovicic discontinuity*     *Back-arc basin*

***When plates collide***
*This illustration shows the type of processes that may be taking place in the subduction zones around Japan, where the Eurasian, Philippine, and Pacific plates are moving together.*

## Accretionary wedge

A wedge of sediments piled up beyond an ocean trench

As a subducting oceanic plate sinks into the asthenosphere, the overlying plate scrapes off ocean floor sediments ▪ from the surface of the sinking plate. These sediments pile up in a great wedge or **accretionary prism**, against the edge of the overlying plate.

## Arc-trench gap

**The region between an island arc and an ocean trench**

There is usually a gap of 62 miles (100 km) or more between the ocean trench where a plate is subducted and the island arc that forms beyond. This gap gradually gets wider as a huge accretionary wedge of sediments builds up. At the eastern end of the Aleutian Islands in the northern Pacific, for example, the gap is up to 354 miles (570 km) wide.

## Hugo Benioff

**American seismologist (1899–1968)**

Hugo Benioff added much to our knowledge of how and why earthquakes occur. In 1927, a Japanese seismologist, **Kiyoo Wadati** (born 1902), showed that many earthquakes start in zones deep in the Earth's crust. In the 1950s, Benioff realized that such zones often lie next to ocean trenches. Benioff later mapped these zones (now called Benioff-Wadati zones).

Hugo Benioff examining an underground seismograph

*Magma burns through the crust to form an arc of volcanic islands*

*The Sea of Japan, which separates Japan from North and South Korea, is a good example of a back-arc basin*

*Japan is an island arc thrown up by subducting plates*

*An ocean trench forms where one plate subducts*

*Direction of plate movement*

*Asthenosphere (part of mantle)*

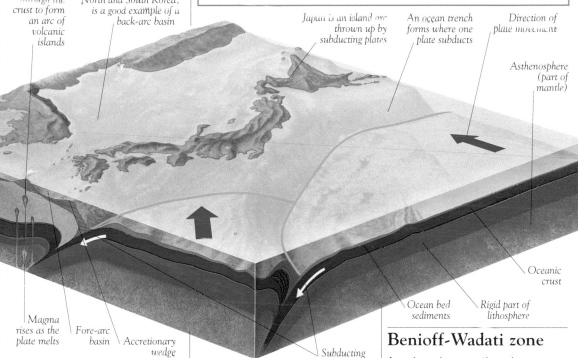

*Oceanic crust*

*Magma rises as the plate melts*

*Fore-arc basin*

*Accretionary wedge*

*Ocean bed sediments*

*Rigid part of lithosphere*

*Subducting plates*

## Fore-arc basin

**The area of shallow sediments in an arc-trench gap**

As an oceanic plate is subducted, an accretionary wedge piles up and forms a crest next to the ocean trench. Between this crest and the island arc is a shallow dip known as the fore-arc basin. This basin slowly fills up with layers of material flung out by the volcanoes of the island arc.

## Back-arc basin

**The area of shallow sediments beyond an island arc**

A back-arc basin is a huge region of shallow seafloor sediments that builds up on the far side of an island arc from the ocean trench. Many of the sediments are washed into the sea by rivers, but they can also come from volcanoes and other sources.

## Benioff-Wadati zone

**A region where earthquakes originate deep underground**

At an ocean trench, earthquakes start close to the surface, but farther away from the trench they start progressively deeper, up to a depth of 435 miles (700 km). Seismologists ■ believe that such deep earthquakes are caused by a subducting plate as it judders down into the asthenosphere. These deep-earthquake regions are always near to ocean trenches.

# Diverging plates

Beneath the world's great oceans, some of the huge tectonic plates that make up the Earth's surface are steadily pulling apart. As they do so, they allow molten rock to rise up from the Earth's interior. This adds new material to the plates, replacing what is "destroyed" when plates collide.

## Median valley

**A long cleft in a mid-ocean ridge**

A median valley, or **rift**, is a crack in the Earth's surface between two diverging plates. At the summit of the Mid-Atlantic Ridge is a deep gash as large as the Grand Canyon in Arizona. It runs along the top of the ridge for almost its entire length.

## Constructive margin

**A boundary between tectonic plates where new plate material is created**

When two oceanic plates ■ pull apart, a mid-ocean ridge forms. Hot molten magma ■ from the asthenosphere ■ continually wells up through the long median valley that runs down the center of the ridge. The magma emerges as lava ■ and solidifies to form new seafloor. The rock near the crest of the ridge is very young, having recently formed, but it gets steadily older farther away. The formation of new oceanic crust ■ and the gradual widening of the oceans is called **seafloor spreading**.

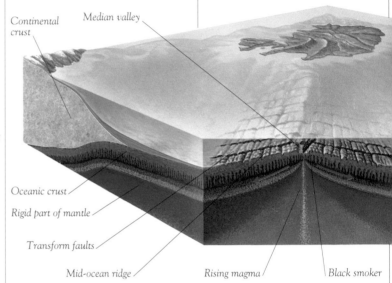

Continental crust
Median valley
Oceanic crust
Rigid part of mantle
Transform faults
Mid-ocean ridge
Rising magma
Black smoker

1   A mid-ocean ridge forms

The central block sinks

Rising magma   2

New seafloor

Magma rises through cracks

Convection currents   3

### The growing oceans
*Seafloor spreading begins where plates pull apart (**1**). Hot magma erupts as lava and solidifies into new seafloor, which is then pushed apart by magma rising beneath (**2**). The ocean widens as the process continues. Transform faults may form along the ridge (**3**).*

## Conservative margin

**A boundary between two tectonic plates that slide past one another**

Some plate margins ■ are neither constructive nor destructive ■, because the plates slide past one another in opposite directions. These are conservative margins, or **transforms**.

Transform fault

As new crustal blocks subside, fresh cracks appear

## Mid-ocean ridge

**A long ridge of mountains that winds along the seafloor**

Mid-ocean ridges occur where the great tectonic plates ■ of the Earth's surface are pulling apart. Mid-ocean ridges are rarely more than about 4,920 ft. (1,500 m) high, but they may snake along the ocean bed for thousands of miles. There is a mid-ocean ridge beneath each of the world's great oceans. The **Mid-Atlantic Ridge**, for example, stretches from the North Pole to the South Pole down the middle of the Atlantic Ocean. The **East Pacific Rise** winds under the Pacific Ocean from Mexico to Antarctica. Mid-ocean ridges are areas of much volcanic ■ and earthquake ■ activity.

**Rising mid-ocean ridge**
*At Thingvellir, Iceland, the rift between the North American and Eurasian plates appears as a long gash in the landscape.*

*Continental crust*

*Sediments*

*Mohorovicic discontinuity*

**The growing Atlantic**
*Iceland sits on top of the Mid-Atlantic Ridge. This illustration shows what may be happening along the ridge as the North American and Eurasian plates gradually pull apart. The ridge – viewed here from the south – continues beyond the northern tip of Iceland.*

# Transform fault

A sideways "tear" in the sea floor

A mid-ocean ridge is not a continuous line, because the curve of the Earth's surface makes it break into a series of short, stepped sections. Each section is slightly offset from the next and separated by a long crack called a transform fault. As the seafloor spreads outward from the ridge, the stepped sections rub against one another. This sets off vibrations, creating earthquakes.

# Fracture zone

A long, narrow belt of ridges and valleys on the seafloor

There are fracture zones running at right angles across each of the mid-ocean ridges. They are about 37 miles (60 km) wide and curve gently across the seafloor, often for thousands of miles. The **Mendocino Fracture Zone** stretches three-quarters of the way across the Pacific Ocean. Fracture zones are thought to be transform faults.

# Triple junction

A point where continents split apart

No one is quite sure how mid-ocean ridges form. Some may start as fracture zones grow larger. Others may begin where a hot magma column, called a **mantle plume**, rises through the mantle and melts through an oceanic plate. This may be happening near the Galapagos Islands in the Pacific Ocean. Many geologists think that a mantle plume may also melt through a continental plate to form a triple junction: it splits the plate three ways and creates huge rift valleys ■. As the rifts widen, new oceans may form.

*Red Sea*                *Gulf of Aden*

**A triple junction?**                *Great Rift Valley*
*The Y shape formed by the Gulf of Aden, the Red Sea, and Africa's Great Rift Valley may be a triple junction. The Red Sea and the Gulf of Aden may eventually grow into huge oceans.*

# Pillow lava

Piles of lava that form under water

Hot magma bubbles up at a mid-ocean ridge and emerges as lava. As soon as it comes into contact with the cold water of the deep ocean, a glassy skin forms around the lava. This brittle surface cracks and allows the still-molten lava inside to ooze out. The process continues as the new lava cools and cracks. It creates a rock formation that resembles a pile of stony pillows or sandbags.

**Stony pillows**
*These globules of pillow lava formed from hot magma that erupted onto the seafloor near the Galapagos Islands in the Pacific Ocean.*

# Black smoker

A hot vent on the sea floor

In some places along a mid-ocean ridge, fluid heated by hot magma gushes out of holes, or vents ■, in the seafloor. Dissolved in the fluid are metal oxides ■ and sulfides ■ that immediately precipitate ■ out of the fluid. This produces thick, black, smokelike plumes that rise from the vents.

# Volcanoes

Volcanic eruptions are perhaps the most awesome of all natural events. When a big volcano erupts, huge underground explosions fling molten rock, red-hot ash, and fiery gases up onto the surface and high into the air, spreading devastation far around.

## Volcano

A gap in the Earth's crust where molten rock and other materials escape onto the Earth's surface

Some volcanoes are just cracks that open up in the Earth's crust ■. Others are holes blasted through mountains. They occur where magma bubbles up through the crust and emerges onto the Earth's surface. **Magma** is hot molten rock created by the partial melting of the crust and mantle ■ at high temperatures far below the ground. Once magma emerges on the surface it is called lava ■.

## Active volcano

A volcano erupting or liable to erupt

There are about 1,300 volcanoes on land around the world thought to be active – that is, likely to erupt at any moment. There are also many volcanoes under the sea, along mid-ocean ridges ■. Some volcanoes, such as those in Hawaii, "simmer" most of the time, steadily oozing lava and hot gas. Others lie **dormant** for centuries but then erupt suddenly and violently. There are also many more **extinct** volcanoes – ones no longer liable to erupt.

### See also

Aquifer 109 • Crust 40 • Lava 55
Mantle 41 • Mantle plume 51
Mid-ocean ridge 50
Subduction zone 48 • Tectonic plate 46

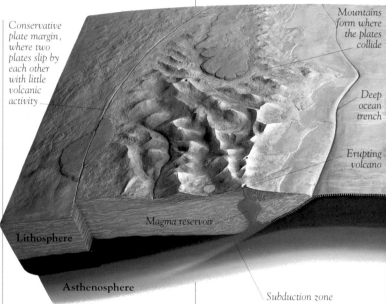

*Conservative plate margin, where two plates slip by each other with little volcanic activity*

Lithosphere

Asthenosphere

*Magma reservoir*

Mountains form where the plates collide

Deep ocean trench

Erupting volcano

*Subduction zone*

## Fissure volcano

A long crack in the Earth's crust through which magma erupts

Fissure volcanoes occur where magma reaches the surface through a series of vertical cracks in the crust. These cracks may form as two tectonic plates pull apart.

*How volcanoes form*
*Volcanoes often erupt in subduction zones, where an oceanic plate slides under a continental plate and into the mantle. They also form where "hot-spots" in the mantle burn through the Earth's crust.*

## Volcanic cone

A conical mountain built up by volcanic eruptions

Where magma erupts from a single hole, or **vent**, it builds up a mound of debris called a **dome volcano**. **Composite cones**, such as Mount Fuji in Japan, are built up from alternate layers of lava and ash. **Ash-cinder volcanoes** form from layers of ash and cinder. **Spatter cones** are small, steep-sided cones made from pancake-shaped lumps of lava thrown out by volcanoes such as those in Hawaii.

## Andesite volcano

A type of volcano liable to erupt violently

The most explosive volcanoes are called andesite volcanoes, because the type of rock they throw out is named after the Andes Mountains where many such volcanoes occur. They are linked with subduction zones ■, where one plate slides beneath another and melts, sending up bubbles of magma. The magma mixes with substances in the overlying plate, making it thick and sticky. This sticky magma clogs up the volcano's mouth, trapping magma below. Pressure builds up until the magma bursts through in a huge explosion. Volcanoes near subduction zones erupt rarely but violently.

## Shield volcano

**A broad, shallow volcanic cone made from runny lava**

The lava that erupts from some volcanoes, such as those in Hawaii, is very runny. Magma tends to ooze from these volcanoes gently, spreading out into a shallow cone or **shield**.

## Hot-spot volcano

**A volcano situated away from tectonic plate margins**

Volcanoes far away from plate margins, such as those of the Hawaiian Island Chain, are associated with very hot areas, or **hot-spots**, in the Earth's mantle – perhaps with mantle plumes ■. A hot-spot is probably stationary, but every so often it burns its way through the moving plate above, to create a line of volcanoes.

*Fuming geyser*
*As steam forms in a water chamber below ground, the mixture of water and steam suddenly explodes, forming a geyser.*

## Geyser

**A hole in the Earth's crust spouting fountains of boiling water**

Geysers occur where hot rock heats up water in an underground chamber, or aquifer ■. When the water boils, it sends out a fountain of boiling water, up to 1,640 ft. (500 m) into the air. **Fumaroles** are small vents that shoot out steam and gas.

## Crater

**A shallow depression at the top of a volcanic cone**

At the top of most volcanic cones there is a broad bowl, or crater, blown out by the eruption. This is often filled with a lake. The largest craters, or **calderas**, can be up to 62 miles (100 km) wide.

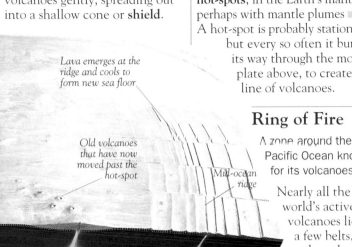

*Lava emerges at the ridge and cools to form new sea floor*

*Old volcanoes that have now moved past the hot-spot*

*Mid-ocean ridge*

*Hot-spot volcano erupting*

*Hot magma rising up to spreading ridge*

## Ring of Fire

**A zone around the Pacific Ocean known for its volcanoes**

Nearly all the world's active volcanoes lie in a few belts, such as the ring around the Pacific Ocean called the Ring of Fire. These belts coincide with the edges of the tectonic plates ■ that make up the Earth's crust.

---

# TYPES OF VOLCANO

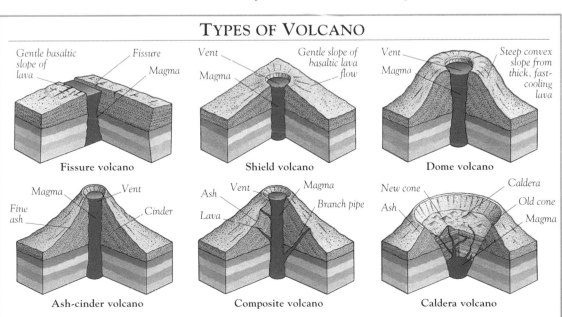

*Gentle basaltic slope of lava* — *Fissure* — *Magma*

**Fissure volcano**

*Vent* — *Magma* — *Gentle slope of basaltic lava flow*

**Shield volcano**

*Vent* — *Magma* — *Steep convex slope from thick, fast-cooling lava*

**Dome volcano**

*Magma* — *Vent* — *Fine ash* — *Cinder*

**Ash-cinder volcano**

*Ash* — *Vent* — *Magma* — *Lava* — *Branch pipe*

**Composite volcano**

*New cone* — *Caldera* — *Ash* — *Old cone* — *Magma*

**Caldera volcano**

# Volcanic eruptions

When a volcano erupts violently, flaming streams of lava usually pour from the summit. Huge clouds of hot ash and steam may billow high into the sky, and burning cinders and rocks may be flung out in all directions, falling over a wide area in a scorching, choking rain.

*Erupting lava*
*Red-hot molten rock is hurled into the air during the eruption of Mauna Loa on the island of Hawaii.*

## Eruption

The sudden emergence of hot material from the Earth's interior

Explosive volcanic eruptions get their power from gas mixed with magma ■. Huge pressures underground cause vast quantities of carbon dioxide gas to be dissolved within the magma. But as the magma rises toward the surface, the pressure falls and it can hold less gas. Small bubbles start to form in the magma. They grow bigger and bigger until they force the magma out through the volcano's ■ vent ■ in a mighty eruption.

### See also

Andesite volcano 52 • Basalt 89
Crust 40 • Hot-spot volcano 53
Magma 52 • Vent 52 • Volcano 52

## Magma chamber

A cavity beneath a volcano where magma collects

All the magma that escapes in a big eruption is believed to accumulate in a massive chamber beneath the ground.

*Pressure forces magma up the main pipe and any branch pipes*

*Branch pipe*

## Plug

A tower of hard rock left by a volcano

The magma that plugs the vents of some volcanoes when it solidifies is very tough. It may be left standing as a tall tower of rock long after the rest of the volcano has been worn away by the effects of the weather. The Puy-de-Dôme in the Massif Central region of France is an example of such a plug, as is the Devil's Tower in Wyoming.

*Ash and gas clouds billow out of the crater*

*Main volcanic pipe or vent*

*The volcano is built up from layers of lava and ash*

*Erupting volcano*
*This cutaway model shows how a composite volcano builds up as magma from the mantle erupts onto the surface.*

*Magma collects in a magma chamber underground before it is forced up to the surface*

## Fire fountain

A jet of magma spouting from a narrow volcanic vent

Hawaiian volcanoes and others with runny basaltic ■ lava, send out jets of magma, up to 660 ft. (200 m) high, which spatter the surrounding ground.

## Scoria

Bubble-filled stones ejected from a volcano

Dissolved gas can sometimes make magma froth. This froth cools into stones of low density, filled with bubbles, or **vesicles**. **Pumice stone** is so bubbly and light that it floats on water.

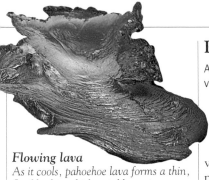

*Flowing lava*
*As it cools, pahoehoe lava forms a thin,*
*flexible skin which wrinkles as it moves.*

# Lava

Molten rock thrown out by a volcano

When magma reaches the surface of the crust ■ it is called lava. The way a volcano erupts depends on how thick and sticky, or **viscous**, the lava is. Sticky, **acidic lavas** are linked with andesite volcanoes ■. Runny **basaltic lavas** are linked with shield and hot-spot volcanoes ■.

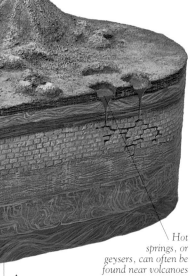

Hot springs, or geysers, can often be found near volcanoes

# Aa

Jagged, chunky lava found in Hawaii and elsewhere

Aa is a Hawaiian word for a type of lava that solidifies into sharp, jagged chunks. Lava may also cool quickly to develop a thin skin, cool enough to walk on when only a few inches thick. If the lava continues to flow underneath, the surface wrinkles into ropelike coils called **pahoehoe**.

# Pyroclast

A fragment from an explosive volcanic eruption

The word pyroclast means "fire-broken." When an andesite volcano erupts and blasts the plug of sticky magma out of the vent, the shattered fragments, or pyroclasts, may be blown far away.

# Pyroclastic flow

A flowing avalanche of hot volcanic ash, cinder, and pyroclasts

Eruptions may release flows of ash, cinder, and pyroclasts. The ash is mixed with gas, so this fiery mass flows down the volcano, almost like water, devastating everything in its path. This is a pyroclastic, or **ash flow**. In 1902, the city of St. Pierre on the Caribbean island of Martinique was incinerated in minutes by such a flow. **Nuée ardente** and **glowing cloud** are terms used to describe a pyroclastic flow that is accompanied by an ash cloud.

# Volcanic sunset

A colorful sunset following a volcanic eruption

Eruptions can send dust and ash up into the stratosphere, where strong winds may scatter them around the world in just a few weeks. The dust can have a dramatic effect on climate and produce spectacular sunsets. The eruption of Mount Tambora in Java in 1815 sent up so much dust that the Sun was obscured around the globe, causing poor summers for two years.

*Volcanic ash plume*
*During the eruption of Mount St. Helens*
*(July 1980), ash was thrown up to an*
*altitude of 11 miles (18 km).*

# Tephra

Fragments thrown into the air by a volcanic eruption

Tephra are pyroclasts thrown high into the air by a violent eruption. The largest fragments are **volcanic bombs**, which measure across 1.3 in.–3.3 ft. (32 mm–1 m). They often have distinctive shapes, such as **bread-crust bombs**, which are covered with crisscross cracks, and rounded **cannonball bombs**. Smaller chunks of tephra are called **lapilli**.

# Volcanic ash

Tephra less than 0.08 in (2 mm) across

Big volcanic eruptions can send huge dust clouds high into the sky. Some may fall like rain far around, covering the ground in a thick, choking blanket. After Sumatra's Mount Toba erupted 20,000 years ago, it covered the island with a layer of ash over 980 ft. (300 m) deep. When Mount Vesuvius erupted in AD 79, the people of Pompeii were buried instantly by ash. Their preserved remains were discovered in the 18th century.

# Volcanic intrusions

Not all volcanic activity is visible on the surface. Much of the molten magma that bubbles up from the Earth's hot interior remains trapped underground. It pushes into the overlying rock, either following existing structures or breaking right through them.

***Exposed intrusion***
*This dike has cut straight through the existing rock. It is situated in the Sierra Nevada Mountains, California.*

## Igneous intrusion

Volcanic rock that has penetrated older rocks through cracks but remains underground

Igneous intrusion is volcanic activity below ground, whereas **igneous extrusions** are visible surface volcanoes ■ and lava ■ flows. If molten magma ■ pushing up underground cannot reach the surface, it may be forced into different-shaped gaps beneath the surface. When the magma eventually cools, it solidifies as igneous intrusions. The surrounding rock enclosing the intrusions is called **country rock**. Sometimes, intrusions become visible when the overlying rock is worn away by erosion, exposing the hard igneous rock beneath. **Pluton** is a term once used to describe all forms of igneous intrusion, of all shapes and sizes. It is now used more specifically to describe a huge, drum-shaped intrusion of granitic ■ rock pushed up close to the surface in a nearly solid state.

## Concordant intrusion

An igneous intrusion that follows existing bedding planes

When magma is runny and cools to form basaltlike ■ rock, the intrusion tends to follow lines of weakness and existing bedding planes ■ within the country rock. Intrusions that mold themselves within gaps in the country rock are said to be concordant. Conversely, **discordant intrusions** such as dikes, cool to form granitelike rock and often break right through existing bedding planes.

## Batholith

A gigantic igneous intrusion of great depth, covering a large area

Batholiths are the largest igneous intrusions, at least 39 sq. miles (100 km²) in area. The largest in North America is the Coast Range Batholith of British Columbia and Washington, with a length of 932 miles (1,500 km). Batholiths are irregular in shape and intrude across the layers of country rock. They often lie at the center of major mountain ranges. Batholiths usually cool slowly to form coarse-grained granitelike rocks. At the surface, they may appear as just a single pluton. Sometimes, however, several plutons far apart on the surface may originate from a single giant batholith. In southwest England, for example, various separate granite domes including Dartmoor, Bodmin Moor, and St. Austell Moor are the surface exposures of the same batholith, uncovered by erosion.

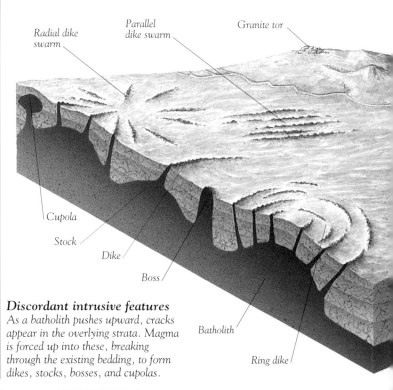

Radial dike swarm

Parallel dike swarm

Granite tor

Cupola

Stock

Dike

Boss

Batholith

Ring dike

***Discordant intrusive features***
*As a batholith pushes upward, cracks appear in the overlying strata. Magma is forced up into these, breaking through the existing bedding, to form dikes, stocks, bosses, and cupolas.*

## Stock

A small igneous intrusion

Small-scale discordant intrusions, less than 16 miles (25 km) across, may simply be offshoots of a batholith. A stock is generally drum-shaped. A **boss** is similar, but with very steep sides. A **cupola** is a dome-shaped extension of a batholith.

## Dike

A thin, wall-like igneous intrusion

Dikes are discordant intrusions. As a batholith pushes up below ground, vertical cracks form in the rock above, cutting completely through existing structures. Dikes form when magma is injected into these cracks. Often, a single batholith may produce dozens of dikes in a **dike swarm**. The swarms may be in a **parallel** or **radial** pattern, as they are on the island of Rhum in Scotland. **Ring dikes** are circular in shape.

## Lopolith

A saucer-shaped igneous intrusion

Lopoliths are concordant intrusions, usually cooling to form basaltlike rock. Smaller lopoliths tend to run into downfolds in the existing rock structure to form bowl-shaped intrusions. Larger lopoliths, sometimes called **megalopoliths**, simply spread out into saucer shapes. The biggest megalopoliths – such as the Duluth outcrop near Lake Superior in Ontario, Canada – can be over 77,000 sq. miles (200,000 km²) in area.

## Phacolith

A shallow, lens-shaped igneous intrusion

Phacoliths are concordant intrusions that are smaller than lopoliths. They settle into the existing rock, forming curved intrusions that either arch up into upfolds or bow down into downfolds.

***Waterfall formed over a sill***
*High Force Waterfall, Teesdale, England has formed where the water has worn away the soft rock beneath the hard sill.*

## Sill

A flat, sheetlike igneous intrusion

Sills are concordant igneous intrusions that flow between the layers of country rock to form a horizontal sheet of igneous rock. The Palisades Sill in New Jersey is a slightly tilted sill. Salisbury Crags in Edinburgh, Scotland, is another.

## Laccolith

A lens-shaped igneous intrusion with a flat base that forces the overlying strata into a dome

Magma that bursts through one layer of rock may spread out beneath the rock layer above. It may then form a laccolith by pushing up into an arched concordant intrusion with a flat base. If this happens in multiple layers and laccoliths are stacked on top of each other, a **cedar-tree laccolith** forms.

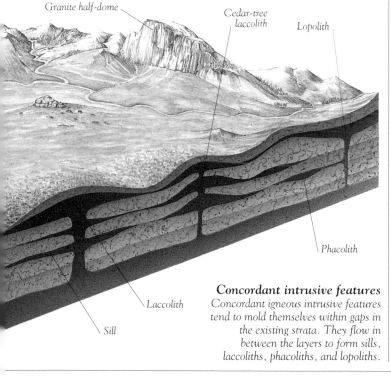

Granite half-dome
Cedar-tree laccolith
Lopolith
Phacolith
Laccolith
Sill

***Concordant intrusive features***
*Concordant igneous intrusive features tend to mold themselves within gaps in the existing strata. They flow in between the layers to form sills, laccoliths, phacoliths, and lopoliths.*

### See also

Basalt 89 • Bedding plane 93 • Granite 90
Lava 55 • Magma 52 • Volcano 52

# Earthquakes

Many things can cause the ground to shake, or tremble, including erupting volcanoes, exploding bombs, and avalanches. But the most dramatic tremors are usually caused by earthquakes, which can shake the ground so violently that buildings collapse and people's lives are endangered.

## Earthquake

A shaking of the ground caused by sudden movements in the Earth's crust

Most earthquakes are so small and gentle that no one notices them. The biggest earthquakes are set off by the movement of tectonic plates ■. At the margins ■ where the plates meet, the edges rub against each other. Some plates slide past each other gently, others may get stuck, and the forces pushing the plates build up. The stress on the rocks eventually makes them crack and judder past each other, sending out vibrations or shock waves through the ground. It is these vibrations, called **seismic waves**, that cause an earthquake.

## Focus

The place below ground where an earthquake starts

Vibrations from an earthquake radiate out from an underground region called the focus or **hypocenter**. Earthquakes are classified according to the depth of the focus. Shallow earthquakes start 0–43 miles (0–70 km) below ground; intermediate earthquakes start 43–186 miles (70–300 km) below ground; and deep earthquakes start at depths exceeding 186 miles (300 km). The deepest earthquake ever recorded started at 447 miles (720 km), but shallow ones usually cause the most damage. Earthquake vibrations are only felt when they reach the surface. They are at their most intense at the **epicenter** – that is, the point on the surface directly above the focus.

## Isoseismic line

A line on a map that links points of equal earthquake intensity

Isoseismic lines form concentric circles around the earthquake's epicenter. As the distance from the focus increases, the intensity of the earthquake decreases.

## Surface wave

A vibration from an earthquake that travels at ground level

Each type of seismic wave has a distinctive pattern of movement that helps seismologists to understand how the earthquake started. Surface waves are slow and powerful, and cause most of the damage in an earthquake. There are two types: **Love waves** move from side to side, while **Rayleigh waves** move up and down, like waves in the sea.

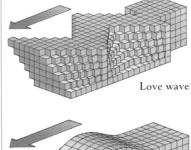

Love wave

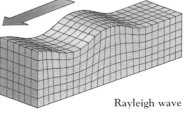

Rayleigh wave

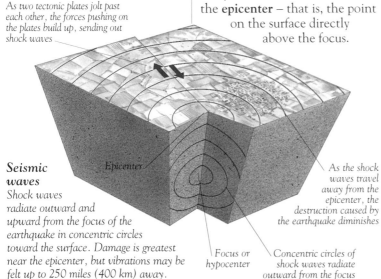

*As two tectonic plates jolt past each other, the forces pushing on the plates build up, sending out shock waves*

*Seismic waves*
*Shock waves radiate outward and upward from the focus of the earthquake in concentric circles toward the surface. Damage is greatest near the epicenter, but vibrations may be felt up to 250 miles (400 km) away.*

Epicenter

*As the shock waves travel away from the epicenter, the destruction caused by the earthquake diminishes*

Focus or hypocenter

Concentric circles of shock waves radiate outward from the focus

*Seismic damage*
*This road collapsed when seismic waves hit Los Angeles, California, during the 1994 earthquake. In all earthquakes, surface waves cause more damage than the deeper body waves.*

# Body wave

A vibration from an earthquake that travels deep underground

**Primary (P) waves** are fast-moving waves that travel through the body of the Earth at 3 miles (5 km) per second. They alternately push and pull on the rocks, stretching and squeezing them, with a movement similar to a shunting train. **Secondary (S) waves** move slightly slower than primary waves, at about 2 miles (3 km) per second. They move the rocks up and down or from side to side, like a flicked jump rope.

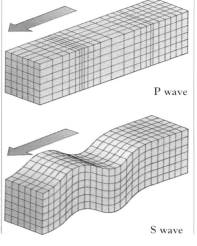

P wave

S wave

# Foreshock

A small tremor before a major earthquake

The initial fracture of the rocks as an earthquake begins may send out a gentle tremor in advance of the main earthquake. There may be minor **aftershocks** hours, days, or even months after the main quake as the rocks settle down.

# Tsunami

A huge sea wave set off by an undersea earthquake

Tsunamis can devastate coastal areas. They travel away from the earthquake's epicenter at speeds of 435 mph (700 kph) or more, but they are barely noticeable on the surface. As they approach the shallows they can build up to heights of over 98 ft. (30 m).

# Seismograph

A device for recording the magnitude of seismic waves

One part of a seismograph stays stationary, while the rest shakes with the seismic waves. The waves are recorded as a trace by a pen on paper, or by a beam of light on photographic paper. Such a trace is called a **seismogram**. The Worldwide Standardized Seismograph Network monitors global seismic activity. Each of its monitoring stations has two or three seismographs, and is synchronized with all the others.

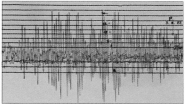

*Recording earthquakes*
*The 1923 earthquake in Tokyo, Japan, was recorded by this seismogram in Oxford, England. The length of the lines shows the magnitude of the waves.*

# Mercalli scale

A scale that shows the intensity of an earthquake by its effects

Earthquakes are given a value on the Mercalli scale from 1–12 in Roman numerals. A Mercalli III earthquake rattles windows, and a Mercalli XII earthquake causes total destruction.

Mercalli scale

| | |
|---|---|
| XII | Total destruction; "waves" seen on ground surface; river courses altered; vision distorted |
| XI | Railway tracks bend; roads break up; large cracks appear in ground; rock falls |
| X | Most buildings destroyed; large landslides; water thrown out of rivers |
| IX | General panic; damage to foundations; sand and mud bubble from ground |
| VIII | Car steering affected; chimneys fall; branches break; cracks in wet ground |
| VII | Difficult to stand; plaster, bricks, and tiles fall; large bells ring |
| VI | People walk unsteadily; windows break; pictures fall off walls |
| V | Doors swing open; liquid spills from glasses; sleepers awake |
| IV | Dishes rattle; standing cars rock; trees shake |
| III | Shaking felt indoors; hanging objects swing |
| II | People at rest upstairs notice the shaking |
| I | Vibrations are recorded by instruments |

1 2 3 4 5 6 7 8 8 9
Richter scale

*Mercalli and Richter compared*
*This graph gives a rough comparison between the Mercalli and Richter scales. Moderate earthquakes may be IV and V on the Mercalli, and 4.3–4.8 on the Richter scale. Severe earthquakes may be VI–X on the Mercalli and 6.2-7.3 on the Richter scale.*

# Richter scale

A scale that measures the magnitude of an earthquake

The Richter scale is logarithmic and open-ended. It currently ranges from 0–8.9, the largest earthquake yet recorded (Chile, 1960). Richter scale readings are taken on a seismograph.

## See also

Global seismology 40 • Plate margin 47
Seismic survey 171 • Tectonic plate 46

# Faults

As the tectonic plates of the Earth's crust jostle together, they often put rocks under such strain that they fracture, producing cracks, or faults, in the rock. Large blocks of rock then slip past each other, breaking up the landscape and creating new mountains and valleys as the blocks are forced up or down.

## Fault

A fracture in rock along which blocks of rock slip past each other

Faults occur mainly in areas called **fault zones**, especially near plate margins ■. The surface along which blocks of rock slip is called a **fault plane**. This is usually clearly defined, despite the rocks on either side being shattered. Faults vary greatly in size, ranging from very small cracks to those involving entire mountain ranges ■. Single earthquakes ■ rarely move rocks more than a few inches, although the San Francisco earthquake in 1906 shifted land either side of the San Andreas fault by more than 20 ft. (6 m). But the cumulative effect of millions of years of earthquakes and plate movement can shift faulted rock hundreds of miles sideways and a few miles up or down. A **fault scarp** is a huge cliff exposed as a massive block is thrown up or down.

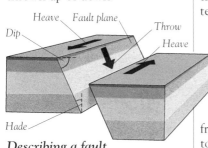

*Describing a fault*
*Geologists measure the dip, hade, throw, and heave of this oblique-slip fault to find out about the deformation of the rock.*

## Throw

The distance upward or downward that fault blocks have moved

The throw is the vertical movement of rock at a fault. The **dip** ■ is the angle of the fault plane to the horizontal. Typically, normal faults are steep and dip at an angle of 65°–90° to the horizontal. The **hade** is the angle of a fault plane to the vertical. The **heave** is the amount the rocks shift sideways.

## Compression fault

A fault caused by the squeezing of rocks in the Earth's crust

Compression faults are caused by rocks being squeezed together, perhaps when two tectonic plates ■ collide. **Tension faults** are the result of rock being pulled apart, maybe when two plates move away, or diverge, from each other. In some faults, there is an element of both tension and compression.

## Normal fault

A fault in which blocks of rock slip straight down

Normal faults occur where tension in the Earth's crust ■ fractures rock and allows blocks to slip straight down – or, in other words, in line with the dip of the fault, which is why they are also called **dip-slip faults**.

## Wrench fault

A fault in which blocks of rocks slip sideways past each other

Wrench faults, also known as **tear faults** or **strike-slip faults**, occur where plates move sideways past one another. This causes blocks of rock to move horizontally past each other. The biggest wrench faults are called **transcurrent faults**. The best known is the San Andreas fault.

*Transcurrent fault*
*The San Andreas Fault in California has been created by the Pacific Ocean plate grinding past the North American plate. The two plates may have moved hundreds of miles past each other.*

## Reverse fault

A fault in which one block of rock slides up over another

Reverse faults occur when compression in the Earth's crust pushes two blocks of rock together so that one overhangs the other. The overhanging rock is called the **hanging wall**, the rock below is called the **footwall**. Reverse faults are less steep and more varied in angle than normal faults. **Thrust faults** are reverse faults with an angle of 45° or less. They may be split into a kind of staircase of level sections called **flats** and steep sections called **ramps**.

## Oblique-slip fault

A fault in which blocks of rock slip up or down, and past each other diagonally

When a wrenching movement in the Earth's crust is combined with compression or tension, blocks of rock may slip diagonally past each other in an oblique fault. If this happens on a massive scale, they are called **transtension** or **transpression faults**.

## Rift valley

A huge, trough-shaped valley created by faulting

Rift valleys are among the most dramatic fault features. The Great Rift Valley of East Africa stretches all the way from Mozambique through the Red Sea and into Israel. The floor of a rift valley is a downthrown block called a **graben**; the walls are normal faults. Most geologists believe they are created by tension as two tectonic plates pull apart. Others believe they are caused by compression, as two reverse faults are thrust up in opposite directions. Some believe they are connected with mantle plumes ■.

## Horst

A block of rock thrown up between normal faults

A horst is the opposite of a graben and may create huge, high plateaus or mountain ranges. The Sinai Desert in the Middle East, the Black Forest in Germany, and the Ruwenzori Mountains in East Africa are all horst blocks.

## Fault breccia

Rock fragments created by faulting

The location of a fault may be revealed by a band of broken rocks that crumbled as the blocks of rock slid past each other.

## FAULT TYPES

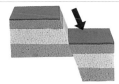

**Normal fault**
*A simple fault in which blocks of rock move up or down.*

**Wrench fault**
*A horizontal shearing across a vertical fault plane.*

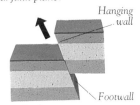

Hanging
wall

Footwall

**Reverse fault**
*One block is forced up and over another block.*

**Rift Valley**
*A long narrow block sunk between two parallel normal faults.*

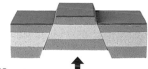

**Horst**
*A horizontal block raised between two normal faults.*

**Complex faults**
*A series of faults may tilt the rocks in many directions.*

# Folds

Rocks generally form in flat layers called strata. However, the great tectonic plates of the Earth's surface move around with such enormous force that, as plates collide, rock strata are often crumpled and twisted into all kinds of shapes.

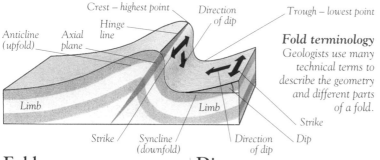

Crest – highest point
Direction of dip
Trough – lowest point
Anticline (upfold)
Axial plane
Hinge line
Limb
Limb
Strike
Syncline (downfold)
Direction of dip
Strike
Dip

**Fold terminology**
*Geologists use many technical terms to describe the geometry and different parts of a fold.*

## Fold

A buckling in the rock strata of the Earth's crust

Folds in rock usually occur where the strata ■ are crumpled up as they are squeezed horizontally and vertically, perhaps by two tectonic plates ■ moving together. Sometimes this occurs on a very small scale, creating "wrinkles" just a few inches long. It may also occur on a massive scale, so that there are hundreds of miles between the crests of the folds. The bend of a fold may be gentle or severe depending on a variety of factors. These include the strength of the forces involved, the ability of the rock to resist being deformed, the arrangement of the rock layers, and the nature of the movement that caused the folding. Horizontal compression of rocks causes buckling, whereas a sudden subsidence may cause rocks to twist rather than fold.

## Dip

The angle in degrees between a tilted layer of rock and the horizontal

In gentle folds, strata may dip at just a few degrees. In severe folding the dip may be as much as 90°. The direction of dip – which way a fold is facing – is measured using a compass. The **strike** is the direction of a horizontal line on the rock layer, at right angles to the direction of dip.

### Heavily folded rock
*The mountain of Picos de Vallibierna, in the Pyrenees Mountains in northeast Spain, shows some heavily folded rock strata.*

## Limb

The strata either side of a fold

When rock strata are folded, they bend around the **hinge line**, which is the "crease" of a fold. The **crest** is the highest point and the **trough** the lowest point of each fold. The limbs of the fold are the rock strata either side of the hinge line.

## Anticline

An arch-shaped fold in rocks

Rock strata may be warped either up or down by folding. An anticline is an upfold. A **syncline** is a bowl-shaped downfold.

## Axial plane

An imaginary plane halfway between the limbs of a fold

When geologists analyze the way rock has been folded, they look for the axial plane of a fold, which "hangs" from the hinge line. The axial plane divides a fold into two more or less equal halves. It helps geologists to distinguish between the different types of fold.

Recumbent fold

## See also

Erosion 98 • Strata 68
Tectonic plate 46 • Weathering 98

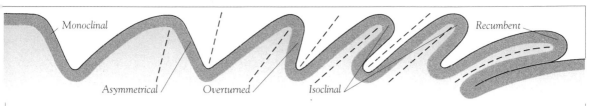

Monoclinal
Asymmetrical
Overturned
Isoclinal
Recumbent

## Different types of fold

*Folds vary in complexity, depending on the intensity of the force causing the deformation. As a fold becomes progressively more deformed, it may pass through the stages from a monoclinal to an asymmetrical, then an overturned, and finally a recumbent fold. Isoclinal folds form after repeated tight folding.*

## Fold attitude

The shape of a fold

Folds may be all kinds of shapes, depending on how forcefully they have been compressed. A simple fold with only one dipping limb is called a **monocline**. A **neutral** or **symmetrical** fold is one where no limb is steeper than another. Often, continued pushing may distort a fold until one limb is steeper than the other, producing an **asymmetrical fold**. When the deformation is intense, the limb may become so steep that it folds right over, producing an **overturn**. If it folds even farther to lie on top of the next fold, so that the axial plane is subhorizontal, it is called a **recumbent fold**. There are some good examples of these in the Alps. Repeated tight folding often produces **isoclinal folds**, which are two or more parallel folds.

## Competent rock

A rock that is rigid compared to neighboring rocks

Different kinds of rock strata bend and fold in various ways. Competent rocks are very rigid compared to the layers of rock above and below, and tend to crack rather than bend. When folded, layers of competent rock usually stay the same thickness. **Incompetent rocks**, however, may behave more like modeling clay, bending and distorting as they are folded. If competence varies greatly from layer to layer, there may be dramatic changes in the shape of the folds, with much more intense folding in the least competent beds. This is called **disharmonic folding**.

## Boudin structure

A layer of rock distorted into a shape like a string of sausages

When a competent layer of rock lies between very incompetent layers, it is not as easily bent and molded, if squeezed or stretched, as the rock around it. This results in the rock becoming pinched and fractured, breaking it into a series of sections that are long and fat, and short and thin, like a string of sausages. *Boudin* is a French word for sausage.

## Belted landscape

A series of ridges and valleys following the line of folded rocks

Gentle folding sets layers of rock at an angle to the surface. Once the forces of weathering ▣ and erosion ▣ have had an effect, the result is a distinctive belted landscape. The softer beds erode faster to create valleys, while the harder beds resist to form long parallel ridges. The ridges, called **cuestas**, are usually asymmetrical in shape. Cuestas have one long, gentle slope following the dip of the rock, called the **dip** or **back slope**. The other, steeper slope is called the **scarp** or **escarpment**. If the layers dip very steeply, both sides of the ridge may be equally steep. This is called a **hog's back**.

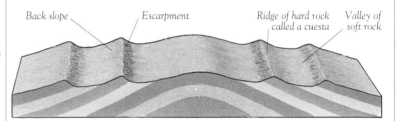

Back slope
Escarpment
Ridge of hard rock called a cuesta
Valley of soft rock

*Belted landscape*
*The parallel ridges and valleys of a belted landscape are caused by the uneven erosion of hard and soft layers of folded rock.*

## Dome

A round upfold, with rock dipping away in all directions

Not all folds in a landscape lie in parallel lines – some run in many different directions. In a few places, the land bows up to form a dome-shaped structure. This may be eroded to create a circular belted landscape.

# Mountain building

Mountains are the world's highest places; Mount Everest in the Himalayan Mountains of Nepal and Tibet is the highest of all at 29,078 ft. (8,863 m). Mountain terrain is usually rugged, with high peaks, steep slopes, and deep valleys.

## Mountain

A steep-sided hill over 2,000 ft. (600 m) high

A few mountains, such as Mount Kilimanjaro in East Africa, are single isolated mountain tops or **peaks**. But most are grouped into **mountain ranges**, like the Jura Mountains in Europe and the Sierra Nevada Mountains in California. Often, a whole series of ranges is connected as a larger chain of mountains called a **cordillera**. The eastern and western cordilleras in the Andes in South America are examples. Most of the world's highest mountains are part of great **mountain systems**, such as the Alps in Europe, the Andes, and the Himalayas, which include various cordilleras, dozens of ranges, and hundreds of high peaks.

### The formation of fold mountains
*This experiment represents what happens when one plate is forced (subducted) below another, crumpling up the crustal rocks. As the layers of sand (representing crustal rocks) are squeezed horizontally, they become progressively more folded so that simple folds may become completely overturned folds called nappes. Eventually fold mountains are formed.*

## Fold mountain

A mountain built up by the crumpling of crustal rocks

Most of the world's great mountain regions were built by the buckling of crustal rocks as a tectonic plate ■ crashed into the edge of a continent. This is why the great fold ■ mountain systems of the world lie along the margins of colliding ■ plates. The Andes, for example, have formed where the Nazca plate runs into South America, and the Himalayas rise where the Indian plate runs into Asia.

## Geosyncline

A vast depression in the Earth's surface

Geologists once believed that fold mountains were formed in geosynclines. These are vast depressions in the Earth's surface along the edges of continents. Here, sediments ■ washed off the land settle to form sedimentary rocks ■. It was thought that the weight of the sediments warped the Earth's crust so much that eventually it pulled in the edges of the geosyncline, crumpling the sediments to create mountains. This idea has since been discredited, and it is now thought that mountains are formed by tectonic plate movement.

*Layers of sand represent layers of crustal rocks*

*First Z-shape fold forms*

**1**

*Second Z-shape fold*

*New folds begin to form and the first set becomes more deformed*

**2**

*Nappe*

**3**

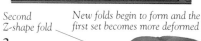

*Fold mountains have been created by repeated folding*

*Simple deformation of sedimentary rock*

*Foothills*

*Nappe*

**4**

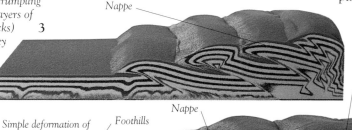

*Eiger and Monch, Swiss Alps*
*These fold mountains have been easily weathered into dramatic peaks because the rock was so fractured by the folding.*

# Lystric fault

A huge, curved slippage of rock in a region of mountain building

When continents collide, the old crystalline basement ■ of one plate is subducted ■ below the other, while the younger rocks on top crumple up to form fold mountains. The crumpled younger rocks can become detached from the basement. The boundary between them is called the **décollement horizon**. Occasionally the strain may snap the younger rocks altogether, creating a huge, curved fault ■ right down to the décollement horizon. This is a lystric fault.

# Block mountain

A mountain created by a massive uplift

Not all mountains are built by folding. When horst blocks ■ are raised high up between two faults or when the land surrounding the faults sinks, tall, flat-topped, block mountains are often formed. Mountains can also be created by volcanoes ■. Some volcanoes, such as Aconcagua in Argentina, are among the world's highest mountains.

# Massif

A very large mountain or rock structure

Huge single mountains, or areas of mountains with similar characteristics, are sometimes described by the French term *massif*. The old crystalline blocks of rock in a mountain system are also called massifs.

# Isostasy

The balance between the height of mountains and the depth of their "roots"

The Earth's rigid continental crust ■ floats on the mantle ■ like a ship on the sea. Just as a boat floats lower in the water if it is heavily laden, so the crust floats lower in the mantle if it is heavy above. High mountain areas sink farther, and so have deeper "roots" to balance their height. When mountains are worn down, they float upward to compensate for the change in weight and maintain the balance, or **isostatic equilibrium**. Similarly, the crust may sink under the weight of an ice sheet ■ and bounce slowly back up again once the ice sheet melts.

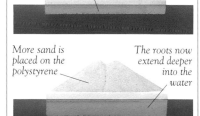

*With little sand on top of it, the polystyrene does not sink far into the water*

*More sand is placed on the polystyrene*

*The roots now extend deeper into the water*

### Height and depth
*In this experiment, sand represents a mountain and polystyrene its crustal "roots." As more sand is placed on the floating polystyrene, the polystyrene sinks farther into the dyed water.*

## Grove Karl Gilbert

American geologist (1843–1918)

Gilbert, one of the great figures of geology around the turn of the century, was one of the first people to distinguish between fold and block mountains. He coined the word "orogeny" to describe the process of mountain building.

# Orogeny

The process of building mountains

Orogeny, or mountain building, is limited to a few specific areas in the world, called **orogenic belts**, usually along the edges of colliding tectonic plates. Two examples of these belts are the Andes and the Himalayas. Although most of the world's mountain ranges are continually getting higher as the tectonic plates collide, mountain building is believed to have been most active during certain episodes in the Earth's history, called **orogenic phases**. Each of these extended over many millions of years. Different phases are identified in different places, such as the Caledonian, Hercynian, and Alpine phases in Europe, and the Huronian, Nevadian, and Pasadenian phases in North America.

# How the Earth began

No one can be quite sure how the Earth began, but billions of years ago there was probably just a vast cloud of hot gas and dust circling around the newly formed Sun. About 4.6 billion years ago, parts of this cloud began to cluster together, forming the Earth and other planets.

*The Earth is born*
*Most scientists believe that the Solar System formed about 5 billion years ago from a vast, contracting cloud of gas and dust. At the center of this cloud was the Sun. Farther out, part of the cloud condensed to form a red-hot ball of molten matter – the Earth.*

## Planetary accretion

The clumping together of fragments of space debris to form a planet

The Earth probably began with the rapid accretion, or bunching together, of tiny pieces of space debris called planetesimals ■. As the Earth formed, space debris continually smashed into it, adding new material, including ice from the edges of the Solar System. Such impacts gave the Earth water and other chemical compounds ■ essential for life.

## Primeval Earth

The Earth during the first millions of years of its existence

For a long time, the surface of the newborn Earth was a mass of erupting volcanoes ■ and smoke. The planetesimals from which the Earth formed were quite cool, but they collided with such force that the Earth became very hot. Radioactive decay ■ of elements ■ heated it further. Iron and nickel melted, and sank to form the core ■. Lighter materials floated up to form the crust ■.

*The Sun was born at the center of a huge, rotating, disk-shaped cloud of dust and gas*

*The Earth formed as part of the cloud condensed*

*An atmosphere formed as the cooling Earth gave off gases and water vapor*

## Primeval atmosphere

The atmosphere of the young Earth

As the Earth stabilized, vast gas bubbles rose up from the interior to form a cloudy atmosphere ■. The clouds were full of water vapor. After less than a billion years, rain began to fall and create the first oceans. Methane and ammonia in the air were soon broken up by sunlight. The hydrogen which they contained escaped into space, leaving carbon dioxide and nitrogen behind.

## Oxygenation

The appearance of free oxygen in the atmosphere

The primeval air lacked oxygen – the gas that animals need to live. Present oxygen levels were reached only about 1 billion years ago, once plants had begun making it by photosynthesis ■. The oxygen also helped form the ozone layer ■, which blocks out the Sun's harmful ultraviolet rays. Without this protection, not even plants could survive on land.

## Unicellular life

Simple living organisms consisting of just one cell

Life probably began about 3.8 billion years ago – perhaps in warm volcanic pools, or in hydrothermal vents ■, where hot water bubbles up under the sea. The first living organisms were **bacteria**, which were made of just a single cell. They lived in water and were able to feed on chemicals. About 3 billion years ago, a type of plantlike bacteria called **blue-green algae** or **cyanobacteria** appeared.

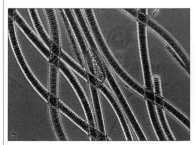

*Oxygen makers*
*Blue-green algae use sunlight for photosynthesis. They began to add oxygen to the early atmosphere.*

## Protist

The first complex living cells

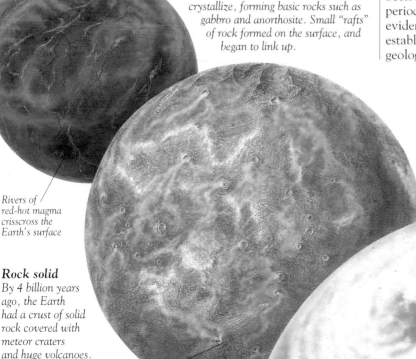
*Amoeba*

Single-celled organisms called protists appeared about 1.5 billion years ago. They have **organelles** (tiny organs) to carry out specialized tasks. Protists are **eukaryotes**, which means they contain a **nucleus** – a central organizing unit enclosed by a membrane. Bacteria are **prokaryotes**, which have no nucleus. The largest protists, called **amoebae** (singular: **amoeba**), are about 0.04 in. (1 mm) long.

## Sponge

A simple, multicellular marine organism

Sponges were among the earliest multicellular organisms to leave fossil █ records. They probably evolved when *Sponge* several specially adapted types of protist joined together. True multicelled organisms, in which the cells are organized into tissues, are called **metazoa** (humans are metazoans). Fossils of early metazoa, such as jellyfish, exist from 700 million years ago.

## Precambrian time

The entire history of the Earth before about 570 million years ago

Little is known about the Earth's first 4 billion years, because the simple organisms rarely formed fossils. Precambrian time is divided into the **Archaean eon** █ (more than 2.5 billion years ago) and the **Proterozoic eon** (570 million–2.5 billion years ago).

## Cambrian explosion

The sudden appearance of complex lifeforms during the Cambrian Period

A huge variety of complex marine life emerged during the Cambrian period █, 510–570 million years ago. This left behind a rich diversity of fossils. There have been numerous fossils from every period since, providing crucial evidence for geologists trying to establish the sequence of the geological column █.

*Semimolten surface*
*As the Earth cooled, minerals began to crystallize, forming basic rocks such as gabbro and anorthosite. Small "rafts" of rock formed on the surface, and began to link up.*

*Water and life*
*Primitive forms of life began to develop about 3.8 billion years ago. By 1 billion years ago the Earth would have had a familiar look from space, with swirling clouds, huge oceans, and vast land masses.*

*Rivers of red-hot magma crisscross the Earth's surface*

*Rock solid*
*By 4 billion years ago, the Earth had a crust of solid rock covered with meteor craters and huge volcanoes.*

*Plumes of smoke and gas rise up from active volcanoes*

*Surface water appeared on Earth about 3.9 billion years ago, and the first oceans formed about a million years later*

# History in rocks

Our knowledge of the Earth's history comes almost entirely from studying the rocks of the Earth's crust. By looking at the distribution of particular rocks, their relationship to other rocks, the kind of fossils they contain, and many other factors, geologists build up a picture of past events.

## Stratigraphy

The study of the distribution and order of rock layers

Stratigraphy is based on the work of William Smith ■. He realized that if two rock layers or **strata** (singular: **stratum**) contain the same range or assemblage ■ of fossils ■, they must be the same age, even if they are different types of rock. Stratigraphers use a variety of other dating methods, including radiometric dating ■.

## Lithostratigraphy

The description of rock layers and their distribution

Lithostratigraphers establish the sequence of rock strata in a particular area, and try to link strata of the same rock found in different areas. A **formation** is a stratum of rock that can be mapped across country. There is usually a sharp change in rock type above and below a formation. Formations can be divided into smaller units called **members**, and members into **beds**, which are the smallest lithostratigraphic units.

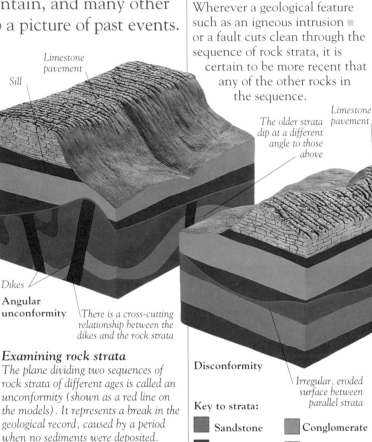

*Limestone pavement*

*Sill*

*Dikes*

**Angular unconformity**

*There is a cross-cutting relationship between the dikes and the rock strata*

### Examining rock strata
*The plane dividing two sequences of rock strata of different ages is called an unconformity (shown as a red line on the models). It represents a break in the geological record, caused by a period when no sediments were deposited.*

## Law of superposition

The principle that a layer of rock is younger than the layer beneath

The law of superposition was discovered in the 17th century by Nicolas Steno ■. Steno realized that layers of sediment ■ are laid down on top of one another, so the oldest strata of sedimentary rock ■ are always at the bottom and the youngest at the top. This is true as long as the beds have not been overturned by folding ■ or faulting ■.

## Law of cross-cutting relationships

An igneous intrusion or a fault is younger than the rocks it cuts through

The law of cross-cutting relationships can provide an important clue to the relative age of geological features. Wherever a geological feature such as an igneous intrusion ■ or a fault cuts clean through the sequence of rock strata, it is certain to be more recent that any of the other rocks in the sequence.

*Limestone pavement*

*The older strata dip at a different angle to those above*

**Disconformity**

*Irregular, eroded surface between parallel strata*

**Key to strata:**

| | |
|---|---|
| ■ Sandstone | ■ Conglomerate |
| ■ Mudstone | ■ Red sandstone |
| ■ Clay | ■ Shale |
| ■ Igneous rock | ╱ Unconformity |

## Chronostratigraphy

The study of the timescale in which rock layers were laid down

Chronostratigraphers try to link rock strata laid down at the same time but in different areas. This process is known as **time-correlation**. There are two basic chronostratigraphic units, called chronomeres and stratomeres.

# Chronomere

A basic unit of geological time

Just as a day is divided into hours, minutes, and seconds, geological time is divided into periods called chronomeres. These are times during which particular processes occurred within the Earth's rocks. The longest chronomere is the **eon**, followed by the **era**, **period**, **epoch**, **age**, and **chron** (the shortest unit). Chronomeres vary in length, and more recent chronomeres tend to be shorter than those in the past. The Palaeozoic era ■, for example, lasted 320 million years, while the later Mesozoic era ■ lasted 184 million years.

*The strata on either side of the unconformity dip at the same angle and direction*

**Parallel unconformity**

# Stratomere

Part of a rock sequence laid down in a particular geological time unit

When examining a rock sequence, chronostratigraphers try to find out during which chronomere the strata were laid down. A **system** is strata of rock laid down in a period. A **series** is strata laid down during an epoch. A **stage** is strata laid down in an age. A **chronozone** is strata laid down during a chron.

# Unconformity

A break or gap in a sequence of rock layers

Where an unconformity occurs, one rock sequence overlays rocks from a completely different sequence. There are several important types of unconformity in sedimentary rocks. An **angular unconformity** is where the lower, older strata dip ■ at a different angle to the younger strata above. This can happen where a folded sequence is worn down by erosion ■ and then buried beneath a new sequence of rock strata. A **disconformity** is an irregular, eroded surface between parallel rock strata. In a **parallel unconformity**, the strata either side of the unconformity dip in the same direction and by the same amount. In a **nonconformity**, a sequence of strata overlies an eroded surface of igneous or metamorphic rock ■.

*Batholith*

*Metamorphic aureole*

**Nonconformity**

# Stratotype

A standard sequence of rock strata

In field work, geologists try to establish standard sequences of rock strata, called stratotypes or **type sections**, with which other sequences can be compared. A **type locality** is the place where a particular stratotype occurs. The **type area** is the region around it.

# Isochronous

A layer of rock known to be the same age everywhere

The identification of isochronous beds is a crucial aid to the time-correlation of rock strata. Beds of lava ■ or volcanic ash ■ are isochronous. So are many glacial deposits. Few rock formations are isochronous over more than a few hundred miles. A **diachronous** bed of rock differs in age from place to place.

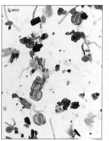

**Plant relics**
*This magnified image shows fossilized pollen grains found in peat. Pollen fossils give clues to an area's ecology in past times.*

# Paleoecology

The study of ancient environments

Scientists use stratigraphy not only to find out about geological history, but also about changes in the environment. Fossils give very valuable clues, as does **pollen analysis**, which is the study of ancient pollen trapped in sedimentary rock. It gives a good idea of the plants and trees that once grew in a place at a particular time, and of the nature of the climate.

# Tektite

Small, tear-shaped lumps of black glass created by meteor impacts

When large meteors crash into the Earth, they splash out showers of tektites. These glass lumps are melted either from the rocks in the Earth or from the meteor itself. If the date of the impact is known, the presence of tektites in rock strata can give a good clue to the age of the rock.

# Fossils

Preserved in many sedimentary rocks are the remains of plants and animals that lived millions of years ago, when the sediments in the rock were first deposited. Like the sediments themselves, these remains were preserved by being turned to stone.

**Seaside fossil**
*The exposed soft rocks of wave-washed cliffs and foreshores are good territory for finding fossils, such as this ammonite.*

## Fossil record

The picture of past life provided by fossil evidence

The softer parts of a dead animal quickly rot away, so most fossils show only the shell or a few isolated bones of the creature. But knowledge of anatomy allows paleontologists ■ to build up a picture of what the living creature was really like. The record of past life given by fossils is not a complete one. For example, only a tiny fraction of all the species that ever lived have been preserved as fossils. Of the fossils that do exist, most are of shellfish that lived in shallow seas. Fossils of soft-bodied creatures – such as insects and worms, and land-living creatures such as mammals – are rare. This is because their remains usually decayed before they could be fossilized.

## Fossil

The preserved evidence of a living organism

Fossils are relics of living things that have been preserved in rock, often for many millions of years. Not all fossils are actual remains of living organisms. Some are fossilized "signs" left behind, such as footprints, burrows, or droppings. These are called **trace fossils** or **ichnofossils**.

**Relic of the past**
*These fossilized leaves are from the giant redwood tree Sequoiadendron.*

## Plant fossil

The preserved remains of vegetation

Plant remains are preserved when the leaves and stems of dead plants are buried very quickly, flattened, and then turned to a thin carbon film. This process is **carbonization**. Coal ■ seams are made from carbonized plants, but only occasionally are individual plants recognizable in the coal.

## Fossilization

The process of fossil formation

When a creature such as a shellfish dies and falls to the sea floor, its soft body tissue quickly rots away, leaving the hard shell behind. If this is buried intact by sediment ■, it may be dissolved away over millions of years by water trickling through the mud. This leaves a shell-shaped hollow known as a **mold**. Minerals ■ in the water, such as silica or iron sulfide, may take the place of the shell and harden to form a **natural cast**. This process is called **replacement**. Sometimes, the buried shell is barely altered by mineral action.

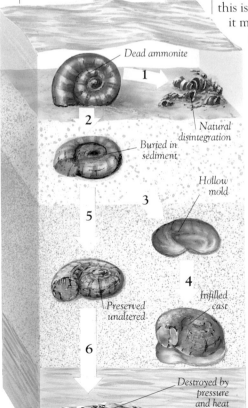

Water

Soft sediment

Compacted sediment

Metamorphic rock

*Dead ammonite*
**1**
*Natural disintegration*
**2**
*Buried in sediment*
*Hollow mold*
**3**
**5**
**4**
*Infilled cast*
*Preserved unaltered*
**6**
*Destroyed by pressure and heat*

**Fossil formation**
*Dead sea creatures may slowly disintegrate on the seabed (**1**) or get buried in soft sediment (**2**). As the sediments compact, minerals may dissolve the remains, leaving a mold (**3**). Other minerals then fill the mold (**4**), forming a cast. Other remains are preserved unaltered in the compacting sediment (**5**). They are destroyed when sedimentary rock is metamorphosed (**6**).*

## Microfossil

A fossil that is clearly visible only under a microscope

Many fossils are too small to see with the naked eye. Microfossils enable paleontologists to date rocks brought up from deep below the Earth's surface by drilling. Larger fossils are usually destroyed by the action of the drill. Microfossils include tiny marine organisms such as **foraminiferans**, minute bivalved **ostracods**, plant spores, and planktonlike **hystrichospheres**.

## Stromatolite

Rocklike structures produced by microorganisms

Stromatolites are found in shallow, tropical seawaters. These dome-shaped layers of sediment are built up very slowly by bacteria called cyanobacteria ▥. They form hard deposits that fossilize very easily. Fossilized stromatolites are the oldest fossils of all. Some, in Western Australia, date back 3.5 billion years and are the earliest evidence of life on Earth.

## Petrifaction

A form of fossilization in which cavities in organic structures are filled with minerals

Bones and shells contain tiny cavities. These bones and shells may be preserved when minerals from groundwater ▥, such as calcite ▥ or silica, are deposited in the cavities. The organic material is slowly turned into stone or other hard substances.

# MAJOR FOSSIL GROUPS

Most fossils found in sedimentary rocks, especially in limestones and shales, are of small, shelled sea creatures. Fossils of mammals and of soft-bodied creatures such as insects or worms are rarer.

### Coral
A small sea creature that usually grows in large colonies

Thecosmilia
*Coral fossil*

### Trilobite
An extinct sea creature with a flexible shell divided into three parts

Paradoxides
*Trilobite fossil*

### Bivalve
A shellfish with a shell of two hinged halves, such as clams, cockles, and mussels

Glycymeris
*Bivalve fossil*

### Crinoid
A sea lily – a creature fixed to the seabed by a flexible stem

Saccocoma
*Crinoid fossil*

### Echinoid
A sea urchin

Micraster
*Echinoid fossil*

### Brachiopod
A type of shellfish with bivalvelike shells, now nearly extinct

Platystrophia
*Brachiopod fossil*

### Graptolite
An extinct sea creature that lived in colonies, probably dangling by threads from drifting seaweed

Rhabdinopora
*Graptolite fossil*

### Gastropod
A creature such as a snail

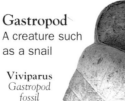

Viviparus
*Gastropod fossil*

### Cephalopod
A free-swimming squidlike shellfish, including the now extinct ammonite and belemnite

Ethioceras
*Cephalopod fossil*

### Vertebrates
All animals with backbones, including fish, mammals, birds, and reptiles such as dinosaurs

Diplomystus
*Vertebrate fossil*

# Geological column

If sediments remained forever undisturbed, it would be possible to cut a column down through the layers to reveal the entire sequence, from earliest times to the present day. Although such a complete column exists nowhere on Earth, it is a valuable way of summarizing the Earth's history.

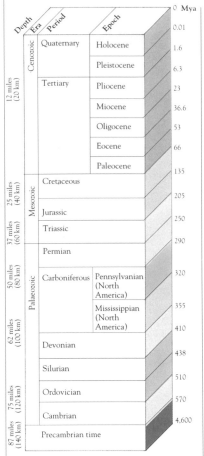

| Depth | Era | Period | Epoch | Mya |
|---|---|---|---|---|
| | | | | 0 |
| | | | | 0.01 |
| | Cenozoic | Quaternary | Holocene | |
| | | | | 1.6 |
| | | | Pleistocene | |
| | | | | 6.3 |
| 12 miles (20 km) | | Tertiary | Pliocene | |
| | | | | 23 |
| | | | Miocene | |
| | | | | 36.6 |
| | | | Oligocene | |
| | | | | 53 |
| | | | Eocene | |
| | | | | 66 |
| | | | Paleocene | |
| | | | | 135 |
| 25 miles (40 km) | Mesozoic | Cretaceous | | |
| | | | | 205 |
| | | Jurassic | | |
| | | | | 250 |
| 37 miles (60 km) | | Triassic | | |
| | | | | 290 |
| | Palaeozoic | Permian | | |
| 50 miles (80 km) | | Carboniferous | Pennsylvanian (North America) | 320 |
| | | | Mississippian (North America) | 355 |
| 62 miles (100 km) | | | | 410 |
| | | Devonian | | 438 |
| | | Silurian | | |
| | | | | 510 |
| 75 miles (120 km) | | Ordovician | | |
| | | | | 570 |
| | | Cambrian | | |
| | | | | 4,600 |
| 87 miles (140 km) | | Precambrian time | | |

**Key:**
Mud
Sandstone
Shale
Limestone
Metamorphic

*Geological rock column*
*If there were a place in which sediments had been deposited continuously since Cambrian times, there would now be a sequence of sedimentary rocks stretching down as far as 100 miles (160 km). The rock types shown along the side are the predominant rocks of each period.*

## Geological column

A visual representation of the divisions of geological time and the order in which rock strata appear

The history of the Earth's rocks is often shown in the form of a vertical column listing the sequence of known rock strata ■ in chronological order. The oldest rock layer appears at the bottom, and the youngest at the top, so each layer becomes a unit of geological time. In reality, the rock sequence is often broken, buckled, twisted, or overturned by tectonic ■ activity. Geologists use evidence such as fossils ■ and unconformities ■ to interpret such a sequence.

## Biostratigraphy

The use of fossils to identify rock strata

Fossils play a crucial part in establishing the geological column, and provide the basis for nearly all time-correlations ■. Over the course of time, new species ■ have evolved while others have died out. The fossil record is sparse before the Cambrian ■ Period (570–510 million years ago), but since then millions of species have come and gone. Only a tiny minority of these species have been preserved as fossils. But the timing of their arrivals and departures provides the best way of comparing the relative ages of sediments ■.

*Geological time chart*
*The first living things were soft-bodied, and left few traces of their existence. The fossil record really begins about 570 million years ago. Sedimentary rocks from every period since can be identified by the fossils they contain.*

**Trilobite (segmented invertebrate)**

**Blue-green algae (unicellular life)**

### Precambrian time

The first, single-celled life-forms such as blue-green algae develop. Later, multicellular soft-bodied animals such as worms and jellyfish appear.

**4,600 million years ago (mya)**

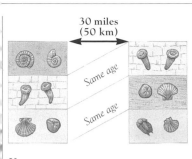

**30 miles
(50 km)**

*Same age*

*Same age*

**Key:**

■ Mudstone    □ Sandstone

■ Shale    ⊞ Limestone

*Using index fossils*
*The presence of an index fossil in two rock strata shows they are the same age, even if they are different types of rock.*

# Index fossil

A fossil used for time-correlation

Index fossils are also called **zone**
**fossils.** For a fossil to be useful for time-correlation, it must be widely distributed, small, easy to identify, and have evolved rapidly, showing clear changes from time to time.

# Worldwide index fossil

An index fossil that can be used to date rocks on a worldwide basis

The best index fossils are **ammonites** (cephalopods ■) of the Jurassic and Cretaceous periods; goniatite ammonites of the Devonian, Carboniferous, and Permian; and graptolites ■ of the Ordovician and Silurian, especially in shales ■. These fossils are widespread, since they are of organisms that floated freely in the sea. Crinoids ■, trilobites ■, and extinct sponges ■ called **archaeocyathids** are useful for the Cambrian, while foraminiferans ■ are useful for the Permian. Gastropod ■ and bivalve ■ species evolved slowly and are limited in range, so they are used only for worldwide time-correlation of recent rock strata.

# Local index fossil

An index fossil that can be used to date rocks locally

Brachiopods ■, cephalopods called **belemnites**, corals ■, fish, freshwater mussels, pollen, and other fossils are used for time-correlation on a local level.

*Ichthyostega*
(amphibian)

Giant tree
fern

*Cooksonia*
(land plant)

Crinoid
(marine animal)

## Cambrian period

There is no life on land. A variety of algae and invertebrates flourishes in the oceans. Mollusks and segmented shelled invertebrates such as trilobites appear.

**570 mya**

## Ordovician period

Crustaceans appear, along with early, fishlike vertebrates. Coral reefs form in the oceans. Southern continents drift toward polar regions. Glaciation of the Sahara.

**510 mya**

## Silurian period

Simple land plants such as *Cooksonia* evolve around shorelines and estuaries. Fish with jaws appear. Some freshwater fish present in rivers and lakes. Continents begin to drift toward one another.

**438 mya**

## Devonian period

Sharks and many other kinds of fish swarm in the seas. The first insects and amphibians, such as *Ichthyostega*, appear. Spore-bearing plants such as ferns and club mosses grow as big as trees, forming the first forests. Desert sandstones form.

**410 mya**

## Carboniferous period

Vast, swampy forests flourish on river deltas. These forests eventually form coal deposits. Amphibians are abundant. The first reptiles evolve from amphibians. Glaciation of Gondwanaland.

**355 mya**

*Continued on next page* ➤

# Charles Lyell

Scottish geologist (1797–1875)

Until the 18th century, most people believed that the Earth was just a few thousand years old, and that it was shaped by catastrophic natural events. Lyell argued that the Earth was in fact very old, and that rocks were shaped gradually by everyday processes. His book *Principles of Geology* marks the beginning of modern geology ■.

# Zone

The basic biostratigraphical unit

In a particular area, sequences of rock strata can be divided up according to the fossils they contain. A sequence containing its own unique range of fossils is called a zone. The zone is named after one of the fossils present – the index ■ or zone fossil.

# Acme zone

The zone of rock strata where an index fossil is most abundant

An index fossil is more abundant in one part of a fossil zone if the species thrived in that particular place or time, or if conditions for preservation were especially good.

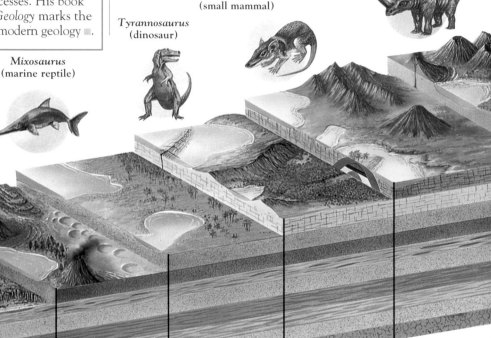

*Arsinoitherium*
(large mammal)

*Crusafontia*
(small mammal)

*Tyrannosaurus*
(dinosaur)

*Mixosaurus*
(marine reptile)

Early
conifers

## Carboniferous period
(*see page* 73)

355 mya

## Permian period

Conifers replace tree ferns. Reptiles diversify. Deserts are widespread.

290 mya

## Triassic period

Mammals appear. Seed-bearing plants dominate. North America and Europe in the tropics.

250 mya

## Jurassic period

Dinosaurs are abundant. *Archaeopteryx*, the earliest known bird, evolves from reptiles. Pangaea splits up.

205 mya

## Cretaceous period

Flowering plants and small land mammals appear. Dinosaurs die out. Oil and gas deposits form.

135 mya

# Biostratigraphical unit

A division of rock layers according to their fossil content

Biostratigraphers ■ classify rock strata ■ by the fossils ■ they contain, rather than by units of geological time or the different types of rock. Biostratigraphical units are called zones and stages.

# Stage

A biostratigraphical unit formed by the grouping of several fossil zones

*Micraster* Chalk is a stage made up of zones of chalk strata of the Cretaceous period. The strata are zoned according to the species ■ of fossilized *Micraster* sea urchin (an echinoid ■) they contain.

# Assemblage zone

A sequence of rock strata in which a particular group of fossils occurs

An assemblage zone is identified by a group or **assemblage** of fossil species. It is usually named after one of the fossils present. It may be further divided into subzones, each with its own index fossil.

◀ *Continued from previous page*

### On top of the geological column

*Despite their dominance of the world today, humans have only existed for an incredibly short period of the Earth's history. Our earliest ancestors evolved from apes 5–10 million years ago, and modern humans (Homo sapiens) appeared about 90,000 years ago.*

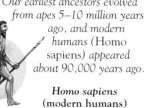

**Homo sapiens (modern humans)**

## Concurrent range zone

A sequence of rock strata defined by the presence of two or more index fossils

A concurrent range zone is where two (or more) key fossil species overlap in the sequence of rock layers, or occur in the same place. **Oppel zones** are similar to concurrent range zones, but they are more loosely defined and so are more useful. The lower boundary of an Oppel zone is the first appearance of an index fossil in the strata; the upper boundary is the last appearance of the second index fossil. (Oppel and concurrent range zones, along with the other zones described in this section, are shown in the diagram on the right.)

## Zonal scheme

The basis on which rock strata are split into zones

Because most creatures can survive only in a limited range of environments, most fossils occur only in a particular facies ▓ of rock. This means that each facies of rock must have a different zonal scheme, according to the creatures that lived at that time and in that particular environment. In Europe, for example, there are three main facies of rocks in the Devonian System ▓, and each facies has a different zonal scheme. The first is Old Red Sandstone, which formed in lakes and estuaries and is zoned by fish fossils. The second, Rhenish rock, formed in shallow sandy seas and is zoned by brachiopods ▓ and corals ▓. The third, Hercynian rock, formed in deep muddy seas and is zoned by ammonites ▓.

### Tertiary period

Large mammals appear. Birds and mammals flourish. Primates evolve and grasslands expand. Himalayas and Grand Canyon form. The continents start to take their present shapes.

**66 mya**

### Quaternary period

Many mammals die out during repeated ice ages. North and South America join together. Vertebrates evolve rapidly as habitats change frequently. Modern humans (*Homo sapiens*) appear.

**1.6 mya**    **0 mya**

## Range zone

The extent of a fossil zone through a sequence of rock strata

The region in which an index fossil or assemblage is found, and how far it extends up and down the rock strata, is a range zone. A small region in which an index fossil occurs is a **local range zone**.

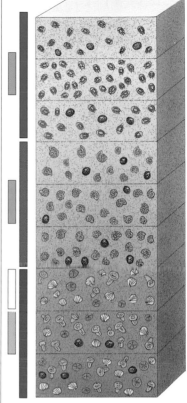

**Key:**

| | | |
|---|---|---|
| ■ | 🦐 | Acme zone of trilobite |
| □ | 🦐 | Range zone of trilobite |
| □ | 🐚🐚 | Concurrent range zone of ammonites |
| ■ | 🐚🐚 | Oppel zone of ammonites |
| □ | 🐚 | Acme zone of bivalve |
| □ | 🐚 | Acme zone of coral |
| ■ | 🐚🐚🐚 | Assemblage zone of coral, bivalve, and echinoid |
| | 🐚 | Other fossils |

### Defining fossil zones

*Biostratigraphers use fossils and their distribution throughout a sequence of rock strata to divide up the sequence into different fossil zones.*

# Absolute dating

Examining the fossils in a band of rock gives a good idea of its relative age – that is, whether it is older or younger than the rocks around it. But fossils cannot accurately indicate the rock's age in years. This is possible only with chronometric or "absolute" dating techniques.

Woman's skull radiocarbon dated to 1,770 years old

## Chronometric dating

Finding the age of rocks in years

It is difficult to determine the exact or **absolute age** of rocks or other ancient objects. Various methods are used, including radiometric dating, varve analysis, and dendrochronology. None of these is very accurate, and the older a rock is, the more inaccurate the dating will be.

## Isotope

A form of an element with a different number of particles in the nuclei of its atoms than other forms of the same element

The most common isotope of the element ■ carbon has 12 particles (6 neutrons ■ and 6 protons ■) in the nuclei ■ of its atoms ■, so it is called carbon–12. "Heavier" carbon isotopes have nuclei that contain 7 (carbon–13) or even 8 neutrons (carbon–14).

*Inside an atom*
*This atom of the carbon–12 isotope has a nucleus containing six protons (red) and six neutrons (gray), orbited by six electrons (blue).*

*Protons and neutrons are clustered together in the nucleus*

*Around the nucleus there are two "shells" of orbiting electrons*

## Radioactivity

The spontaneous disintegration of unstable isotopes

The atoms of heavy isotopes such as uranium–238 have unstable nuclei. As soon as they form, they begin to disintegrate into lighter isotopes. The nuclei may emit **alpha particles** (groups of two protons and two neutrons), **beta particles** (electrons ■) and high-energy **gamma rays**. This process is called **radioactive decay**.

## Half-life

The time it takes for half the atoms in a radioactive isotope to decay

Radioactive isotopes decay at a constant rate. It is possible to work out how long a substance has been decaying – that is, how long ago it formed – from the proportion of the original isotope left in the substance. It is impossible to measure an isotope once all its atoms have decayed, so scientists measure the half-life – the time it takes for half its atoms to decay.

## Radiometric dating

Finding the age of rocks by measuring radioactive decay

A rock may contain several radioactive isotopes. The age of a rock can be calculated by measuring how much of one of the **parent isotopes** has decayed into lighter **daughter isotopes**.

## Radiocarbon dating

Radiometric dating that relies on the decay of the isotope carbon–14 to date organic remains

Carbon–12 and carbon–14 are present in all living things in the same ratio, but carbon–14 decays into nitrogen–14 when an organism dies. After 5,730 years, half the carbon–14 is left; after another 5,730 years, a quarter is left; and so on. Scientists work out how long ago the organism died from the ratio of carbon–14 to carbon–12 atoms. It is accurate for objects up to 30,000 years old, but cannot be used for anything older than 70,000 years.

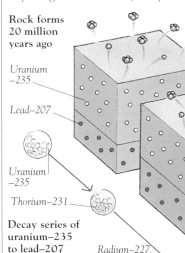

Rock forms 20 million years ago

*Uranium –235*

*Lead–207*

*Uranium –235*

*Thorium–231*

**Decay series of uranium–235 to lead–207**

*Radium–227*

## Fission-track dating

Radiometric dating using tracks left in rock by the decay of uranium atoms

As uranium–238 decays, it emits alpha and beta particles that leave traces, or **fission tracks**, in the rock. A rock's age is calculated by counting the tracks in a particular area. It works best for the minerals mica ■, titanite ■, **epidote**, **zircon**, and **apatite** in igneous ■ and metamorphic rocks ■.

## Uranium-lead dating

Radiometric dating that relies on the decay of uranium isotopes into lead isotopes

Natural uranium contains two unstable isotopes: uranium–238 and uranium–235. Both decay into isotopes of lead through long chains of disintegrations called **decay series**. Traces of isotopes from these series are found in the mineral zircon in granitic ■ rocks. Especially useful for dating is the decay of uranium–235 to lead–207 and of thorium–232 to lead–208. Uranium-lead dating works well for rocks older than 20 million years; **thorium-lead dating** is best for rocks older than 50 million years.

*Uranium-lead dating*
*This artwork sequence shows the decay series of uranium–235 through to lead–207, and how the proportions of these two isotopes in a rock can tell geologists how old the rock is.*

**10 million years ago**

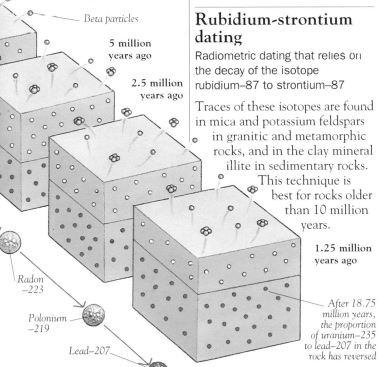

— *Alpha particles*

— *Beta particles*

**5 million years ago**

**2.5 million years ago**

**1.25 million years ago**

*Radon –223*

*Polonium –219*

*Lead–207*

— *After 18.75 million years, the proportion of uranium–235 to lead–207 in the rock has reversed*

## Potassium-argon dating

Radiometric dating that relies on the decay of the isotope potassium–40 to argon–40

Traces of potassium–40 and argon–40 are detected in the minerals mica, pyroxene ■, and feldspar ■ in metamorphic and igneous rocks, and in **glauconite** in sedimentary rocks ■. This technique is best for rocks more than one million years old.

**Laboratory dating**
*This scientist is using potassium-argon dating to find the age of volcanic rocks.*

## Rubidium-strontium dating

Radiometric dating that relies on the decay of the isotope rubidium–87 to strontium–87

Traces of these isotopes are found in mica and potassium feldspars in granitic and metamorphic rocks, and in the clay mineral illite in sedimentary rocks. This technique is best for rocks older than 10 million years.

## Willard Frank Libby

American chemist
(1908–1980)

Early in his career, Libby worked on the "Manhattan Project" to develop the atomic bomb. In 1947, Libby and his colleagues at the Institute of Nuclear Studies in Chicago, Illinois, discovered how the radioactive isotope carbon–14 can be used to establish the age of organic remains. For this discovery, Libby was awarded the 1960 Nobel Prize for Chemistry.

## Dendrochronology

A dating technique using tree rings

Dates in the recent past can be established by counting the number of annual growth rings in the trunks of old trees. The width of these rings also gives clues to climatic conditions in the past.

## Varve analysis

A dating technique that relies on deposits in lakes in front of glaciers

**Varves** are two-layered beds of sediment in proglacial lakes ■. As glacial ice melts in the summer, streams of meltwater ■ flow into the lake and deposit sediment, which is topped by a thinner layer in the winter. Dates in the most recent ice age can be established by counting the number of varves.

# Evolving continents

The story of much of the Earth's past is locked in the ancient rocks of continents. Helped by sophisticated radiometric dating techniques, paleontologists and geologists are discovering more and more of this story, slowly building up a picture of the way the continents have evolved.

## Continental core

The ancient heart of a continent

Continents have ancient cores surrounded by bands of progressively younger rock. This pattern is particularly clear in North America, where the rocks of the Canadian Shield (more than 2.5 billion years old), are ringed by younger rock structures.

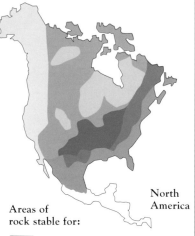

Areas of
rock stable for:

- 2.6 billion years or more
- 1.6–2 billion years
- 1.3–1.5 billion years
- 0.9–1.1 billion years
- 0.3–0.6 billion years
- 0.2 billion years
  or less (still unstable)

*Growth of the African and North American continents*
*These maps show the age of the rocks that make up North America and Africa. Younger tracts around the cores of continents were made either from equally old rocks reworked by tectonic activity, or from rocks that emerged more recently from the Earth's mantle.*

## Continental growth

The gradual enlargement of continents through the eons

Continents probably began as small areas of land ringed by deep ocean trenches ■. As island arcs ■ formed and crashed into these microcontinents, so new bits were "welded" on and the continents grew – mainly in short bursts of activity around 2.7, 1.8, and 1 billion years ago.

## Craton

A large section of continent that has remained stable for more than an eon

All but a small proportion of the Earth's continental crust ■ had formed by 1 billion years ago. Although tectonic activity has reshaped the continents considerably since then, large areas called cratons – typically basements ■, continental shields, or ranges of ancient fold mountains – have been stable for a very long time.

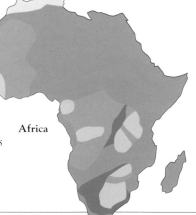

North
America

Africa

## Continental shield

A large area of exposed ancient rock

On every continent, there are large areas or "shields" of very ancient Precambrian ■ crystalline rock exposed at the surface. Such areas include the Canadian Shield, western Australia, and all of Finland. They are often highly metamorphosed ■ and folded. Where the shields are covered by a thin layer of recent sedimentary rock, they are called basements.

*Ancient conglomerate rock*
*This conglomerate in Isua, Greenland, contains ancient pebbles similar to the Isua Pebble, which was once thought to be the oldest rock in the world.*

## Acasta gneiss

The oldest rock in the world

The Earth's most ancient rocks are found near the poles, in places such as Greenland, Canada, and Antarctica. Radiometric dating ■ techniques have shown Acasta gneiss rocks from Canada to be 3.9 billion years old. Previously, the **Isua Pebble**, a pebble of volcanic ash found near Isua in Greenland, was thought to be the oldest rock, at 3.812 billion years old. Meteorites are about 4.6 billion years old – about as old as the Earth itself.

## Gneiss terrain

A large expanse of ancient metamorphosed rock

In places such as Greenland, there are extensive areas of rock that have been transformed or metamorphosed by intense heat and pressure into gneiss.

# Anorthosite

An ancient igneous plutonic rock found on the Moon

Gneiss terrains often contain areas of an ancient plutonic igneous rock called anorthosite, which is composed almost entirely of plagioclase feldspar. The Moon's surface is formed almost entirely of these rocks, which suggests that they form very early in any planet's history.

# Greenstone belt

An ancient metamorphic rock formation

Embedded in the ancient granite and gneiss terrains of South Africa and Australia are strange greenstone belts. These are islands of very twisted, ancient rock metamorphosed from basaltic lava and topped by sediments ■. They are between 3.5 and 2.5 billion years old. No one knows exactly how these unusual structures formed. But because greenstone belts often contain pillow lavas ■, some geologists believe that they are ancient pieces of oceanic crust that formed under the sea in back-arc basins ■ as the continents grew larger.

# Angara

An ancient continent consisting of much of modern Asia

About 1 billion years ago, the continents of the world may have been amalgamated into one giant land mass. Tectonic activity split it into three main pieces: Angara, consisting of much of what is now Asia (apart from India); **Euramerica**, consisting of northern Europe, North America, and Greenland; and Gondwanaland ■, which at this time included Africa, Antarctica, South America, Australia, and India. For 500 million years they drifted apart, but by 220 million years ago, they had joined up again as Pangaea ■.

## See also

Back-arc basin 49 • Basement 40
Crust 40 • Eon 69 • Gondwanaland 46
Island arc 48 • Metamorphism 96
Ocean trench 48 • Pangaea 46
Pillow lava 51 • Precambrian time 67
Radiometric dating 76 • Sediment 92

*Euramerican landsapes*
*As the continents drifted over the globe, their landscapes changed dramatically. These pictures show how New York may have looked in past ages.*

**0.5 million years ago: a freezing polar landscape**

**250 million years ago: New York is on the equator, with a hot, desert landscape**

**300 million years ago: New York is in the tropics, with a landscape dominated by warm, swampy forests**

# Rocks

Although rocks are usually covered by soil and vegetation, or by sediments and water, they can be found beneath every square inch of the Earth's surface – under plains and valleys, hills and mountains, lakes and oceans.

## Rock

A large mass of mineral matter

Rocks make up the solid mass of the Earth's crust. They are usually very hard and, once formed, last for millions of years. The oldest known rocks are at least 3.9 billion years old – almost as old as the Earth itself. There are three main rock types, called igneous rock ■, sedimentary rock ■, and metamorphic rock ■.

## Acid rock

Rock containing at least ten percent quartz

Acid rocks have more quartz than basic rocks, and are 65 percent silica, making them lighter in color. They are often called **felsic** (*fel*dspar and *silica*) rocks. **Intermediate rocks**, between acid and basic rocks, are 50–65 percent silica.

## Basic rock

Rock containing no quartz

Igneous rocks and the rocks derived from them can be classed as basic, intermediate, or acid rocks, according to their chemical content. Basic or **dark rocks** contain no quartz ■. They contain up to 50 percent silica, along with significant amounts of feldspar ■, iron, and magnesium. They are sometimes called **mafic** (*ma*gnesian and *fer*ric) rocks. **Ultrabasic rocks** contain less silica than basic rocks.

### The rock cycle

*New rock material is constantly pushed up from the Earth's mantle by volcanoes and igneous intrusions to form igneous rock. This is just one stage in the rock cycle.*

*Magma emerges as lava, and solidifies to form rock*

Volcano

Rising magma melts the surrounding rock

Heat and pressure change sedimentary rock into metamorphic rock

## Rock cycle

The continuous rearranging of the rocks in the Earth's crust

Igneous rocks form when hot magma ■ solidifies. When exposed on the Earth's surface, these rocks are worn down by weathering ■ and erosion ■ into tiny fragments. Wind and water carry the fragments out to sea, where they settle in layers on the seabed. They slowly turn into sedimentary rocks as they are buried deeper. These rocks are either worn away to form new sedimentary rocks, or are transformed by pressure and heat into metamorphic rocks. Exposed metamorphic rocks are in turn worn away to form new sedimentary rock.

Sediment

Sedimentary rock

Igneous rock

Metamorphic rock

Magma

### See also

Cementation 92 • Crystallization 88
Erosion 98 • Feldspar 83 • Gneiss 97
Granite 88 • Igneous rock 88
Lithification 92 • Metamorphic rock 96
Metamorphism 96 • Mica 82 • Magma 52
Quartz 83 • Sedimentary rock 92
Schist 97 • Slate 97 • Weathering 98

Key

■ **Melting**

■ **Crystallization**
(*cooling and solidification*)

■ **Metamorphism**
(*heat and pressure*)

■ **Weathering and erosion**
(*breakup, transport, and deposition*)

■ **Lithification**
(*compression and cementation*)

### Recycled rock

*The rock cycle is an endless process in which rock material is continually being recycled as the rocks of the Earth's crust are created and destroyed.*

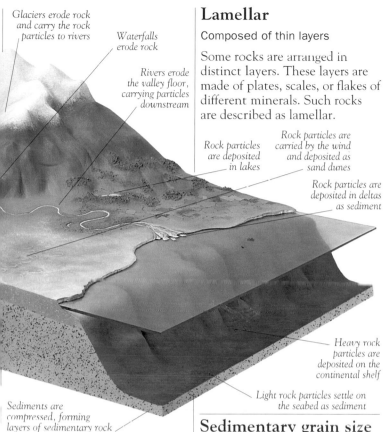

Glaciers erode rock and carry the rock particles to rivers

Waterfalls erode rock

Rivers erode the valley floor, carrying particles downstream

Rock particles are deposited in lakes

Rock particles are carried by the wind and deposited as sand dunes

Rock particles are deposited in deltas as sediment

Heavy rock particles are deposited on the continental shelf

Light rock particles settle on the seabed as sediment

Sediments are compressed, forming layers of sedimentary rock

## Lamellar

Composed of thin layers

Some rocks are arranged in distinct layers. These layers are made of plates, scales, or flakes of different minerals. Such rocks are described as lamellar.

## Igneous grain size

The size of crystals in igneous rock

Rocks consist of **grains** or crystals of different minerals. Granite ▦, for example, consists of crystals of quartz, various feldspars, and mica ▦. An igneous rock made of grains bigger than 1.2 in. (30 mm) across is said to be **very coarse grain**; 0.2–1.2 in. (5–30 mm) is **coarse grain**; 0.04–0.2 in. (1–5 mm) is **medium grain**; less than 0.04 in. (less than 1 mm) is **fine grain**. A rock with a grain size of zero is **glassy**.

**Coarse-grained igneous gabbro**

## Sedimentary grain size

The size of particles in sedimentary rocks

On the **Udden-Wentworth scale**, a **boulder** is a particle more than 10 in. (256 mm) across; a **cobble** is 2.5–10 in. (64–256 mm); a **pebble** is 0.08–2.5 in. (2–64 mm); **sand** is 0.003–0.08 in. (0.065–2 mm); **silt** is 0.00008–0.003 in. (0.002–0.065 mm); and **clay** is less than 0.00008 in. (less than 0.002 mm). On other scales, **gravel** is particles of a similar size to pebbles.

## Matrix

The fine-grained material of a rock that holds coarser grains together

Many rocks have a few coarse grains embedded in a mass or matrix of fine grains. The matrix in sedimentary rocks is a **cement**, which binds the coarse grains together. In igneous rocks the matrix is called the **ground mass**.

## Rock texture

The size, shape, and pattern of grains in a rock

Examining the texture of a rock is usually the simplest way of identifying it, because each type of rock has a different size, shape, and arrangement of grains. Rock texture also determines the feel of the rock (rough, smooth, gritty, and so on) and its strength.

## Glassiness

A smooth, shiny texture like glass

Certain rocks, or minerals within rocks, have a glassy appearance. Glassiness occurs when molten rock cools so rapidly that there is no chance for crystals to form. It is most common in igneous rocks.

## Foliation

The creation of a banded structure within rocks

Extreme heat and pressure can align the different minerals in a rock to form parallel bands called **laminations**. This process, called foliation, occurs most often in igneous and metamorphic rocks. Slates ▦ and gneisses ▦ are good examples of foliated rocks.

## Schistosity

A strong, banded rock texture

In medium to coarse grained metamorphic rocks, foliation can create very distinctive bands of mineral crystals. Schistosity occurs when crystals grow under intense pressure. A rock with schistosity is called a schist ▦.

**Close-up of folded schist**

# Minerals

All rocks contain crystals of naturally occurring chemicals called minerals. Each type of rock is made from a particular combination of minerals – sometimes just one, sometimes half a dozen or more. These minerals give the rock its character.

## Mineral

### A naturally occurring chemical

A mineral is an element ■, or a compound of different elements. There are more than 1,000 minerals, but only a few are common. A table of common minerals appears on page 85. A mineral can be identified by a number of key properties, which are described on pages 84–85, as well as by its crystal system ■ and habit ■. Tests for magnetism and radioactivity ■ are also used. An **acid test** involves testing a mineral with a drop of dilute hydrochloric acid. Calcite, for example, fizzes as it gives off carbon dioxide gas, while galena gives off hydrogen sulfide, which smells of rotten eggs.

## Silicates

### Minerals made of oxygen and silicon combined with metallic elements

**Almandine garnet**

Silicates are the most abundant of all mineral groups. Because of this, geologists divide minerals into silicates and **nonsilicates**. Silicates are generally hard, transparent or translucent, and insoluble in acid. Silicates are often grouped according to the shape of their molecules ■, which contain one silicon atom ■ and four oxygen atoms. There are more than 500 different silicates, including olivine, **pyroxene**, **garnet**, and the gem ■ beryl.

## *Mineral springs*

*Hot springs from the Earth's interior bring calcite solutions to the surface at the Minerva Terrace in Yellowstone National Park, Wyoming. As the water cools, layer upon layer of calcite is deposited, forming spectacular terraces.*

## Sulfides

### Minerals made of sulfur combined with metallic and semimetallic elements

**Pyrite**

Sulfides form one of the largest groups of nonsilicate minerals. They are also among the most valuable minerals, because they contain many useful metals in the form of ores ■. For example, **galena** (lead ore) is the lead sulfide, **cinnabar** (mercury ore) is mercury sulfide, **pyrite** (iron ore) is iron sulfide, and **sphalerite** (zinc ore) is zinc sulfide.

## Micas

### A group of flaky silicate minerals

Micas are an important mineral group, usually forming very flaky, sheetlike structures. The small, dark grains in granite ■ are mica. In its **biotite** and **muscovite** forms, mica is common in gneiss ■ and schist ■, as well as granite.

**Muscovite mica**

## Amphiboles

### Silicate minerals that contain the elements iron and magnesium

Many amphiboles are described as **ferromagnesian**, meaning that they contain iron and magnesium. Aluminum, calcium, and sodium may also be present. The best known amphibole is **hornblende**, a mineral common in igneous rocks ■.

**Hornblende**

# Sulfates

Minerals made of sulfur and oxygen combined with metallic elements

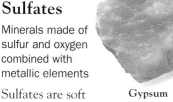
Gypsum

Sulfates are soft minerals that are often left behind when mineral-rich water evaporates. The most common sulfate is **gypsum**, which occurs as an evaporite ▦. Gypsum is hydrated calcium sulfate – that is, calcium sulfate containing water. **Barite** (barium sulfate) is deposited as veins in rock when underground jets of mineral-rich hot water, called **hydrothermal vents**, dry up.

# Olivines

Glassy-looking silicate minerals containing iron and magnesium

Olivines form thick, wedge-shaped crystals and are usually dark green in color. Their molecules have a more simple structure than those of amphiboles. Olivines are especially important in basic rocks ▦ and are thought to be a major constituent of the oceanic crust ▦ and the Earth's mantle ▦.

# Oxides

Minerals made of oxygen combined with other elements

Corundum

Oxides are one of the most important groups of nonsilicate minerals. Some oxides are useful metal ores. They include iron ores such as **hematite** and **magnetite** (iron oxides), and tin ores such as **cassiterite** (tin oxide). **Corundum** (aluminum oxide) occurs as the gems ruby and sapphire. **Quartz** (silicon dioxide) is one of the most abundant of all minerals.

# Carbonates

Minerals made of carbon and oxygen combined with metallic or semimetallic elements

When carbon and oxygen combine they form **carbonate**. Carbonate minerals include **calcite** (calcium carbonate), which makes up the bulk of limestones ▦ and marbles ▦, and **dolomite** (calcium magnesium carbonate). Most carbonates can be identified by the fact that they dissolve in hydrochloric acid.

# Feldspars

Silicate minerals that contain calcium, sodium, potassium, and aluminum

Feldspars are the most important group of rock-forming minerals, and are found in many igneous and metamorphic rocks ▦. The most common are **plagioclase feldspars** (silicates of sodium and calcium) and **orthoclase feldspars** (potassium aluminum silicate). Plagioclase feldspar is a major constituent of gabbro ▦, and orthoclase feldspar of granite.

**Albite – a plagioclase feldspar**

# Essential minerals

The minerals that identify a rock

In every rock, there is a combination of minerals that gives the rock its character and identity. These are called the essential minerals. In granite, for example, the essential minerals are quartz, feldspar, and mica. But rocks often contain traces of additional minerals, called **accessory minerals**. In granite, wedge-shaped crystals of the silicate **titanite** often occur as accessory minerals.

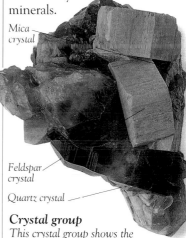
Mica crystal

Feldspar crystal

Quartz crystal

**Crystal group**
*This crystal group shows the essential minerals of granite – quartz, feldspar, and mica.*

# Amygdale

A mineral formed in a gas bubble that is trapped as lava solidifies

If gas bubbles, or vesicles ▦, are left behind when lava solidifies, they may eventually fill in with minerals such as quartz or calcite.

## See also

Atom 42 • Basic rock 80 • Crystal habit 87
Crystal system 87 • Element 42
Evaporite 95 • Gabbro 90 • Gem 166
Gneiss 97 • Granite 90 • Igneous rock 88
Limestone 94 • Molecule 42 • Mantle 41
Marble 97 • Metamorphic rock 96
Oceanic crust 40 • Ore 167
Radioactivity 76 • Schist 97 • Vesicle 54

*Continued on next page* ➤

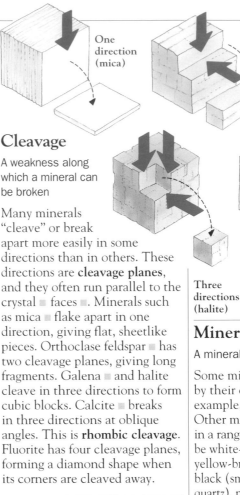

One direction (mica)

Two directions (feldspar)

**Cleavage patterns**
*Cleavage planes are caused by the way atoms are arranged in the mineral.*

Three directions (halite)

Four corners broken off

Four directions (fluorite)

*Diamond shape*

## MOHS' SCALE

Everyday equivalent in parentheses

1 Talc

2 Gypsum *(fingernail)*

3 Calcite *(bronze coin)*

4 Fluorite *(iron nail)*

5 Apatite *(glass)*

6 Feldspar *(penknife blade)*

7 Quartz *(steel knife)*

8 Topaz *(sandpaper)*

9 Corundum

10 Diamond

## Cleavage

A weakness along which a mineral can be broken

Many minerals "cleave" or break apart more easily in some directions than in others. These directions are **cleavage planes**, and they often run parallel to the crystal ■ faces ■. Minerals such as mica ■ flake apart in one direction, giving flat, sheetlike pieces. Orthoclase feldspar ■ has two cleavage planes, giving long fragments. Galena ■ and halite cleave in three directions to form cubic blocks. Calcite ■ breaks in three directions at oblique angles. This is **rhombic cleavage**. Fluorite has four cleavage planes, forming a diamond shape when its corners are cleaved away.

## Fracture

A break in a mineral that does not follow a cleavage plane

Minerals with no cleavage pattern break unevenly. The pieces may be **conchoidal** (shell-like), **hackly** (jagged), or **splintery**.

## Specific gravity (SG)

A measure of a mineral's density

The density of a mineral can help geologists to identify it – metals ■, for example, are much denser than nonmetals. Density is calculated by dividing the mineral's mass by its volume. But the density of an irregular lump of mineral is hard to calculate, so geologists measure its specific gravity instead. This is the ratio of its mass to the mass of an equal volume of water.

## Mineral color

A mineral's color in natural light

Some minerals can be identified by their color. Olivine ■, for example, is usually dark green. Other minerals, however, occur in a range of colors. Quartz ■ can be white-gray (milky quartz), yellow-brown (citrine), brown-black (smoky quartz), pink (rose quartz), purple-violet (amethyst ■), or even colorless (rock crystal).

## Streak

The color of a mineral when ground to a powder

A mineral's color may vary, because of impurities and the different ways in which it forms. However, a mineral's streak usually stays the same. The color of a mineral's streak is found by rubbing it across the surface of an unglazed porcelain tile.

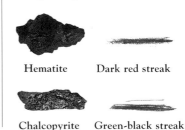

Hematite — Dark red streak

Chalcopyrite — Green-black streak

## Hardness

A mineral's resistance to being scratched

A mineral ■ can be given a rating on **Mohs' scale of hardness**. This scale, devised by the German geologist **Friedrich Mohs** (1773–1839), goes from 1 (talc, very soft) to 10 (diamond ■, very hard). A mineral scratches any other mineral with a lower rating.

◄ *Continued from previous page*

## See-through mineral

*This block of Iceland spar calcite is highly transparent, but it gives a double image of objects placed behind it.*

## Transparency

The way in which light passes through a mineral

Some minerals, such as Iceland spar calcite, are almost as **transparent** as glass – that is, it is possible to see right through them. Others, such as fluorite, are milky or **translucent**. They let some light through, but objects cannot be clearly seen through them. The rest, such as galena, are **opaque**, and let no light through at all.

## Luster

The way in which light reflects off the surface of a mineral

Some minerals have a **glassy** or **vitreous** luster, and glisten like broken glass. Others have a **metallic** luster, and shine like metal. In addition to glassy and metallic, the most commonly used terms to describe luster are **pearly**, **silky**, **adamantine** (like diamonds), **waxy** or **greasy**, **splendent** or **spectacular** (reflects like a mirror), and **dull** (reflects light poorly). Some minerals such as opal have a shimmering rainbow sheen, like oil on water. This is called **iridescence**.

Iridescent opal

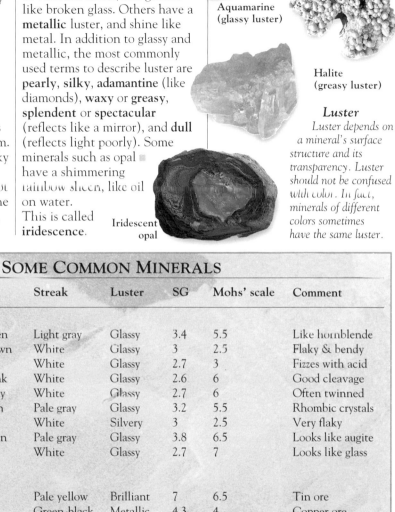

Hydrozincite (pearly luster)

Aquamarine (glassy luster)

Halite (greasy luster)

*Luster*
*Luster depends on a mineral's surface structure and its transparency. Luster should not be confused with color. In fact, minerals of different colors sometimes have the same luster.*

## SOME COMMON MINERALS

| Mineral | Color | Streak | Luster | SG | Mohs' scale | Comment |
|---|---|---|---|---|---|---|
| **Rock-forming** | | | | | | |
| Augite | Black-green | Light gray | Glassy | 3.4 | 5.5 | Like hornblende |
| Biotite mica | Black-brown | White | Glassy | 3 | 2.5 | Flaky & bendy |
| Calcite | White | White | Glassy | 2.7 | 3 | Fizzes with acid |
| Orthoclase feldspar | White-pink | White | Glassy | 2.6 | 6 | Good cleavage |
| Plagioclase feldspar | White-gray | White | Glassy | 2.7 | 6 | Often twinned |
| Hornblende | Dark green | Pale gray | Glassy | 3.2 | 5.5 | Rhombic crystals |
| Muscovite mica | Colorless | White | Silvery | 3 | 2.5 | Very flaky |
| Olivine | Olive green | Pale gray | Glassy | 3.8 | 6.5 | Looks like augite |
| Quartz | Milky | White | Glassy | 2.7 | 7 | Looks like glass |
| **Mineral ores** | | | | | | |
| Cassiterite | Black | Pale yellow | Brilliant | 7 | 6.5 | Tin ore |
| Chalcopyrite | Brass | Green-black | Metallic | 4.3 | 4 | Copper ore |
| Galena | Lead gray | Lead gray | Metallic | 7.5 | 2.5 | Lead ore |
| Hematite | Gray-red | Dark red | Dull | 5.2 | 6 | Iron ore |
| Magnetite | Iron black | Black | Metallic | 5.2 | 6 | Iron ore |
| Malachite | Bright green | Pale green | Dull | 4 | 3.5 | Copper ore |
| Pyrite | Gold | Green-black | Metallic | 5 | 6.5 | Iron ore |
| Sphalerite | Dark brown | Pale brown | Resinous | 4 | 4 | Zinc ore |
| **Other minerals** | | | | | | **Uses** |
| Barite | Colorless | White | Variable | 4.5 | 3 | White paint |
| Fluorite | Pale purple | White | Glassy | 3.1 | 4 | Enamel |
| Gypsum | White-yellow | White | Variable | 2.3 | 2 | Cement, plaster |
| Halite | Colorless | White | Glassy | 2.2 | 2.5 | Chemicals |

**Background image:** *a crystal of olivine*

# Crystals

Although it may not appear so to the naked eye, much of the Earth's surface is made of crystal, because many rocks contain crystalline minerals. There is an almost infinite variety of crystals, but all have regular, geometrical shapes.

*The angle is read from this scale*

**Goniometer**

*Topaz crystal*

*Angle being measured*

*Measuring faces*
*Above, a goniometer is being used to measure the angles of a crystal's faces.*

## Crystal

A solid, regular, angular, smooth-faced form of a mineral

Crystals are usually made entirely of a single element ■ or compound ■, although patches of other substances may sometimes be found embedded within them. Crystals form geometrical shapes, with smooth faces, straight edges, and symmetrical corners. This is because they are built up from a regular framework, or lattice, of atoms ■. Crystals form as a molten solid cools, or as liquid evaporates from a solution containing a dissolved mineral. The slower a crystal forms, the larger its size. A crystal grows as more and more atoms join onto the basic lattice.

*Naturally forming crystals*
*This huge outcrop of sulfur crystals has formed at the mouth of a volcanic vent called a fumarole. The crystals form as emerging sulfur-rich gases cool down.*

## Crystallography

The study of crystals

Scientists study the structure and properties of crystals by testing them with chemicals, by examining them under very powerful microscopes, and by investigating their effect on light or X-rays shone through them.

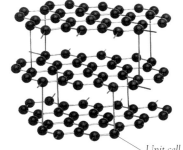

*Unit cell*

*Graphite lattice*
*Graphite crystals have unit cells of hexagonally arranged carbon atoms. The unit cells in the lattice are arranged in layers that are held together weakly, making graphite a very soft mineral.*

## Crystal lattice

The atomic structure of a crystal

A well-formed crystal is regular and symmetrical, but the actual shape of a crystal depends upon the way its atoms are arranged. All crystals are made of a three-dimensional framework called a lattice. The smallest complete piece of a lattice is a group of atoms called a **unit cell**. Each crystal is built up from identical unit cells, repeated again and again. Unit cells can interlock in 32 different ways, called **crystal classes**, to form the basic lattice.

## Crystal face

A flat plane on a crystal's surface

Crystal faces intersect at set angles to form well-defined edges. In all crystals of the same mineral ■, the angles between corresponding faces are always the same. These angles, which are measured by an instrument called a **goniometer**, are determined by the arrangement of the crystal's atoms. Crystal faces are created naturally as the crystal grows. The flat surfaces produced when gems ■ are cut and polished are not true crystal faces. When the faces of certain crystals are treated with chemicals, regular marks or **etch figures** may develop. These are used to identify the crystal system to which the crystal belongs.

## Crystal symmetry

The regular arrangement of a crystal's faces

Crystals are described in terms of their symmetry. An **axis of symmetry** is an imaginary line through a crystal's center. If the crystal is rotated 360° about this line, it always appears perfectly symmetrical. A **plane of symmetry** is an imaginary plane that divides a crystal into two identical halves. Cubic crystals are the most symmetrical. They have 12 axes of symmetry and nine planes of symmetry.

# Crystal system

A basic geometrical shape formed by crystals

All crystals can be placed, according to their symmetry, into one of six crystal systems: **monoclinic**, **triclinic**, **cubic**, **tetragonal**, **orthorhombic**, and **hexagonal** or **trigonal**. Crystals of the same mineral always belong to the same crystal system. However, they do not always look alike, because within each system there may be many variations or **forms**. A crystal in the cubic system, for example, could be cube-shaped, but it could also be an octahedron (an eight-sided diamond shape), a dodecahedron (a twelve-sided shape, like a cube with its corners cut off), and a number of other variations.

# Crystal habit

The characteristic appearance of a crystal or a mass of crystals

Crystals are rarely perfectly formed, so it is often much easier to describe a crystal by its habit than to find out which crystal system it belongs to. Crystal habit is often determined by the conditions under which the crystal grows. Some terms used to describe habit are **dendritic** (treelike), **prismatic** (prism-shaped), **lenticular** (lens-shaped), **acicular** (needlelike), **bladed** (blade-shaped), **reniform** (kidney-shaped), and **massive** (no definitive shape).

*Sharp habit*
*This impressive mesolite crystal from Bombay, India, is a good example of the acicular habit, which produces sharp, needlelike masses.*

## CRYSTAL SYSTEMS

The blue diagrams show crystal systems alongside real examples

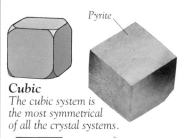
Pyrite

Emerald

**Cubic**
*The cubic system is the most symmetrical of all the crystal systems.*

**Hexagonal/trigonal**
*These two systems are grouped because of their similar symmetry.*

Gypsum

Axinite

**Monoclinic**
*One of the most common systems; less symmetrical than the cubic system.*

**Triclinic**
*The least symmetrical of all the crystal systems.*

Idocrase

Barite

**Orthorhombic**
*This system often produces prismatic crystals.*

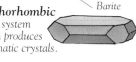

**Tetragonal**
*This system produces crystals more elongated than cubic crystals.*

*The slender crystal "needles" are very fragile, but so sharp that they can pierce the skin*

# Crystal color

The color of a crystal in natural light

Some crystals are nearly always the same color because they contain atoms that absorb certain colors of light. These are **idiochromatic** crystals. Sulfur crystals, for example, are usually yellow. **Allochromatic** crystals occur in a range of colors. The different colors result from impurities or variations in the crystals' atomic structure. Quartz ■ and beryl ■ form allochromatic crystals.

## See also

Atom 42 • Beryl 166 • Compound 42
Element 42 • Fumarole 53
Gem 166 • Mineral 82 • Quartz 83

# Extrusive igneous rocks

When molten magma bubbles up from the Earth's interior and erupts from volcanoes as lava, it is incredibly hot. As the lava starts to cool, crystals begin to appear. The more it cools, the more crystals form. Eventually it becomes a solid mass of hard, crystalline igneous ("fiery") rock.

### The Giant's Causeway
*This rock formation in County Antrim, Northern Ireland, is made of about 40,000 basalt columns, each 3–7 ft. (1–2 m) high. It was part of a huge lava flow that erupted million of years ago.*

## Igneous rock
Rock that forms as molten magma or lava solidifies

The oldest igneous rocks date back at least 3.6 billion years, while the youngest are being formed even now. There are over 600 types of igneous rock. Each one has its own grain pattern and mineral ▪ composition. This is determined by the nature of the magma from which the rock forms and how quickly it cools.

## Extrusive igneous rock
Rock that forms when lava erupts onto the Earth's surface

Extrusive igneous rock is also called **volcanic rock**, because it forms from lava ▪ thrown out by erupting volcanoes. Rock that forms below ground in an igneous intrusion ▪ is called intrusive igneous rock.

## Igneous minerals
The chemical components of igneous rocks

Igneous rocks are made mainly of silicates ▪. Silica-rich rocks are acid ▪ and pale in color. Those containing less silica are dark and basic ▪. The main silicates in igneous rocks are orthoclase feldspar ▪, plagioclase feldspar, quartz ▪, biotite mica ▪, olivine ▪, amphibole ▪, and pyroxene. Each type of rock contains different proportions of these minerals. Rhyolite, for instance, is about 30 percent orthoclase feldspar, 28 percent quartz, 20 percent plagioclase feldspar, with small amounts of mica and biotite.

## Crystallization
The growth of crystals as igneous rock forms from cooling magma

Every mineral "freezes out" and crystallizes at a particular temperature. Olivine crystallizes at 2,200°F (1,200°C), while quartz only freezes out when the temperature is 1,560°F (850°C).

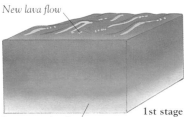

*New lava flow*

*Lava is too hot for crystals to form*

**1st stage**

*Feldspar crystals form first*

*The surface of the lava cools quickest*

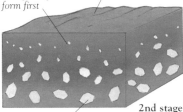

*Larger crystals form farther from surface*

**2nd stage**

*Mica crystals form after further cooling*

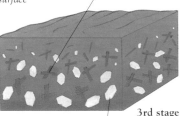

*Denser crystals sink down*

**3rd stage**

*Quartz crystals make up the ground mass, binding the rock together*

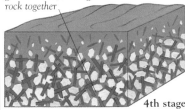

**4th stage**

### How crystals form in rhyolite
*When lava cools, mineral crystals freeze out at different stages. Feldspar forms first, followed by mica. Shapeless quartz crystals form last, filling in the gaps.*

## BASALTIC ROCKS

Basaltic or basic igneous rocks are dark in color; the larger the grains, the deeper they formed in the Earth's crust.

Gabbro
(coarse-grained)

Dolerite
(medium-grained)

Basalt
(fine-grained)

## Grain texture

The size and structure of grains in igneous rock

Igneous rock can be identified by grain size ▦ as well as by mineral content. Larger crystals ▦ grow in igneous rock when magma ▦ and lava cool slowly. Volcanic rock forms from lava that cools rapidly on the surface to give glassy or fine-grained rocks. Intrusive rocks that form deep below ground cool much slower to give coarser-grained rocks. Rocks in minor intrusions tend to be medium-grained. For most types of fine-grained volcanic rock, there is a coarse-grained and a medium-grained equivalent with a similar mineral makeup. The rock rhyolite, for example, is similar in mineral content to granite ▦ (coarse-grained) and **microgranite** (medium-grained).

### *Towering columns*

*The Devil's Tower in Wyoming is a cluster of rock columns that rises 867 ft. (264 m) into the air.*

## Basalt

A dark-colored, fine-grained volcanic rock

About 80 percent of all volcanic rocks are basalt rocks. They form from very runny lavas that spread out far around a volcano. Because this lava cools very quickly, basalt rocks are also very fine-grained – so fine-grained, in fact, that the grains can often be seen only under a microscope. Basalt rocks are made mainly from plagioclase feldspar and augite, with or without olivine. Basalts rich in olivine are common in the lavas of Pacific island volcanoes. Basalts lacking olivine are called **tholeiitic basalts**. They make up much of the oceanic crust ▦.

## Columnar rock

A volcanic rock that splits into columns as the lava cools

As a basalt lava flow cools, it contracts, and fractures may appear in the rock. This often splits the rock into remarkable hexagonal columns like the Giant's Causeway in Northern Ireland and the Devil's Tower in Wyoming.

## Andesite

A dark-colored, fine-grained, silica-rich volcanic rock

Andesite

Andesite is the second most abundant volcanic rock after basalt. It is almost as dark as basalt and has a similar mineral content, although it contains more silica. It is common in the Andes of South America and in the island arcs ▦ of the Pacific Ocean.

## Rhyolite

A light-colored, fine-grained volcanic rock

Rhyolite is acid rock. It forms from sticky lavas that pile up around volcanic vents ▦. It is similar to granite in its mineral makeup, as are the shiny black **obsidian** and the dark green **pitchstone**, which both have a glassy texture.

## Trachyte

A gray, fine-grained volcanic rock

Trachyte

Trachyte is an intermediate rock ▦, between basalt and rhyolite, that is rich in feldspar. Trachyte is found where lava erupted as continental plates pulled apart, such as along Africa's Great Rift Valley. Lava flow often leaves distinct bands in the rock. This is the rock's **trachytic texture**.

## Tuff

Medium-grained volcanic rock formed not from lava but from volcanic ash deposits

Tuff

Volcanic rocks that form from pyroclastic ▦ material are called **pyroclastic rocks**. Tuff is lithified volcanic ash ▦, with a grain size of less than 0.08 in. (2 mm).

# Intrusive igneous rocks

Molten magma does not always erupt on the Earth's surface and form volcanic rock. Intrusive igneous rocks may form as magma solidifies underground. They are only exposed on the surface if the overlying rock is worn away.

## Intrusive igneous rock

A rock that forms when magma solidifies far below ground

Two types of igneous rock form underground. **Hypabyssal rocks** form just below the Earth's surface, usually in dikes ■ and sills ■. **Plutonic rocks** form deep beneath the ground in plutons ■ and batholiths ■. All igneous rocks that form below ground cool more slowly than those that form on the surface, so they tend to have coarser grains. Plutonic rocks are the most coarse-grained of all igneous rocks.

### Granite dome
*The massive Half Dome in Yosemite Valley, California, is part of a huge granite batholith that has been exposed to form the Sierra Nevada mountain range.*

## Granite

A light-colored, coarse-grained igneous rock

**Hornblende granite**

Granite is the most common plutonic rock. There are many different types of granite, including finer-grained **aplite** and very coarse-grained **pegmatite**. Granite is the coarse-grained equivalent of rhyolite ■. It is made largely of quartz, with varying amounts of orthoclase or plagioclase feldspar ■, and a little biotite or muscovite mica ■. Granite is nearly always found in areas of mountain ■ building.

## Gabbro

A dark, coarse-grained igneous rock

Gabbros are the second most common group of plutonic rocks. Gabbro is the coarse-grained equivalent of basalt ■. It contains large black crystals of augite, combined with pale feldspar crystals and a little olivine ■. This gives it a mottled appearance. Gabbros usually form in giant igneous intrusions ■ called lopoliths ■. The Bushveld in South Africa and the Duluth lopolith near Lake Superior, Canada, are good examples.

## Dolerite

A dark-colored, medium-grained igneous rock

Dolerites are the medium-grained, hypabyssal equivalent of basalt and gabbro. They can be distinguished from basalt by their slightly larger crystals, which give the rock a subtly mottled appearance. Dolerites often form in dikes and sills such as the Palisades Sill in New Jersey, and the Great Whin Sill in northern England.

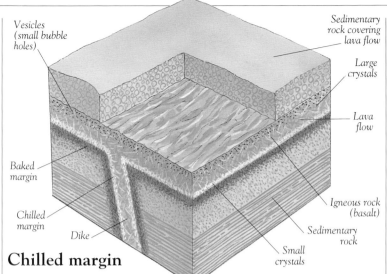

Vesicles (small bubble holes)

Sedimentary rock covering lava flow

Large crystals

Lava flow

Baked margin

Chilled margin

Dike

Igneous rock (basalt)

Sedimentary rock

Small crystals

# Chilled margin

**The rapidly cooled edge of an igneous intrusion**

Igneous intrusions cool slightly faster along the edges that are in contact with the cold country rock ▨ around them. This means that the rock formed in this cool edge, or chilled margin, is finer-grained than that in the rest of the intrusion. The heat of the intrusion "cooks" the country rock alongside the cool edge and changes it into metamorphic rock ▨, forming a **baked margin**.

# Xenolith

**A fragment of old rock caught in a new igneous intrusion**

As an igneous intrusion forms it may trap pieces of "foreign" rock, such as fragments of country rock from the wall of the intrusion. These fragments, called xenoliths, may be partly changed, or metamorphosed, by heat and pressure.

Coarse grains of newer granite

Finer grains of older lava

**Xenolith**
*The dark center of this xenolith is lava, surrounded by a pink granite edge.*

*Chilled margins*
*Intrusions have chilled margins. If there are vesicles in the rock instead, it shows that the lava reached the surface as an extrusion, even if it is now covered by a layer of new rock.*

# Peridotite

**A dark, coarse-grained igneous rock**

Peridotite is a dense, ultrabasic ▨ plutonic rock. It is made almost entirely of dark ferromagnesian ▨ minerals such as olivine, augite, and hornblende. **Dunite** is similar to peridotite, but it contains slightly more olivine and less augite. Both of these rocks are greenish brown. They are often found at the base of gabbro intrusions or in areas of mountain building. They may form a large part of the Earth's upper mantle ▨.

# Syenite

**A grayish, coarse-grained igneous rock**

**Syenite**

Syenite is the coarse-grained plutonic equivalent of trachyte ▨. It is quite rare and probably forms when gabbro magma is contaminated by impurities. Syenite's silica content is intermediate ▨ between gabbro and granite, which it may resemble.

# GRANITIC ROCKS

Granitic or acidic igneous rocks are light-colored. The larger the grains, the deeper they formed.

White granite (coarse-grained)

Quartz porphyry (medium-grained)

Rhyolite (fine-grained)

# Diorite

**A light colored, coarse-grained igneous rock**

Diorite

Diorite is the coarse-grained, plutonic equivalent of andesite ▨, and forms when granitic magma is contaminated by impurities. It often forms in offshoots of large granite intrusions.

## See also

Andesite 89 • Basalt 89 • Batholith 56
Country rock 56 • Dike 57 • Feldspar 83
Ferromagnesian 82 • Igneous intrusion 56
Intermediate rock 80 • Lopolith 57
Magma 52 • Mantle 41
Metamorphic rock 96 • Mica 82
Mountain 64 • Olivine 83
Pluton 56 • Rhyolite 89 • Sill 57
Trachyte 89 • Ultrabasic 80

# Sedimentary rocks

Almost 90 percent of the Earth's crust is made from igneous rock, but 75 percent of the world's land surface is covered with thin layers of debris or sediments. These sediments settle on the beds of oceans, lakes, and rivers, and are compacted over millions of years to form sedimentary rock.

## Sedimentary rock

Rock formed from the debris of both other rocks and living matter

Three types of sedimentary rock exist: clastic, organic ■, and chemical ■. Many sedimentary rocks form from debris, or **sediments**, deposited on the ocean floor. Sediments can also build up on land, on beaches, in glacial moraines ■, desert sands, river deposits, and so on. Each sedimentary environment gives a certain type of rock, and different rocks laid down at the same time in different places are known as **facies**. Sedimentary rocks may contain fossils ■, which help geologists to date them.

## Diagenesis

The process that turns loose sediments into rock

Soft sediment is turned into hard rock over millions of years when the sediments are near the surface, and are under relatively low pressures and temperatures (unlike metamorphism ■). It happens as sediments are buried beneath other layers of sediment and become gradually hardened by compaction and cementation. **Lithification** is like diagenesis. It involves cementation but not necessarily burial or compaction.

## Compaction

The slow squeezing of sediments to form hard rock

As sediments pile up on top of each other, they are gradually squeezed. Exactly how much they are squeezed depends on the type of sediment. Mud may be compacted to as little as a tenth of its original thickness as it changes into mudstone, while sand is squeezed very little as it changes to sandstone. Sediments often contain a great deal of water, but this is gradually squeezed out during compaction.

## Cementation

The binding together of compacted sediments

As sediments are compacted, the matrix ■ of fine silt and clay fuses and helps to bind the larger particles together. The sediments are also cemented together by chemicals left by the water in the original sediment. The most common cements are calcite ■, silica (which gives a very hard rock), and iron compounds (which give rock a rusty red color). The strength of the cement controls how strong the rock is. Weak, poorly cemented sandstones are said to be **friable**.

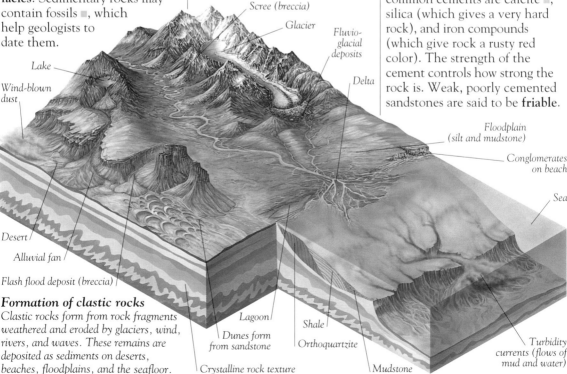

Scree (breccia)

Glacier

Fluvio-glacial deposits

Lake

Wind-blown dust

Delta

Floodplain (silt and mudstone)

Conglomerates on beach

Sea

Desert

Alluvial fan

Flash flood deposit (breccia)

Lagoon

Shale

Dunes form from sandstone

Orthoquartzite

Crystalline rock texture

Mudstone

Turbidity currents (flows of mud and water)

**Formation of clastic rocks**
*Clastic rocks form from rock fragments weathered and eroded by glaciers, wind, rivers, and waves. These remains are deposited as sediments on deserts, beaches, floodplains, and the seafloor.*

*Cross-bedded sandstone*
*Heavily eroded, multicolored sandstone in Arizona.*

# Bedding plane

A boundary between one layer of sedimentary rock and another

Bedding planes are visible as lines in the rock and mark a break in the laying down of the sediments. Some rocks have planes just a fraction of an inch apart that divide thin beds called **laminae**, and create a pattern called **lamination**. Laminae are ripple marks made by currents in the water in which the sediments were deposited. **Cross-lamination** or **cross-bedding** occurs when the water current flowed in different directions at different times. In **graded bedding**, grains are graded in size, with fine grains at the top and larger ones below. This most commonly occurs in turbidity currents when a large load of mixed sediments is dumped at once, allowing heavy particles to settle out first. **Massive rocks** are rocks with no bedding planes at all.

# Clastic rock

Rock made of older rock fragments from weathered and eroded rock

Clastic rocks are classified by the size of the particles from which they are made into clays or lutites, sandstones or arenites, and conglomerates or rudites.

# Clay

Fine-grained sedimentary rock

Sediments made from very small particles, less than 0.002 in. (0.05 mm) in diameter, are known as **lutites**. These particles are normally the result of chemical weathering and usually only settle out of water in very still places such as lagoons and lakes. The smallest particles of all are clay, less than 0.00008 in. (0.002 mm) across and invisible to the naked eye. Clays form **argillaceous rocks**. **Silts, shales**, and **mudstones** have slightly bigger particles.

Mudstone

# Sandstone

Medium-grained sedimentary rock

Sedimentary rocks made from medium-sized grains, between 0.002 in. (0.06 mm) and 0.08 in. (2 mm) across, are called **arenites** or **arenaceous rocks**. The particles in these rocks can be seen quite clearly by the naked eye and the rocks have a rough feel. The **orthoquartzite** sandstones, made largely of quartz grains deposited in a shallow sea, are the largest group. **Arkoses** are pinkish sandstones containing a high proportion (35 percent) of feldspars.

# Graywacke

Medium-grained sedimentary rock with a substantial clay matrix

Graywacke

Graywackes are arenites in which the sand particles are embedded in clay minerals and flakes of mica. They may be laid down in graded beds by turbidity currents.

# Conglomerate

Coarse-grained sedimentary rock

Sediments made from particles more than 0.08 in. (2 mm) across are called **rudites**. They include conglomerates and **breccias**. Conglomerates contain large rounded pebbles made of quartz or metaquartzite. They probably formed on beaches, where the wave action rounded the pebbles. Breccias contain large angular fragments – perhaps from screes or from flash floods in deserts.

## See also

Calcite 83 • Chemical sediment 94
Flash flood 117 • Fossil 70
Load 112 • Matrix 81 • Moraine 124
Metamorphism 96 • Organic sediment 94
Turbidity current 134 • Weathering 98

## Organic sediment

A sedimentary rock made from the remains of plants and animals

Most sedimentary rocks contain fossils ▪, but some rocks are made almost entirely from the remains of living things. **Biogenic rocks** form from the whole remains of living things. Reef limestones, for example, are formed by colonies of coral ▪. **Bioclastic rocks** are made from the fragmented remains of living things and include shelly limestone and chalk.

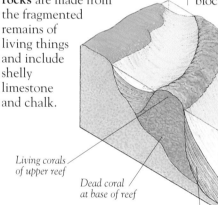

Living corals of upper reef

Dead coral at base of reef

Coral broken from reef

Debris from reef (animal and plant remains)

***Formation of biogenic sedimentary rocks***
*Most reef limestones tend to form in shallow waters from the compressed debris of coral reefs.*

## Chemical sediment

A sedimentary rock made from chemicals dissolved in water

Many minerals, such as calcite ▪, dissolve easily in water. These dissolved minerals may precipitate – that is, come out of solution to be left as deposits, or **precipitates**. Precipitates may build up within other sediments, or they may form rocks by themselves.

## Limestone

A sedimentary rock made mainly from calcite

Some limestones are organic in origin, others are chemical. But all limestones are held together by large amounts of carbonate ▪ cement ▪, especially calcite (or **lime**), as well as magnesium carbonate. Most limestones, such as shelly limestone and chalk, are bioclastic; some, such as reef limestone, are biogenic; while others, such as oolitic limestone, are chemical.

## Reef limestone

Limestone formed from biogenically produced carbonate

Reef limestones are made from the hard calcite skeletons of marine organisms, such as corals, that grow in colonies in warm seas. Reef limestones often occur within layers of shelly limestones. They are harder than shelly limestones and may be left protruding as small hills, called **reef-knolls**, as the shelly limestone is worn away.

## Chalk

A white, very pure form of limestone

Chalk is almost pure calcite. It is a powdery, fine-grained rock. Some chalks are made largely of tiny calcite disks. These disks were produced by a tiny plant called a **coccolith**, which once lived in shallow seas. Other chalks are made mainly from broken shells and some are almost entirely chemical in origin. Some chalks contain bands or **nodules** of very hard **flint**, a form of silica.

**Flint nodule**

## Shelly limestone

A limestone made from sea shells

Shelly limestones are made mainly from broken shells or skeletons of sea creatures, which are rich in calcite. The most common remains are crinoids ▪ or sea lilies, brachiopods ▪, and corals. The shells and remains make up 75 percent of the rock, and are often still recognizable. The rest of the rock is clay mud and calcite.

## Lime mud

Calcite mud precipitated from sea water

In some warm, quiet ocean shallows, calcite can precipitate directly from sea water to form a fine white mud called **micrite**, or lime mud. Micrite is the matrix ▪ in some shelly limestones, but it can also form a rock on its own.

◄ *Continued from previous page*

## LIMESTONES

Limestones vary from coarse-grained pisolitic and shelly limestones to very fine-grained chalks.

**Shelly limestone (coarse-grained)**

## Oolitic limestone

Limestone made from sand grains or shell fragments coated with calcite

In certain shallow seas, small silt grains and shell fragments are rolled to and fro by the waves through lime mud. As they roll, they become coated in calcite and develop into tiny spheres called **ooliths**. They are usually less than 0.04 in. (1 mm) in diameter, and may look like fish roe. This process is taking place now on the Bahama bank off the coast of Florida. Oolitic limestone is made from these ooliths. Larger varieties of these spheres are called **pisoliths** and form coarser-grained **pisolitic limestones**.

**Oolitic limestone (medium-grained)**

### White chalk cliffs
*The Seven Sisters chalk cliffs in Sussex, England, were formed from sediments deposited when the area was below the sea.*

## Evaporite

A sediment left behind when salty water evaporates

As salty water evaporates, it precipitates its dissolved minerals as evaporites. This can happen when lakes dry up, such as the Great Salt Lake in Utah. However, it usually happens on a larger scale when seawater evaporates in lagoons. The main minerals involved are halite, also known as rock salt, and gypsum, which is used in plaster of paris. But the type of sediment created depends on the temperatures involved and the concentration of mineral salts within the water.

**Chalk (fine-grained)**

## Magnesian limestone

A limestone in which calcite has been replaced by dolomite

Some of the calcite in limestone may be converted to the mineral dolomite ▦ (calcium magnesium carbonate). This process, called **dolomitization**, creates magnesian limestones or **dolostones**.

## Tufa

A sedimentary calcite deposit formed around a spring

Tufa forms around cool springs with calcite-rich water. In limestone regions, tufa fills in cavities and builds stalactites ▦ and stalagmites ▦. Around hotter springs a harder, denser type of tufa deposit called **travertine** is laid down. This is usually very pale in color and is often used as a marble substitute by sculptors.

*Land*

*In the lagoon, water sinks as it becomes denser, until evaporites precipitate*

*Sea*

*Halite*

*Gypsum with anhydrite*

*Dolomitized carbonate*

*Sand barrier partially shuts out the open sea*

### Evaporite formation in a lagoon
*The minerals are precipitated in a certain sequence, with calcite first, followed by dolomite, gypsum, and halite.*

### See also
Brachiopod 71 • Calcite 83
Carbonate 83 • Cement 81 • Coral 71
Coral reef 135 • Crinoid 71 • Dolomite 83
Fossil 70 • Gypsum 83 • Matrix 81
Stalactite 103 • Stalagmite 103

# Metamorphic rocks

When rocks are baked by the heat of molten magma or squeezed by the movements of vast tectonic plates, they are altered beyond recognition. They become, in effect, new rocks, called metamorphic rocks, after the Greek word *metamorphosis*, which means transformation.

## Metamorphic rock

Rock formed by the alteration of other rocks

**Metamorphism** can transform sedimentary ■, igneous ■, and metamorphic rocks by heat and pressure. Rocks can be heated if they are near the molten magma ■ of an igneous intrusion ■ or if they are deeply buried, where the temperature is higher. Rocks can be squeezed if they are in zones where tectonic plates are converging, or if they are buried deep beneath overlying material.

## Recrystallization

The growth of new crystals during metamorphism

Heat and pressure alters rocks in two ways. They change the mineral content by causing minerals to react together to form new ones. They also change the grain ■ texture, by altering the size, shape, and alignment of the mineral crystals. These changes involve the destruction of old crystals and the production of new ones. This is a process called recrystallization.

**Mica schist**       **Gneiss**

*Crystal metamorphism*
*The shape and alignment of crystals are altered as schist is changed into gneiss.*

## Contact metamorphism

The alteration of rocks situated next to igneous intrusions

Contact metamorphism happens when rocks are altered by coming into contact with the heat of an igneous intrusion. The affected zone around a batholith ■ is called an **aureole**. Just how much the rocks in the aureole are changed depends on how big the intrusion is and how far they are from the hot magma.

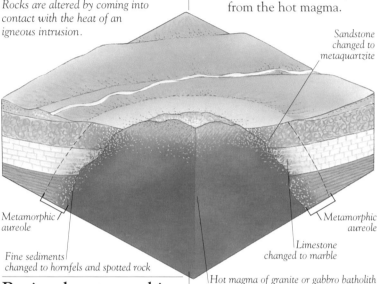

*Contact metamorphism*
*Rocks are altered by coming into contact with the heat of an igneous intrusion.*

*Sandstone changed to metaquartzite*

*Metamorphic aureole*

*Fine sediments changed to hornfels and spotted rock*

*Metamorphic aureole*

*Limestone changed to marble*

*Hot magma of granite or gabbro batholith*

## Regional metamorphism

The alteration of rocks on a large scale as continents collide

Regional metamorphism occurs when rock is crushed and baked deep beneath mountains thrown up between colliding continents. The enormous pressure can give metamorphic rock a distinct foliated ■ texture, with clear schistosity ■. According to the difference in temperature, regional metamorphism is divided into low, medium, and high grades.

## Dislocation metamorphism

The alteration of rocks by faulting

Dislocation metamorphism is a minor form of metamorphism caused when rocks are crushed during faulting ■. It creates rock fragments called fault breccia ■.

*Regional metamorphism*
*Rock is changed on a large scale at depth, under great pressure during the formation of mountains. Metamorphism decreases with distance from the mountain range.*

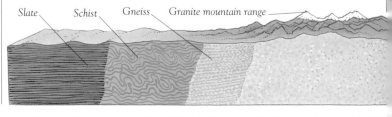

*Slate*    *Schist*    *Gneiss*    *Granite mountain range*

# Marble

A rock made by the metamorphism of limestone

Both regional and contact metamorphism can recrystallize the calcite  in limestone, turning it into marble. Pure limestones are changed into brilliant white marbles that look like shiny sugar. Muddier limestones usually turn into marble with colored streaks and patches caused by the recrystallization of clay minerals.

Marble statue c.2500 BC

# Hornfels

A rock made by contact metamorphism of mudstone and shale

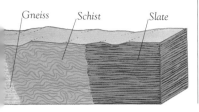

Pyroxene hornfels

Metamorphism of fine-grained mudstones  and shales  can alter the clay minerals within them in different ways, according to the pressure and temperature. In contact metamorphism, the heat close to the intrusion is enough to completely recrystallize the rock into hornfels. Farther away, only some of the minerals are recrystallized, giving **spotted rocks**. Nearer the heat of the intrusion, the spots are crystals of the silicate mineral **andalusite**; farther away they are crystals of biotite mica  and andalusite.

Gneiss    Schist    Slate

# Slate

A rock made by low-grade regional metamorphism of mudstone and shale

Slate is made when shale or mudstone is subject to low-grade regional metamorphism, which involves high pressure, but low temperatures. The pressure realigns the clay minerals of mica and chlorite into smooth, flat layers. The rock remains fine-grained.

# Schist

A rock made by medium-grade regional metamorphism of mudstone and shale

Medium-grade regional metamorphism involves high pressures and moderately high temperatures. This turns mudstone and shale into schist with distinct parallel bands of muscovite or biotite mica, and occasional nodules of garnet . The grain size of schist is larger than that of slate.

# Gneiss

A rock made by high-grade regional metamorphism of shale and mudstone

High-grade regional metamorphism takes place beneath mountain roots, where the pressure is immense and the temperature is extremely high. This completely transforms mudstone and shale into gneiss. The rock is totally recrystallized to form bands of alternating light and dark minerals. The dark layers are rich in micas, amphiboles , and pyroxenes ; the lighter bands contain quartz  and feldspar . Gneiss is thought to make up much of the upper part of the Earth's continental crust .

## METAMORPHIC ROCKS

Intensely metamorphosed rocks have large grains and strong banding.

Gneiss (coarse-grained)

Schist (medium-grained)

Black slate (fine-grained)

# Metaquartzite

A rock made by the metamorphism of sandstone

Metaquartzite

Loose-grained sandstone is metamorphosed by pressure and heat into hard metaquartzite. The space between the grains is filled with recrystallized quartz.

## See also

Amphibole 82 • Batholith 56 • Calcite 83
Continental crust 40 • Fault 60
Fault breccia 61 • Feldspar 83
Foliation 81 • Garnet 82 • Grain 81
Igneous intrusion 56 • Igneous rock 88
Magma 52 • Mica 82 • Mudstone 93
Pyroxene 82 • Quartz 83 • Schistosity 81
Sedimentary rock 92 • Shale 93

# Weathering

Although rock is solid, it does not last forever. When it is exposed on the Earth's surface, assault by wind and other physical or chemical processes gradually breaks it down, eventually turning even the hardest granite into soft clay. Below ground, water seeping past rocks can slowly eat them away.

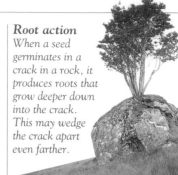

*Root action*
*When a seed germinates in a crack in a rock, it produces roots that grow deeper down into the crack. This may wedge the crack apart even farther.*

## Weathering

The gradual breaking down of rocks

Rocks are broken down by a combination of mechanical, chemical, and organic processes. Usually, only rocks very near the surface are affected, but water filtering through the ground can weather rocks as far down as 600 ft. (185 m). In general, the more extreme the climate is, the faster weathering takes place.

*A sculpted landscape*
*Weathering and erosion have carved the sedimentary rock in Bryce Canyon, Utah, into amazing pillars.*

## Erosion

The wearing down and removal of rock

Weathered rock may stay in the place where the original rock was exposed. But moving glacial ■ ice, rivers and streams ■, the sea, and wind ■ can all wear rock down and carry it away. This process is erosion. The material is carried to another site and deposited as sediment. **Denudation** is the combined result of weathering and erosion. Over thousands or millions of years, denudation can destroy even the toughest rock.

## Biological weathering

The breaking down of rock by living organisms

Growing tree roots exert pressure on the rocks around them, and may force open cracks in the rocks. Similarly, the actions of burrowing animals such as rabbits may expand existing cracks. But geologists now think that acids produced by these organisms – particularly once they are dead and decaying – play a much more important part in weathering. **Chelation** is a process in which rocks are eaten away by acids from soil humus ■.

# Mechanical weathering

The breaking down of rocks by physical processes

Mechanical weathering breaks a rock into smaller and smaller pieces. Each piece of weathered rock has the same characteristics as the original. This differs from chemical weathering ■, in which a rock's chemistry is altered. Mechanical weathering is caused by changes in temperature or pressure, or by wind-blown sand. **Salt weathering** occurs when salt crystals form as water evaporates from cracks and pores in the rock. The pressure exerted by growing crystals can break down the rock.

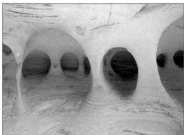

**Honeycomb weathering**
*This strange sandstone formation results from salt weathering and wind erosion.*

# Frost shattering

The fracture of rock by repeated frosts

Frost shattering is also called **freeze-thaw action**. When water that has filtered through cracks and pores in rock freezes, it expands by almost a tenth. This puts enormous pressure on the surrounding rock. At –8°F (–22°C), ice can exert a pressure of 6,614 lb. (3,000 kg) on an area the size of a postage stamp. Repeated freezing and thawing gradually opens cracks and pores wider, breaking up the rock. This process is most effective in moist areas where the temperature continually fluctuates above and below freezing. Such fluctuations are called **freeze-thaw cycles**.

**Scree slope**
*This mass of angular rock fragments fell from the frost-shattered peaks above.*

# Scree

Rock debris from frost shattering

Severe frost shattering produces huge piles of rock fragments called scree. Scree litters the slopes of mountain areas, and piles up at the bottom of rock and hill faces to form **scree slopes**. Frost can also shatter mountain tops into jagged peaks. On high mountains and in cold regions, frost shattering can leave a large boulder-strewn area called a **blockfield** or **felsenmeer**.

# Dilation

The fracturing of rocks caused by the removal of overlying rock or ice

Dilation, or **unloading**, occurs when a heavy layer of ice melts, or a thick rock layer is removed by erosion. The sudden reduction in pressure allows the exposed rock layers to expand more than the rock below, causing them to flake loose. **Sheeting** is when this pressure-release process splits the upper surfaces of rock into large sheets.

**Yosemite domes**
*The spectacular flaky granite domes in Yosemite National Park, California, are called exfoliation domes, but they are actually caused by a form of dilation called sheeting.*

# Insolation weathering

The breaking down of rocks by sunshine in hot environments

Desert rocks expand in the heat of the day and contract in the cool of the night. Some geologists have suggested that this process, called insolation or **thermoclastis**, may cause the rock surface to fracture. But it is probably less significant than other weathering processes, such as arid weathering ■.

# Exfoliation

A weathering process in which rock flakes off in "leaves"

Exfoliation was once thought to be a type of insolation weathering, because it is common in warm, dry areas. It is now thought to be caused by the growth of salt crystals in water that seeps into the rock. Exfoliation makes the surface of boulders flake off in concentric layers, like the skins of an onion, so it also known as **onion-skin weathering**. This term is often wrongly used to describe spheroidal weathering ■. Large flaking granite domes are called **exfoliation domes** but they are really caused by dilation.

*Continued on next page* ➤

## HYDRATION

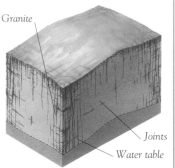

*Granite*

*Joints*

*Water table*

*1 A large, jointed mass of granite lies just below the surface.*

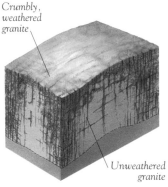

*Crumbly, weathered granite*

*Unweathered granite*

*2 The granite is weathered as water trickles down through the joints, softening the rock chemically.*

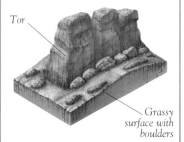

*Tor*

*Grassy surface with boulders*

*3 A granite tor is revealed as the weathered rock is washed away.*

### See also

## Hydration

The breakdown of rocks as they absorb water

Some rock minerals ■ absorb water, making them swell and soften, thereby weakening the rock. This is as much a mechanical weathering ■ process as a chemical one.

## Chemical weathering

The breaking down of rocks by chemical reactions

Chemical weathering usually involves water. For example, many substances dissolve in rain water to form weak acids. These acids slowly soften rocks and dissolve the minerals that cement rock grains together.

## Basal weathering front

The lower limit of chemical weathering underground

Water seeping through cracks can chemically weather rocks below ground. The basal weathering front marks the boundary between the deeper, sound rock and the weathered rock above. In tropical Africa, this may be 160–200 ft. (50–60 m) below ground.

## Carbonation

The chemical breakdown of rocks by carbonic acid

When carbon dioxide in the air dissolves in rain water, it forms a weak carbonic acid that can eat away limestone ■ very quickly.

## Oxidation

The chemical breakdown of rocks as they react with oxygen

Oxygen from the air or dissolved in soil water may react with rock minerals to form chemical compounds called oxides and hydroxides. This makes the rock likely to crumble more easily.

## Hydrolysis

The chemical breakdown of rocks as they react with water

Water reacts with some rock minerals to form insoluble clay minerals. This weakens the structure of the rock. It is most effective in rocks with a high feldspar ■ content, such as granite ■. **Spheroidal weathering** occurs when water seeps below ground and breaks down rocks by hydrolysis. This produces round, flaky boulders, which is why spheroidal weathering is often mistaken for exfoliation ■.

**Flaky boulders**
*Spheroidal weathering formed these granite boulders in the Sahara Desert.*

## Weathering rate

The speed at which rock is broken down

Weathering is more rapid in rocks that contain weaknesses. Chemical weaknesses include the calcite ■ in limestone and the feldspar in granite. Cracks, joints, pores ■, and bedding planes ■ are physical weaknesses. Permeable ■ rocks are especially vulnerable to the action of water. Weathering rates also depend on the climate. Warm, moist climates encourage fast chemical weathering, while cold, moist climates encourage frost shattering ■. Warm, dry climates inhibit all kinds of weathering. Another major factor is **aspect** – that is, the direction the rock faces relative to the prevailing weather. Rocks facing away from the Sun, for example, are more prone to frost shattering.

◄ Continued from previous page

# Rock landscapes

Landscape varies dramatically from place to place, as different rocks are weathered in different ways. Each major rock type produces its own particular type of landscape – from gently rounded chalk hills to spectacular limestone gorges and caverns.

*Granite tor*
*Tors and kopjes are thought to be the result of the gradual uncovering of rock that has already been partially weathered underground.*

## Granite landscape

Typical scenery in granite areas

Granite ▪ scenery varies with the climate ▪. In cold regions, granite's resistance to mechanical weathering ▪ leaves dramatic, exposed peaks. But granite's high feldspar ▪ content makes it particularly prone to chemical weathering ▪. Furthermore, its joint pattern enables hydration ▪ to carry on below ground. When this rock is exposed, it forms rocky outcrops called **tors**. Tors are usually found on top of smooth, grassy hills. **Kopjes** are torlike features found in the tropics ▪.

## Sandstone landscape

Typical scenery in sandstone areas

Sandstone ▪ is a permeable ▪ rock that allows water to seep through easily. In sandstone landscapes, most water soaks into the ground rather than flowing overland. This makes the landscapes quite angular, because they are not rounded by overland flow ▪.

*Sandstone cliffs*
*Sandstone landscapes are often dramatic, such as these cliffs in Provence, France, because they are not worn down by running water.*

## Basalt landscape

Typical scenery in basalt areas

Basalt ▪ scenery is very varied, but in some basalt lava ▪ flows the lava cools to form hexagonal pillars, like those on the Giant's Causeway in Northern Ireland.

## Chalk landscape

Typical scenery in chalk areas

Chalk ▪ is chemically similar to limestone ▪, but it is much softer. This gives chalk landscapes a more rounded appearance than limestone ▪ or karst ▪ landscapes. There are often **dry valleys** or **bournes**, which resemble river valleys and yet do not contain rivers. They may have been formed by rivers in times when the climate was much wetter. There are also large semicircular basins called **combes**, which may have been formed by gelifluxion ▪ in colder times or as a spring ▪ gradually cut back into a hill.

## Solution hollow

A small depression in chalk rock

Water falling onto chalk seeps into the ground but then soaks away as it spreads evenly through pores ▪ in the rock. The result is that chalk areas rarely have the same elaborate networks of caverns ▪ and swallow-holes ▪ as limestone regions. But small dips called solution hollows often form as rain eats away the rock.

*Continued on next page* ➤

***Chinese karst***
*The clusters of steep, narrow, limestone towers that make up the Guilin Hills in China are dramatic karst forms.*

# Limestone landscape

A type of scenery created by chemical action on limestone rock

Streams and rainwater absorb carbon dioxide gas from the soil and air, turning it into a very weak acid called carbonic acid. Where limestone ■ is close to the surface, the action of this acid on the rock (called carbonation ■) can create spectacular scenery. This type of landscape is often called **karst**, because the best example of it is the Karst Plateau near Bosnia's Dalmatian plateau. But there are also major karst areas in other parts of the world, including southern China, Laos, southeastern US, Australia, Malaysia, northern Britain, and France's Massif Central region. Karst produces caverns, steep hills or "towers," pillars, cliffs, and flat "pavements." Karst develops best in wet climates.

## See also

Bedding plane 93

Carbonate 83 • Carbonation 100

Chemical weathering 100 • Climate 154

Limestone 94 • Water table 108

# Doline

A round hollow in limestone scenery

As water flows into a swallow-hole or ponor, the surrounding rock is steadily dissolved. This forms a funnel-shaped hollow, called a doline, up to 330 ft. (100 m) across. Sometimes, a doline gets so big that it merges with other dolines nearby to form a giant hollow called an **uvala**.

# Swallow-hole

The point where a stream disappears underground in limestone scenery

Limestone is among the most permeable of all rocks because of its well-developed joint system. This means that there is very little surface water in karst landscapes, as most streams flowing onto limestone quickly disappear below ground. A swallow-hole, or **sinkhole**, is the point at which a stream disappears. This may be just a place where the stream seeps into the ground and dries up. But chemical weathering ■ of the rock may widen and deepen these seepage points into great vertical shafts called **ponors**, or **potholes**. Spectacular waterfalls, often hundreds of yards deep, may flow down the ponors.

*The stream disappears below the surface into a swallow-hole*

*A pothole forms as the water wears away the rock around the swallow-hole*

*Impermeable rock*

*The stream tumbles into the cavern below as a waterfall*

*Stalactites*

*Stalagmites*

*Pillar*

*Cavern*

*Current level of the water table*

◄ *Continued from previous page*

# Stalactite

A tapering mineral deposit hanging from the ceiling of a cave

When water drips through the roof of a limestone cavern, calcium carbonate ▓ dissolved in the water may form a long, icicle-shaped deposit that hangs from the cave ceiling. This is known as a stalactite. As water drips from the stalactite, some carbonate is deposited on the floor, building up a pinnacle called a **stalagmite**. The stalactite and stalagmite may eventually meet to form a **pillar**.

### Cavern cross-section

*Many limestone areas are riddled with caverns. These caverns develop where water penetrates the surface rock. They sometimes follow the bedding planes along which water seeps, often at the level of the water table.*

*Cracks in the limestone widen as water seeps along the bedding planes*

*A limestone pavement forms as rock is eaten away along joint lines*

*Clints*

*Grykes*

# Cavern

A large cavity underground

As water trickles down through joints in limestone rock, the acid in the water gradually dissolves the rock and widens the joints to form ponors. When ponors open up below ground they form small cavities called **caves**, or larger ones called caverns. Eventually, a cavern roof may become so weak that it collapses. This produces a large hole in the ground called a **polje**, and leaves the cavern floor dotted with mounds of rubble called **hums**.

# Limestone pavement

An area of flat limestone dissected by deep grooves

On a limestone surface, water usually sinks through cracks in the rock and into the ground. But chemical weathering of rock joints can create a striking surface formation called a limestone pavement. This area of bare, flat rock is dissected by deep grooves. The grooves are called **grykes** and the "paving stones" are **clints**.

*Cliff*

*A dry, abandoned tunnel called a gallery is left behind when the level of the water table falls*

*Cave mouth*

*Emerging stream*

*Impermeable rock*

# GORGE FORMATION

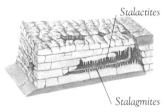

*Limestone*

*Impermeable rock*

*Fault line*

**1** *Below the surface, the stream eats away the limestone along the fault line*

*Stalactites*

*Stalagmites*

**2** *As the water follows the bedding planes, it opens up caves and caverns*

**3** *The water enlarges and links up the caves and caverns, forming a huge cavity*

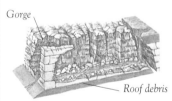

*Gorge*

*Roof debris*

**4** *Eventually, the limestone roof falls in, leaving a deep rocky chasm called a gorge*

# Gorge

A deep, narrow valley with cliff walls

If an entire system of interlinked caverns collapses, it creates a long, rocky-walled valley called a gorge. But in some big gorges, there is no evidence of rubble from collapsed cavern roofs. Some experts think these gorges were cut by powerful rivers when the climate ▓ was much wetter.

# Hills & hillslopes

Hills look permanent enough, but none lasts forever. They are constantly worn down by the weather, running water, moving ice, landslides, and various other "agents of erosion." Slowly but relentlessly, over thousands or even millions of years, valleys broaden and hills are worn flat.

## Mass movement

The downhill movement of rock and weathered material

Weathered ■ material can slide downhill as soon as it is detached from the underlying rock. It usually accumulates and moves down as a single mass. Some mass movements happen gently all the time. Others happen only if the material "fails" – that is, if it becomes too steep or too weak to hold up. A slope of loose material can only be so steep before it fails. The maximum angle of a slope is called the **angle of rest** or **angle of repose**. **Quicksand** is a mass of loose, wet sand that becomes fluid when disturbed by a sudden vibration, so that heavy objects sink into it.

*Rock fall*
*In a rock fall (1), fragments break away from the face of a steep slope.*

1

## Landslide

A sudden collapse of a large mass of hillside

Landslides may be set off by an earthquake ■, by saturation with heavy rain, or by crashing waves. They are clearly visible in sea cliffs ■, but inland they are usually hidden under vegetation. If joints in the rock are weakened by chemical weathering ■, not only the regolith, but also solid rock may fall in a **rock slide** or a **rock fall**. An **avalanche** is a massive fall of snow and ice.

2

## Hill

An area of high ground, usually less than 2,000 ft. (600 m) high

Hills are not only lower than mountains ■; they also tend to be more rounded in outline, with gentler slopes. This is because hills are usually in less dramatically folded terrain than mountains. Hills are often worn into smooth shapes by running water, while most mountain heights are broken into jagged ridges by frost. A highland area bordered by steep, descending slopes is a **plateau**.

3

*Slip plane*

*The slipping blocks often break into stepped sections*

*An "apron" of rock debris builds up at the base of the slope*

*Rock slide*
*In a rock slide (2), a mass of rock moves rapidly down a slope. Rock slides are more dangerous than rock falls because they take place on lower slopes, which are usually nearer to human settlements.*

*Cones of rock debris, or scree, form at the foot of the cliff*

*The rocks range from small fragments only inches across to large slabs several yards across*

*Cliff face*

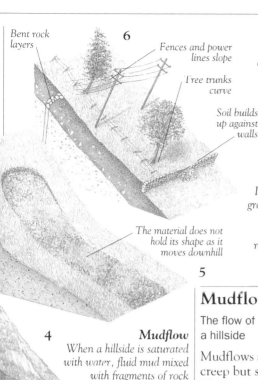

**6**

Bent rock layers

Fences and power lines slope

Tree trunks curve

Soil builds up against walls

*The material does not hold its shape as it moves downhill*

**4**

**5**

### Soil creep

*It is impossible to watch soil creep happening (6), but its effects can be clearly seen. They include tilted fences, walls, and power lines, curving tree trunks, and displaced rock layers.*

### Earthflow

*In an earthflow (5), the wet ground breaks up and tumbles down the slope, forming a tonguelike shape with a rounded end. Earthflows are most common on slopes of clay, silt, and sand.*

### See also

Chemical weathering 100
Earthquake 58 • Mountain 64 • Scree 99
Sea cliff 129 • Weathering 98

## Regolith

A layer of crumbling, weathered material

As rock is steadily broken down by the weather, a layer of loose, weathered material called the regolith builds up on top of the solid, unweathered rock beneath. The lower layer of rock is known as the **bedrock**. On plateaus and flat, lowland regions called **plains**, the regolith can stay in place for millions of years, and may be very deep in places. But on hills, the material slips gradually or suddenly down the slope under the influence of gravity. The regolith is rarely very thick on steep hillsides, because it slips away almost as fast as the rock is weathered. The regolith is generally thicker toward the foot of a slope. In damper regions, it is the regolith that gives a hill its generally rounded shape.

**Mudflow**
*When a hillside is saturated with water, fluid mud mixed with fragments of rock may rush downhill as a muddy torrent (4).*

*The mud flows down existing paths and spreads out at the base of the slope*

*A "toe" forms at the foot of the slope*

**Rotational slide**
*In a rotational slide (3), large blocks move along a concave underlying surface.*

## Slip plane

The undersurface of a landslide

In a typical landslide, the slope collapses and slides down in a curve, a little like jelly sliding from a spoon. The curve down which the slope slides is called the slip plane. The sliding mass of hillside has a semicircular motion along this concave slope. Such movements are known as **rotational slides**. In a **single slide**, there is just one slip plane; in a **multiple slide** there is a whole series. When the slope is very wet and crumbly, the slip planes may merge into a messy **slump**.

## Mudflow

The flow of weathered material down a hillside

Mudflows are faster than soil creep but slower than landslides. They occur when parts of the regolith get soaked through and rush rapidly downhill. The wetter the material, the faster it flows. The fastest, wettest flows are mudflows; the slowest, driest flows are **earthflows**.

## Soil creep

The gradual downhill slide of weathered material

Even on the gentlest slope, the regolith may creep slowly downhill, especially in damper, colder regions. The regolith swells up as it absorbs water or as ice forms in its pores. Then, when it dries out again or the ice melts, it shrinks and moves slightly farther down the slope. Soil creep is also known as **heave**. Little ridges, or **terracettes**, on grassy slopes may be signs of soil creep – or they may just be animal tracks made over many centuries.

**Terracettes**
*On some grassy slopes, a ribbed pattern of terracettes may be seen. These stepped features are 8–24 in. (20–60 cm) high. Experts are not sure whether terracettes are caused by soil creep – the slow downhill movement of regolith – or by animals treading the easiest route up the hill over many years.*

*Continued on next page* ➤

*Upper convexity (curved)*

*Lower concavity (gently curved)*

*Toe slope*

# Slope profile

The shape of a hillside, seen side on

Hillsides are so varied in shape that it is difficult to describe their slope profile accurately. Geomorphologists ■ usually divide the slope into a series of slope units called **straight segments** and **curved elements**.

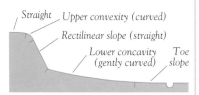

*Straight* — *Upper convexity (curved)*

*Rectilinear slope (straight)*

*Lower concavity (gently curved)* — *Toe slope*

**Typical compound slope profile**
*This imaginary slope profile breaks a slope down into its constituent parts.*

# Slope decline

The theory that a slope gets gentler as it is worn down over time

The theory of slope decline was suggested by William Morris Davis ■ in 1899. He argued that a slope's upper sections are weathered ■ more than the lower sections, because the lower sections are protected by a layer of weathered material called regolith ■. So, as slopes gradually wear down, they get steadily less and less steep.

**Slope decline**
*The slope gets gradually gentler all along its length. The upper section is worn down faster than the lower one.*

**Convexo-concave profile**
*This convexo-concave slope is on chalk downland in Oxfordshire, England.*

# Rectilinear slope

A straight section in a slope

On some hills, it is possible to identify straight or nearly straight sloped sections. These rectilinear slopes usually occur between the hillside's upper convex section and its lower concave section. Occasionally the rectilinear slope is a steep, almost bare rock face, called a **free face**. It is so steep that regolith cannot accumulate there and falls away freely.

# Slope replacement

The theory that the steep sections of a slope get shorter over time

Slope replacement theory was proposed in 1924 by Walther Penck ■. He argued that slopes did not slowly decline, and suggested that a slope's upper sections stay equally steep as they are weathered. But as the weathered material piles up below, the upper sections of the slope get shorter while the gentler lower sections get longer.

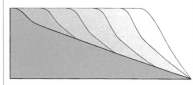

**Slope replacement**
*As the slope is worn back, the gentle lower section gets longer as the steeper upper slopes get shorter.*

# Convexo-concave slope

A slope with a rounded top and dished lower section

In damp regions, slopes are rarely straight. Many have two curved elements: a convex (arched) upper section, getting steeper away from the summit, and a concave (dished) lower section, sloping more gently toward the foot. The regolith slowly moves downhill, mainly by soil creep ■. As it moves away from the summit, it piles up and makes the slope steeper. Lower down the slope, material is moved mostly by overland flow ■. As rain runs off the upper section and down the slope, it carries away material from the lower section and makes it increasingly shallow.

# Parallel retreat

The theory that a slope remains equally steep as it is worn back

In drier regions, slopes may be worn back rather than worn down, so they retain the same shape. This theory is known as parallel retreat, because when each section of a slope is worn back, it stays at exactly the same angle.

**Parallel retreat**
*The slope keeps its shape as it is worn back, except for the lower concavity, which gets steadily longer.*

◀ Continued from previous page

# Water on the land

Rain and snow rarely stays where it falls on the land. Some seeps into the ground, some is taken up by plants, and some evaporates. Water also runs away over the ground into streams and rivers to flow eventually into lakes and oceans.

*Interception of rainwater*
*This rainwater has been intercepted by falling on the branch and leaves of a tree.*

## Meteoric water

Water that has fallen as rain, snow, or other forms of precipitation

Nearly all the water on the Earth's surface has fallen from the atmosphere ■ as rain ■ or snow ■. Such water is called meteoric water. Some rainwater settles on vegetation before reaching the ground or being evaporated. This process is called **interception**. Only a tiny proportion of surface water is **juvenile water**, which is water that wells up from the Earth's interior as hot springs ■. Even less is **connate water**, which is seawater or freshwater trapped in pores in the rock as it was formed.

## Porosity

The capacity of a rock to hold water in spaces within the rock

Some rocks are like sponges, with holes or **pores** into which water can seep. Porosity is measured as the volume of pores compared to the volume of solid rock. Porosity varies greatly from less than 1 percent in slate ■ to more than 30 percent in gravel ■. If a rock is very porous, water can usually seep through it very easily.

*Liquid is held in the spaces between the gravel particles*

*Liquid has seeped into the spaces between the sand particles in the top layer*

**Gravel**

**Sand**

*The liquid remains on top of the clay and does not pass through at all*

**Clay**

### Porosity experiment

*This experiment shows the difference in porosity between gravel, sand, and clay. Gravel is the most porous and water infiltrates very quickly. Sand is more porous than clay, which does not allow any of the water through, so it remains on top.*

## Permeability

A measure of the ease with which water can seep through rock

The permeability of a rock is how easily water passes through it. Sand ■ and gravel are highly **permeable**; clay ■ does not allow water to pass through it, so it is **impermeable**. Limestone ■ is highly permeable even though it is not very porous, because it has large cracks that allow water to run through it.

*All the liquid is retained within the sand*

*Container with hole in base*

*Some liquid is retained in the gravel and some passes through*

**Gravel**

**Sand**

*Liquid can only pass through the impermeable clay if there is a hole in it*

### Permeability experiment

*Gravel is more permeable than sand. Clay is usually highly impermeable because dense clay particles prevent water from passing through, except where there is an existing hole in the clay.*

**Clay**

## Infiltration

The process of water soaking into the ground

Most rainwater soaks or infiltrates into the soil ■ and into permeable rocks. **Percolation** is when water soaks right through and emerges elsewhere. The **infiltration rate** is the speed at which water soaks into the ground, and is dependent on factors such as the permeability of the soil and the plant cover.

*Continued on next page* ➤

## Runoff

Water running away from where it falls

When rain falls, most of the water drains into the ground or runs over the surface. Runoff is the amount of water running away from where it falls in any area. All the rest evaporates where it falls or is taken up by plants. Either way, it eventually returns to the atmosphere, because water taken up by plants is emitted from pores and evaporates in a process called **transpiration**. The combination of transpiration and direct evaporation is called **evapotranspiration**.

**What happens to rainwater**
*When rainwater hits the surface of the ground, some sinks into it, some flows over the surface, and some is taken up by plants, later returning to the atmosphere.*

## Groundwater

All the water below ground

Groundwater is all the water that seeps into spaces and pores ■ in rock. Up to a level called the **water table**, rock is always completely saturated. Water in this **saturation zone** is called **phreatic water**, and rarely moves. Groundwater may extend to 3,300 ft. (1,000 m) below the water table. Above the water table is the **aeration zone**, which is rarely completely saturated. Water here is called **vadose water** and is always seeping up or down.

## Throughflow

Water running through the ground

As water seeps into the regolith ■, it often meets a more compacted layer which impedes its flow. This causes some groundwater to flow along through the ground instead of down, perhaps following small tunnels in the ground. This is called throughflow, and is the major source of water for rivers in cold, moist climates.

*Overland flow*
*During a rainstorm in Yorkshire, England, a large amount of water has collected on the surface of the ground and is now flowing over it.*

## Overland flow

Rainwater running over the surface of the ground

Rainwater runs off over the land when the ground becomes saturated, or when the rain falls too fast to infiltrate ■. When rain is light, the water runs in tiny rivulets. But when rain is heavy, the rivulets join together in a thin sheet that floods across the land. This is sometimes called **sheetwash**.

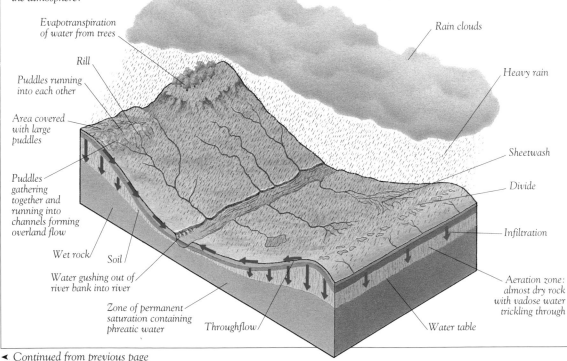

Evapotranspiration of water from trees

Rill

Puddles running into each other

Area covered with large puddles

Puddles gathering together and running into channels forming overland flow

Wet rock

Soil

Water gushing out of river bank into river

Zone of permanent saturation containing phreatic water

Throughflow

Rain clouds

Heavy rain

Sheetwash

Divide

Infiltration

Aeration zone: almost dry rock with vadose water trickling through

Water table

◄ *Continued from previous page*

# Spring

A natural emergence of water from the ground

Where the water table meets the surface – perhaps at the foot of a slope – water comes bubbling out of the ground. If there is only an indistinct trickle of water it is called a **seep**. If there is a gushing flow it is called a spring. If there are many springs in a row, they are called a **spring-line**.

*Bubbling springs*
*These springs of freshwater are bubbling up through the sand and mud on the beach at Wide Bay, Queensland, Australia.*

# Catchment area

The region from which a river gathers all the surface runoff

Scientists studying runoff divide the landscape into different areas, according to where the water runs to. The area supplying a river with water is called the river's catchment area or **watershed**. A **drainage basin** is a region from which all rivers flow into a single river. The boundary between two drainage basins is called a **divide**. In other parts of the world, the word watershed is synonymous with the word divide. An **interfluve** is the band of high ground separating two rivers that are part of the same drainage basin.

# Artesian basin

A rock structure providing a natural reservoir for water

When layers of sedimentary rock ■ are folded into a depression or **basin**, groundwater may run toward the bottom and provide a natural reservoir. An **aquifer** is a layer of permeable rock that can store water. If the aquifer lies in a basin between two impermeable layers, the water in the aquifer will be under high pressure because of the weight of water pushing down into the basin. If a hole is bored through from the surface to the aquifer, this pressure sends water gushing up to the surface. This is called an **artesian well**.

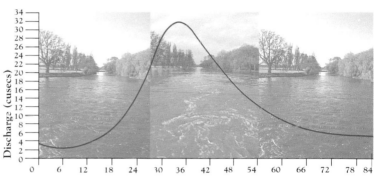

*Storm hydrograph*
*This graph shows the discharge of a river throughout a storm. The photographs show the River Ouse, near Huntingdon, England, before, during, and after a flood.*

# Stream flow pattern

The pattern of flow in a river

Some streams and rivers flow only after heavy rainstorms or during the wet season, and dry up in between. These are called **intermittent streams**. If the stream flows all through the year, it is called a **perennial stream**. With perennial streams, a steady flow of groundwater, usually throughflow, keeps the river flowing between rainstorms.

# Discharge

The rate at which a river flows

The discharge of a river is the amount of water flowing past a particular point each second. It is measured with a flow meter ■ in cubic meters per second or **cusecs**. In most rivers in wet areas, the discharge is relatively steady throughout the year; in drier areas, the discharge can vary widely. The **base discharge** is the minimum flow of water moving in a river. **Peak discharge** is the maximum flow of water in a river. **Bankfull discharge** is the flow when the banks of a river are about to brim over. **Flood discharge** is when a river is so full that it bursts its banks in a **flood**.

# Storm hydrograph

A graph showing the flow in a river after a storm

After a rainstorm, the water level in a river rises, dropping back to normal once the storm is over. This changing pattern of flow can be plotted on a storm hydrograph. Because rainwater takes time to flow overland and through the ground to the river, there is a delay or **lag time** for the flow to rise to its peak. This delay varies between rivers. The graph typically shows the flow rising rapidly to the peak – the **rising limb** – and sinking slowly down to its base flow. This slow decline is the **recession limb**.

# River patterns

The shape of rivers on the landscape is variable. Some form branching networks, for example, while others form regular patterns. Some have no obvious pattern at all. The way a river develops depends on the nature and history of the ground over which it flows.

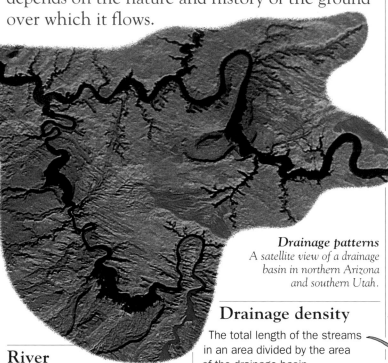

*Drainage patterns*
*A satellite view of a drainage basin in northern Arizona and southern Utah.*

## River

**Water flowing downhill in a channel**

Rivers vary enormously in size, from little more than a trickle to gigantic torrents. The smallest rivers of all are called **rills**. They only run for a short time after it has rained and are thought to be an intermediate stage between overland flow ■ and a real river. Names such as **stream** and **brook** are used for small rivers.

### See also

Batholith 56 • Belted landscape 63
Dip 62 • Dome 63 • Fault 60 • Fold 62
Head 113 • Hydrology 13 • Ice sheet 120
Overland flow 108 • Tectonic plate 46

## Drainage density

**The total length of the streams in an area divided by the area of the drainage basin**

Hydrologists ■ use the concept of drainage density to describe river patterns more precisely. Drainage density is often highest in rainy, mountainous areas.

## Drainage pattern

**The way rivers are arranged on the landscape**

The pattern of rivers in an area varies according to a number of factors, such as the type of rocks and soil, the climate, and human activity. The pattern is thought to be established early on in an area's history and changes little thereafter. A **confluence** is where two streams join. A **tributary** is a small river that joins a larger one.

## Stream order

**A way of describing the status of a tributary**

Every section of a stream can be assigned a place or order in a hierarchy, according to its tributaries. A **first order stream** is the section of a stream from its head ■ to the first confluence with another stream. Two first order streams meet to form a **second order stream**. Two second order streams meet to form a **third order stream**, and so on. Two streams of equal order need to join to produce a stream of a higher order; the order remains the same if a lower order stream joins a higher order one. Drainage basins can be described in terms of the highest order stream within them.

*Stream order*
*This fourth order stream shows how first order streams are the most numerous followed by second, third, and fourth.*

## Accordant drainage

**A drainage pattern directly related to the dip of the underlying rock strata**

In some regions, the rock structure has had a direct influence on the courses of the rivers. This is called accordant drainage. **Discordant drainage** is a drainage pattern not related to the dip ■ of the underlying rock.

# DRAINAGE PATTERNS

Annular

Dendritic

Trellised

Parallel

Radial

Deranged

## Antecedent drainage

A drainage pattern that is maintained as land is uplifted

Discordant drainage patterns may be antecedent or superimposed. Antecedent drainage is when a region of rock is slowly uplifted and rivers cut straight down through the rock as fast as it rises; the original drainage pattern is maintained regardless of the structure of the rising rock. Gorges like the Grand Canyon in Arizona probably formed in this way. **Superimposed drainage** is where the drainage adapts so totally to the overlying rock structure that it keeps its shape even as it cuts down into quite different structures.

## Annular drainage

A ring-shaped drainage pattern

Over circular underground rock structures such as batholiths ▥, the drainage network may develop into a series of concentric rings.

## Dendritic drainage

A branching treelike drainage pattern

In areas of uniform rock, with little distortion by folding ▥ or faulting ▥, the rivers develop a random branching network that looks similar to a tree. This is why it is called dendritic, from the Greek word *dendron* meaning tree.

## Trellised drainage

A rectangular drainage pattern

In some areas, the rock structure steers the drainage pattern so that streams flow parallel to each other and tributaries join almost at right angles. This trellised drainage pattern is typical of belted landscapes ▥, where streams flow along bands of softer rock or in line with the dip of the rock. Sometimes, the joint pattern in the rocks can create a **rectangular drainage** pattern, which is similar to trellis drainage, but the pattern is much less distinct. **Parallel drainage** is where the streams are steered in a virtually parallel course by the structure of the rock – perhaps by parallel folds.

## Radial drainage

A spokelike pattern of rivers

Rivers tend to flow away from the summit of a dome ▥ or a volcano in all directions, creating a spokelike pattern of drainage that radiates from a certain point.

## Deranged drainage

An irregular broken drainage pattern

When an ice sheet ▥ melts, the drainage pattern left behind may be broken and irregular. There may be many marshes, lakes, and short streams. This is because the rivers follow the irregularities in the glacial deposits, and have had little time to adjust to the underlying rock structure.

## Consequent stream

A stream following the original slope of the region

When a new land surface is thrown up by tectonic activity ▥, some streams called consequent streams will follow the shape of the land, perhaps also following the dip of the rock strata below. **Obsequent streams** flow in the opposite direction to the dip of the rock. **Subsequent streams** carve out a course – along a band of softer rock or a weakness – at right angles to the original slope of the land.

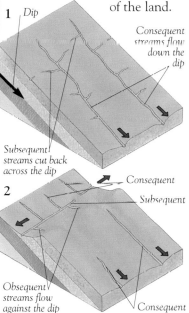

**1** Dip

Consequent streams flow down the dip

Subsequent streams cut back across the dip

**2**

Consequent

Subsequent

Obsequent streams flow against the dip

Consequent

***How obsequent streams develop***
*The subsequent streams in the top picture (1) carve out a valley into which obsequent streams then flow (2).*

## River capture

When a stream cuts back and takes over another stream network

A tributary of one stream may cut back so far that it cuts across another stream network, thereby diverting the waters into its own network. The sharp bend where the captured stream is diverted is called the **elbow of capture**. The short valley left dry by the capture is called a **wind gap**.

# Rivers

Rivers gradually mold the land, eroding material in some places and depositing it in others. As they wind through the landscape, they carve out deep valleys in solid rock, and carry huge amounts of silt that are eventually laid down to form vast plains.

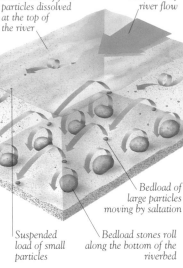

Solute load of fine particles dissolved at the top of the river

Direction of river flow

Bedload of large particles moving by saltation

Suspended load of small particles

Bedload stones roll along the bottom of the riverbed

*Transportation of load*
*The way load is carried within a river depends on the size of the particles.*

## Channel

The long trough in which a river flows

A channel that winds or has a rough bed makes water flow more slowly, because friction between the water and the bottom, or **bed**, interferes with the flow. Similarily, water flows faster in a narrow, deep channel than in a shallow, wide one. Hydrologists ■, who study river flow, use a variety of terms to compare channel shape. The **wetted perimeter** is the distance from the waterline of one bank, across the bed, and up the other bank to the waterline. The **hydraulic radius** is the ratio of the river's cross-sectional area to the length of its wetted perimeter.

## Flow

The way a river moves along within its banks

Flow meters ■ have shown that streams probably run fastest downstream. In the upper reaches, the flow is slowed by friction because the stream is shallow and tumbles over a rough bed – although in places, it goes through fast-flowing sections called **rapids**. Friction is lower downstream, where the river flows between smooth banks of silt ■. **Laminar flow** is very smooth flow, where the water flows in parallel layers without mixing. However, the flow in most rivers is usually **turbulent flow**, which means it whirls and eddies around tiny bumps in the river bed.

## Stream erosion

The way a river wears away its bed and banks

Streams wear away, or erode, their banks and beds, continually widening and deepening them. They do this in a number of ways. **Corrasion** is the way the river scrapes particles of gravel, sand, and small boulders across the bed. Erosion caused by corrasion is called **abrasion**. **Potholing** is when the fragments of load are whirled around in eddies, "drilling" round holes in the river bed. **Hydraulic action** occurs when bits of the bed and bank are loosened by the sheer force of moving water. It is much less important than corrasion. **Solution** is when the material of the river bed simply dissolves. **Attrition** is the wearing down of particles as they hit other particles within the stream.

*Erosion of a riverbank*
*As the river runs past the bank, it cuts into it, picks up material, and carries it away. The bank may be left overhanging.*

## Load

All the material carried within a river

There are three main types of load. The **bedload** is stones and large particles washed along the riverbed. Some of these larger particles may bounce along the bed by a process called **saltation**. The **suspended load** is fine particles that float within the water. The **solute load** is material dissolved in the water. The load varies according to the type of terrain the river flows through and the speed of the flow. Most material is carried during short periods of flooding ■. Rivers such as the Yellow River in China sweep along billions of tons of sediment ■ when in flood.

## Stream transportation

The carrying away of eroded material by a river

The amount of material a river carries varies according to the flow. **Competence** is the size of the largest particle a river can carry. **Capacity** is the maximum weight of load a river can carry.

## Long profile

A graph plotting a river's height

The start of a river is the **source** or **head**. The end and lowest point is the **mouth** or **base level**, which may be the sea or a lake. A long profile is a graph showing the height of a river above the base level all the way along its course. Typically, a profile shows that the stream is steep near the source and slopes more and more gently toward the mouth. This is because tributaries downstream increase the flow of water, and allow the river to run faster and more easily over shallower slopes.

## Graded profile

A river course in which erosion and deposition are balanced

Every river constantly interacts with its channel – as some parts are eroded, so sediments are laid down or **deposited** in others. As the flow changes, so does the balance between erosion and deposition, altering the shape of the channel. Most rivers progress toward a graded profile, in which erosion and deposition are balanced along the river course. Once it reaches this stage, the channel's shape changes only if this balance is upset.

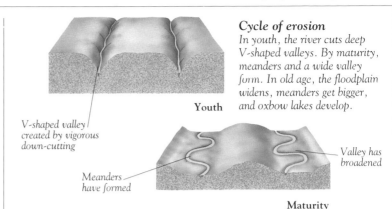

### Cycle of erosion
In youth, the river cuts deep V-shaped valleys. By maturity, meanders and a wide valley form. In old age, the floodplain widens, meanders get bigger, and oxbow lakes develop.

**Youth**

V-shaped valley created by vigorous down-cutting

Meanders have formed

Valley has broadened

**Maturity**

Oxbow lakes have formed

Broad peneplain

Monadnocks

Meanders are very pronounced

**Old age**

## Rejuvenation

An increase in river erosion after a change to the land surrounding the river

When land is uplifted, or the base level of a river drops, the river is rejuvenated and cuts vigorously downward. This sudden increase in erosion creates a sharp **knickpoint**, where the river suddenly steepens as it begins cutting downward and backward. As the rejuvenated river cuts downward, the old valley floor may be left behind as a **river terrace**. Sometimes, the river may follow the original course exactly, cutting down very deeply, creating **incised meanders**.

### Incised meander
*The San Juan River in Utah has developed a deeply cut, incised meander.*

## Cycle of erosion

A theoretical series of stages through which landscapes evolve

The cycle of erosion theory states that rivers and landscapes have their own life cycle, developing over time through certain stages after rejuvenation. These stages are known as **youth**, **maturity**, and **old age**. In youth, rivers cut vigorously down, forming narrow V-shaped valleys ▓. In maturity, rivers widen and deepen, and slopes get gentler as they are worn away. In old age, valleys broaden into wide plains called **peneplains**, and slopes are reduced to isolated hills called **monadnocks**. Some people suggested that rivers exhibited these stages along the length of their course, rather than over time – with youthful upper reaches and old lower reaches. It is now realized the story is much more complex than either of these theories suggest.

### See also
Flood 109 • Flow meter 18 • Hydrology 13
Sediment 92 • Silt 81 • V-shaped valley 114

*Continued on next page* ➤

# River valley

A valley carved out by a river

With the aid of weathering ■ and mass movement ■, rivers gradually carve out deep valleys. In the upper reaches, rivers wind between a series of hills called **interlocking spurs**, and the valleys are narrow, steep-sided, **V-shaped valleys**. The valleys usually broaden out downstream.

# Waterfall

A vertical fall in a river or stream

The gentle slope of a river may be interrupted by a waterfall. Waterfalls may form over a band of hard rock such as a sill ■. In this case, the water speeds up because of reduced friction as it falls over the edge of the hard rock. The river erodes the soft rock below, leaving the hard band untouched. Boulders swirl around at the base of the fall creating a deep pool called a **plunge pool**. Waterfalls may also form over coastal cliffs, at fault scarps ■, at the end of hanging valleys ■, and at the sharp edge of a plateau. Angel Falls in Venezuela is the world's highest fall at 3,212 ft. (979 m). **Cataracts** are a series of rapids.

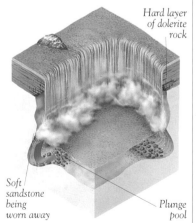

*Hard layer of dolerite rock*

*Soft sandstone being worn away*

*Plunge pool*

**Formation of a waterfall**
*As a river flows over a layer of hard rock, the soft rock below is slowly worn away. In time, the hard rock may collapse, causing the waterfall to retreat upstream.*

# River cliff

A steep bank created when a river cuts into the side of its valley

As rivers carve out their valleys, they erode mainly downward, but where the river meanders they wear sideways as well. This often creates steep undercut slopes called river cliffs, as the foot of the valley side is worn away. Rivers can also wear backward in a process called **spring-sapping**.

# Floodplain

A broad, flat river valley in the lower reaches of a river

Downstream, a river often flows over wide plains of sediment ■ or **alluvium**. This alluvium is washed down from the hills and spreads out over the valley floor in times of flood ■. The floodplain of the Amazon River in South America is hundreds of miles wide. Rivers may sometimes flow across the floodplain between raised banks. These banks, called **levees**, are formed in times of flood when the river drops much of its load ■ as it spills over the top of its channel. Tributaries called **yazoos** may flow next to a levee, unable to join the main stream.

# Oxbow lake

A crescent-shaped lake on a river floodplain

As the river wears away at the outside bend of a meander, the neck of the meander gets continually narrower. Eventually, the river breaks through the neck of the meander, cutting it off. Bars of sediment dam up water in the old cutoff meander, creating an oxbow lake.

*Tributary river*

*Rill (small tributary)*

*Spring-source*

*Waterfall*

*Plunge pool*

*V-shaped valley with steep sides*

*Interlocking spurs*

*Rapids*

*The valley broadens as the river begins to wind*

*Slip-off slope on inside of meander*

**A river course**
*Rivers often start to flow in the mountains. The flow is turbulent high up the valley where the gradient is steeper, the bed rockier, and the river narrower. The river widens downstream, as does the valley into a floodplain.*

# Riffle

A sand or gravel bar on a riverbed

All along its length, a riverbed goes up and down in a series of deep **pools** and shallow riffles where sand or gravel collects.

◄ *Continued from previous page*

# Meander

A looplike bend in a river

All rivers have a tendency to wind. As a river nears the sea, it winds more often, forming regular horseshoe-shaped bends called meanders. Meanders are typical of the lower reaches of a river, but can form wherever the valley is broad and the slope gentle. The biggest meanders form where the river is wide and the material in the banks and bed is fine. Meanders form due to the way a river erodes and deposits material, creating pools and riffles. The riffles may grow further, leading to the formation of a meander. Meanders may also be partly caused by the way water in the river spirals between banks.

## TYPES OF RIVER DELTA

Mississippi: Bird's foot delta

Nile: Arcuate delta

Niger: Modified cuspate delta

# Helicoidal flow

The corkscrewing motion of water through a river channel

Water in a river not only flows downstream but across the river channel as well, creating a kind of spiraling corkscrew motion called helicoidal flow. This occurs because water tends to flow fastest on the outside of meanders, wearing away at the bank. Water flows more slowly on the inside of bends or **slip-off slopes**, and material tends to be deposited here in bars called **point bars**.

# Delta

A fan-shaped, low-lying area of deposits at a river mouth

As a river enters the sea, it suddenly slows down. Its capacity for carrying sediment falls immediately and it may drop the sediment in a huge fan of alluvial deposits called a delta. Often, the river splits up into many smaller branches called **distributaries**. **Arcuate deltas**, such as the Nile delta in Egypt, have a curved, arc-shaped coastline. **Bird's foot deltas**, such as the Mississippi delta, have a ragged coastline shaped a little like a bird's foot. They are formed from the levees of the distributaries. **Cuspate deltas**, such as the Tiber in Italy, are kite-shaped because material is deposited evenly either side of the main channel.

# Estuary

A river mouth broadening into the sea

Rivers usually widen as they flow into the sea, forming broad, often very fertile inlets called estuaries.

## See also

Fault scarp 60 • Flood 109
Hanging valley 123 • Load 112
Mass movement 104 • Sediment 92
Sill 57 • Weathering 98

*River cliff*

*Riffle*

*The river flows between smooth banks of silt*

*Meander*

*Pool in river bed*

*Point bar*

*High bank on outside of meander*

*Braiding*

*Eyot (small island)*

*Yazoo tributary*

*Floodplain with alluvial deposits*

*Sea*

*Delta*

*Deposited sediment*

*Anastomosis*

*Oxbow lake*

*Cutoff neck*

*Levee*

*Distributary*

# Dry landscapes

The processes that shape the landscape in areas where there is little or no rain differ from those at work in moist regions. Dry landscapes, where there is rarely a covering of soil or the action of rivers to soften the contours, are mainly bare rock, sharp cliffs, and dry valleys.

**Encrusted rock**
*The evaporation of water by the Sun produces a hard crust on the top of desert rock, protecting the surface from weathering. But chemical action still manages to eat away at the rock around and below the crust, producing this characteristic mushroom shape.*

## Desert

An area with little or no rainfall

A desert is an area where rainfall is very rare, such as the Sahara in Africa or the Atacama in South America. So deserts are dry (**arid**) regions. The amount of water lost through evapotranspiration ■ often exceeds the amount received from precipitation ■. Vegetation cover is sparse or absent, allowing the ground surface to be exposed to the atmosphere. Temperatures in deserts are usually extreme. Many deserts are among the hottest places in the world. But others are very cold, such as the ice deserts of the Arctic and Antarctic, where rainfall is little higher than in the Sahara.

## Arid weathering

The weathering process in areas of low rainfall

It was once thought that in hot deserts the Sun's heat was mainly responsible for breaking down rocks; a form of weathering called insolation ■. But it is now known that chemical weathering ■ is also an important weathering process in deserts. It produces many different features, including **mushroom rocks (zeugen)**, such as Pedestal Rock, Utah. Even so, desert weathering rarely produces enough fine-grained material to create soils ■, so desert surfaces – with the exception of sandy deserts – are generally bare rock.

## Desert crust

A hard surface deposit of minerals in the desert

Water evaporates very quickly in deserts, leaving behind dissolved minerals ■ that produce a hard crust on the surface. **Desert varnish** is a hard glaze of minerals on exposed desert rock surfaces. It consists mainly of iron oxides and manganese oxides, and is bluish black in color. **Duricrusts** are thicker, and include **calcretes** made from calcium carbonate ■, **gypcretes** made of gypsum ■, and **silcretes** made of silica.

**Desert landscape**
*This barren, rocky desert is Monument Valley, bordering Arizona and Utah. The lack of moisture causes the vegetation to be sparsely spaced.*

Butte that has been eroded to a thin spike

Butte

Mesa

Eroded boulder

# Wadi

A gorgelike, generally dry valley in desert areas

As rain is rare and infiltration ▪ is low in deserts, streams seldom flow all the time. Most streams are intermittent, flowing only occasionally. These dry desert streambeds are called **dry washes** or **arroyos**. In the Sahara and Arabia, rare torrents of rain form narrow gorges called wadis. These are usually dry but after a storm fill with water in a **flash flood**.

*Wadi Kelt*
*This wadi in Israel has cut deep through the existing rock.*

# Bajada

A ramp of sand deposited by rivers along mountain edges in the desert

Where flash floods form wadis in hills that emerge onto plains, they deposit fan-shaped mounds of alluvial ▪ material rather like deltas ▪. If many streams produce such fans, they may merge into one single ramp called a bajada.

# Desert wash

A thin flood of water after a rainstorm in the desert

The lack of soil and the presence of hard crusts prevents rain from infiltrating well into the ground. After a storm, water spreads over the land in a thin sheet called a desert wash, or **sheet flood** ▪.

# Inselberg

An isolated, steep-sided mountain often seen in desert regions

In many desert areas, isolated peaks rise like castles from the surrounding plain. These inselbergs probably form by parallel retreat ▪ of the steep, clifflike face of the mountain. They maintain this shape because they are never covered with soil or weathered material (regolith ▪) like hills in cooler and wetter regions. Uluru (Ayers Rock) in Australia is an inselberg.

# Mesa

An isolated, flat-topped, steep-sided desert mountain

Mesas and further eroded versions called **buttes** form in a different way from inselbergs. They were once part of a wide plateau that was worn back by river erosion when the climate was wetter.

# Desert pavement

A large, flat crust of bare pebbles and stones

In some deserts – particularly in the Sahara – there are large flat areas covered by pebbles and stones. **Hamada** is an area strewn with boulders and larger stones; **reg** is an area blanketed in gravel. One theory is that reg and hamada form when the wind blows away fine material, leaving behind the bigger stones. These may become cemented into a crust called a desert pavement. There are similar pavements, called stone pavements, in periglacial ▪ landscapes.

*Buttes and pediments*
*These buttes rise up out of the flat plain. They rest on the underlying sloping pediment. They are called Mitten Rocks in Monument Valley, bordering Arizona and Utah.*

# Pediment

A shallow rock ramp along mountain edges in the desert

Many desert landscapes are characterized by steep bare slopes and cliff faces, with shallow ramps at the foot called pediments. Pediments often occur at the base of mesas and inselbergs. They look like bajadas but are made from solid rock, rather than river deposits. It is not known quite how pediments form but they may be caused by parallel retreat of the slope or by desert wash.

# Bolson

A closed basin in the desert region of Mexico and southwest US

Desert streams and desert wash rarely flow all the way to the sea, because they are so intermittent. Instead, they often flow into salty lakes called **playas** in the middle of drainage basins ▪ called bolsons. Bolsons are usually surrounded by bajadas.

*Continued on next page* ➤

## Aeolian action

Erosion, transportation, and deposition by the wind

Aeolian action or **wind action** is very effective in deserts because there are few plants to slow the wind and bind the dry, light surface material in place. It was once thought that desert landscapes were essentially wind-formed. Later research suggested that major landforms were shaped by water, and wind only superficially altered the surface. However, recent satellite pictures of the Atacama and Saharan deserts have revealed long narrow, parallel ridges and grooves that could only have been sculpted by the wind. These ridges, called **yardangs**, are aligned with the prevailing wind ■ direction and can be hundreds of yards high and dozens of miles long. They form as the wind scoops out the soft rock, leaving hard ridges behind.

## Aeolian transport

The movement of material by the wind

Material is carried along on the wind in various ways. The finest dust and silt grains, up to 0.006 in. (0.15 mm) across, may be carried along in **suspension**, hanging in the air. Slightly bigger grains, 0.006–0.08 in. (0.15–2 mm) across, may be bounced along by a process called **saltation**. In saltation, grains move along in short hops of a few yards, rarely traveling far above the ground. The biggest grains may be rolled and jogged along the ground, a process called **surface creep**.

***Loess deposits in China***
*The Ordos Plateau in Inner Mongolia, is an example of loess deposits.*

## Loess

Fine yellow sediment probably deposited by the wind

Wind action is important not only in deserts, but wherever light, dry material is exposed, such as in coastal regions and along glacial margins. Deep loess deposits that cover vast areas of China, central Europe, and Siberia are believed to have formed when strong winds carried away sediment created during the last ice age ■. Loess swept along by the Huang-He River in China gives the river its more familiar name, the Yellow River. **Badlands** are areas of intensely dissected landscape. They often develop on loess and other loose material like shale and clay.

## Deflation

The blowing away of fine surface dust by the wind

Strong winds can quickly blow away fine, dry material such as sand, silt, and clay, and carry it long distances before dropping it. This is called deflation. Once the fine material has been blown away, a gravel-strewn area of sparse vegetation called a **surface of deflation** may be left behind.

## Deflation hollow

A basin blown out by the wind

Deflation can blow out fine material forming huge hollows, such as the vast Qattara and Kharga depressions in Egypt. In the Qattara the wind has scooped out a hollow 199 miles (320 km) long, and 440 ft. (134 m) below sea level. The wind may even scoop out a hollow so deep that it reaches the water table ■, and creates an **oasis** ■ – a valuable pocket of moisture in the desert.

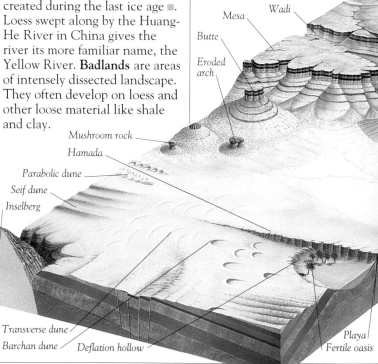

Wadi
Mesa
Butte
Eroded arch
Mushroom rock
Hamada
Parabolic dune
Seif dune
Inselberg
Transverse dune
Barchan dune
Deflation hollow
Playa
Fertile oasis

◄ *Continued from previous page*

# Dust storm

A thick, whirling cloud of dust whipped up by the wind

Warm winds in the desert such as the Arabian **Simoom** can whip up huge dust clouds that reduce visibility to almost zero and bring very hot, electrically charged air. Thousands of tons of dust are lifted to over 10,000 ft. (3,000 m) as the storm ▓ moves across the desert either in a thick wall or as a **vortex** – a rapidly whirling spiral. **Dust devils**, also known as willy-willies ▓, are small, short-lived dust vortexes that whirl along at 20 mph (30 kph), about 1,640 ft. (500 m) high. They are created by local heating of the ground.

# Ventifact

A stone shaped by the wind

The wind constantly bombards pebbles and stones in the desert with sand and dust, sculpting them into angular shapes called ventifacts. They are often shaped into three-sided stones called **dreikanter**.

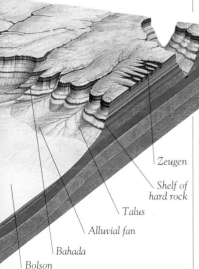

*Zeugen*
*Shelf of hard rock*
*Talus*
*Alluvial fan*
*Bahada*
*Bolson*

**Desert landforms**
*Desert landscapes tend to be dramatic because they are not softened by vegetation cover. They are sculpted by the wind, extreme temperatures, and rare but torrential rains.*

**Sand dune**
*The vast sand seas of the Sahara desert have been blown into many huge sand dunes, such as this one in Algeria.*

# Sand dune

A mound of wind-blown sand in the desert or on coasts

In deserts such as the Sahara and the Arabian desert there are vast areas of sand called **sand seas** or **ergs**. The Great Eastern Erg of Algeria covers an area larger than France. Here, the largest dunes are ridges called **draa**, which may be over 980 ft. (300 m) high and many miles long. There are many kinds of dune. Dune type depends on the amount of sand available, the variability of wind direction, and the amount of vegetation cover. Dunes are often named for their shape, such as **star dunes**, **crescent dunes**, **sword dunes**, and **parabolic dunes**. Crescent dunes include small **lunettes**, which form near playas ▓, and larger **barchan** dunes. Barchans form on hard surfaces and creep along several yards a year as the wind blows sand from one side to the other. Dunes are also named according to their alignment with the wind. **Seifs** or **longitudinal dunes** are aligned parallel to the prevailing wind. **Transverse dunes** are ridges lying across the wind.

## SOME DUNE TYPES

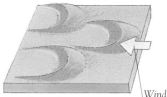

**Barchan dune** Wind direction
*Barchans form where sand is sparse and the wind direction is constant.*

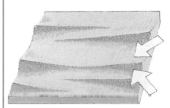

**Seif dune**
*Seifs form where sand is sparse and the wind comes from two directions.*

**Transverse dune**
*Ridges form at 90° to the strongest wind direction where sand is abundant.*

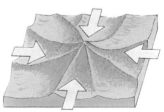

**Star dune**
*Large dunes form where the wind blows from all directions.*

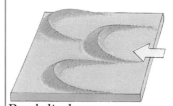

**Parabolic dune**
*These are common on coasts. The two arms are often stabilized by vegetation.*

# Glaciers & ice sheets

At the poles and in high mountainous regions, vast areas are covered in ice: some by ice "rivers" called glaciers, and some by extensive layers of ice called ice sheets. At times in the past, called the ice ages, the area under ice was much larger and the ice left dramatic marks on the landscape.

*Jagged glacier*
*The John Hopkins Glacier in Alaska has been broken into many crevasses as it winds its way down the valley.*

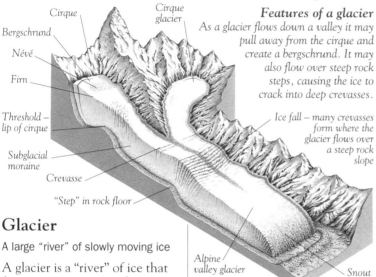

Cirque

Cirque glacier

Bergschrund

Névé

Firm

Threshold – lip of cirque

Subglacial moraine

Crevasse

"Step" in rock floor

Alpine valley glacier

Ice fall – many crevasses form where the glacier flows over a steep rock slope

Snout

**Features of a glacier**
*As a glacier flows down a valley it may pull away from the cirque and create a bergschrund. It may also flow over steep rock steps, causing the ice to crack into deep crevasses.*

## Glacier

A large "river" of slowly moving ice

A glacier is a "river" of ice that forms in mountains and creeps down a valley until it melts. As it moves, the ice cracks into deep fissures called **crevasses**. Along the back of the hollow or cirque ■ where a glacier often begins, the ice may pull away from the wall to form a very deep crack called a **bergschrund**. The lower end of a valley glacier is called the **snout** or **terminus**.

## Ice sheet

A vast layer of ice

Ice sheets usually cover an area as large as a continent. They are sometimes called **continental ice sheets**. **Ice caps** are smaller domes of ice covering a mountain. The polar and Greenland ice masses are also referred to as ice caps. An **iceberg** is a huge mass of ice floating in the sea, broken off from an ice sheet or glacier.

## Valley glacier

A glacier flowing down through an existing valley

There are many different types of glacier. Valley glaciers flow down through existing river valleys under the influence of gravity. **Outlet valley glaciers** are valley glaciers flowing away from the edge of an ice sheet or ice cap. **Cirque glaciers** are small glaciers that form quite quickly in cirques, high in the mountains, and then flow down through the valley below. **Alpine valley glaciers** are valley glaciers formed by the merging of several cirque glaciers. **Piedmont glaciers**, such as the Malaspina glacier in Alaska, are broad glaciers that form where several valley glaciers join as they emerge from the mountains.

## Névé

Freshly fallen snow on a glacier

A glacier forms when new snow ■, or névé, is compacted by its own weight into denser snow or **firn**. During this process of **firnification**, air is squeezed out. As snow piles up, the firn is compacted further and turns into opaque **glacier ice**.

## Glacial mass budget

The balance between new ice and melting ice on a glacier

Glaciers grow by **accumulation** – the buildup and compaction of new snow. At the same time, ice is lost by **ablation** – that is, melting and evaporation. The difference between accumulation and ablation is the glacial mass budget. If the budget is positive (accumulation exceeds ablation) the glacier advances. If it is negative (ablation exceeds accumulation) the glacier retreats. Usually, glaciers have a negative budget at the foot (the **ablation zone**) and a positive budget at the top (the **accumulation zone**).

## See also

Cirque 122 • Pleistocene Epoch 72
Snow 149 • Solar radiation 140

## Glaciation

The covering of the land by ice during an ice age

The effects of glaciation are very widespread. During the last ice age, for example, ice extended far south from the North Pole over continental Europe and Russia, and into North America as far south as Illinois and Indiana. Ice caps grew even in New Zealand and South America

## Ice movement

The way glaciers move

Glaciers move in two main ways. **Warm-based glaciers** (with a base temperature of about 32°F, 0°C) move mainly by **basal slip**. This is when the whole glacier slides as one unit when the base melts – perhaps due to the pressure of ice above. **Cold-based glaciers** (with a base well below 32°F, 0°C) move mainly by **internal deformation**. This is when a glacier slips and its surface flows faster than its base. Layers of ice then slide over each other. In most glaciers there is a mixture of both movements.

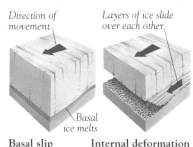

*Direction of movement*

*Layers of ice slide over each other*

*Basal ice melts*

Basal slip　　Internal deformation

*The way ice moves*
*Glaciers move by sliding over melted ice or by layers of ice sliding over each other.*

## Ice age

A cold period in the Earth's history when the ice sheets were much larger

There is plenty of evidence to show that the Earth has been much colder at times in the past, and that ice sheets extended far south into North America and Europe. These ice ages may have been caused by **Milankovich cycles** – changes in the amount of solar ▓ energy reaching the Earth due to the wobbling of the Earth's axis. Each ice age is marked by several very cold periods called **glacial maxima**, broken by warmer periods called **interglacials**. The most recent ice age was in the Pleistocene Epoch ▓, which started 2 million years ago and ended 10,000 years ago. But ice ages occurred at various other times during the Earth's history, such as the **Huronian ice age** 2.4 billion years ago in Canada.

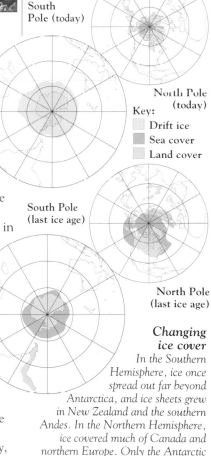

South Pole (today)

North Pole (today)

Key:
　Drift ice
　Sea cover
　Land cover

South Pole (last ice age)

North Pole (last ice age)

*Changing ice cover*
*In the Southern Hemisphere, ice once spread out far beyond Antarctica, and ice sheets grew in New Zealand and the southern Andes. In the Northern Hemisphere, ice covered much of Canada and northern Europe. Only the Antarctic (holding 90 percent of the world's ice) and Greenland ice sheets now remain.*

# Glacial erosion

Glaciers move along very slowly, but their sheer weight and size gives them enormous power to mold the landscape. They carve out wide valleys, gouge great bowls in the mountainside, and slice away entire hills and valleys as they move on relentlessly.

## Glacial entrainment

Rocks and rock fragments caught up in a glacier and carried away

Rocks were once thought to be carried away by a process called **plucking**, in which ice freezes around well-jointed blocks and rips lumps of rock from the ground. Few people now believe this is feasible, but a glacier ■ may freeze around rock fragments already loosened by frost shattering ■ and "entrain" them, or carry them off. For the ice to refreeze around a rock, it first has to melt, which takes place by **regelation**. This is where the pressure of the ice above lowers the melting point of the ice below, turning it into water. The water runs downhill until the pressure lessens and the melting point rises, so that refreezing occurs.

## Glacial abrasion

The wearing down of rocks as they are scratched by rocks in a glacier

Rocks and gravel caught up in the base of a glacier make it grind away at the rocks beneath. Glaciated areas are characterized by polished rocks and scratch marks called **striations**.

***Cirque with a tarn***
*Cyfrwy arête rises up to the backwall of Cwm Y Gaddir on the north flank of the mountain Cadre Idris, Wales. A tarn has formed in the cirque or cwm.*

## Cirque

An armchair-shaped hollow scooped out by ice

A cirque – also known as a **cwm**, **corrie**, or **kar** – is one of the most common features of glaciated uplands. Cirques are hollows with a steep backwall (headwall) and a raised rock lip or barrier at the front called the **threshold**. This rock lip often traps a lake or **tarn** within the cirque after the ice has gone. Cirques probably start to form where névé ■ piles up in a small depression. As the glacier develops, it cuts deeper and deeper into the rock, gouging out a large hollow.

## Arête

A sharp ridge between two cirques

Cirques rarely occur on their own. There may be groups of them around a single mountain. As cirque glaciers ■ cut backward into the mountain, the ridges between the cirques become narrower and sharper, leaving just a knife-edge ridge called an arête between them. The summit of the mountain is eventually cut away to a sharp peak called a **horn peak** or a **pyramidal peak**. A famous example of a horn peak is the Matterhorn in Switzerland.

## Roche moutonnée

An ice-molded rock with one smooth side and one rough side

Roche moutonnées are large rocks shaped by the action of ice. They have a smoothly polished, gentle "upstream" side called the **stoss**, and another more rugged "downstream" side called the **lee**.

## U-shaped valley

A huge, broad valley carved out by a glacier

Over tens of thousands of years, glaciers carve out huge troughs, which deepen, widen, and straighten the existing river valley. Unlike V-shaped ■ river valleys, they form a distinctive, wide U-shape.

***Classic U-shaped valley***
*Glen Rosa is a wide U-shaped valley on the Isle of Arran, Scotland.*

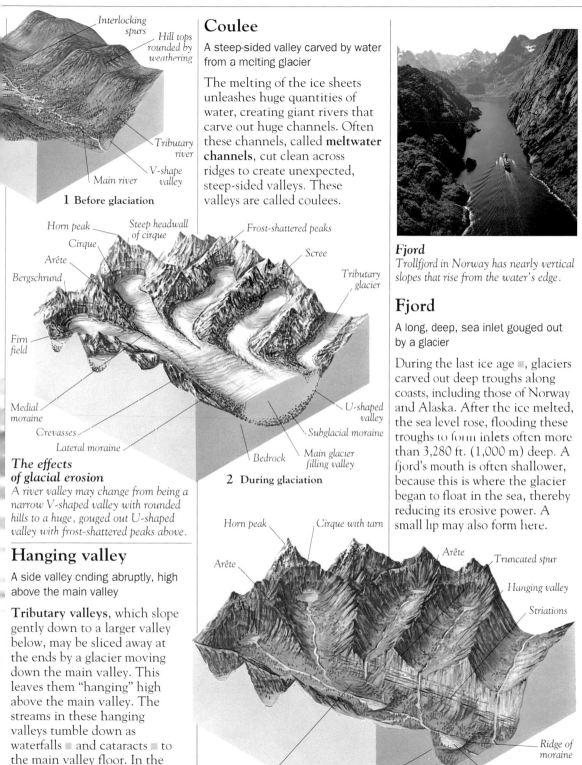

**1 Before glaciation**

*Labels:* Interlocking spurs · Hill tops rounded by weathering · Tributary river · V-shape valley · Main river

## Coulee

A steep-sided valley carved by water from a melting glacier

The melting of the ice sheets unleashes huge quantities of water, creating giant rivers that carve out huge channels. Often these channels, called **meltwater channels**, cut clean across ridges to create unexpected, steep-sided valleys. These valleys are called coulees.

**The effects of glacial erosion**
*A river valley may change from being a narrow V-shaped valley with rounded hills to a huge, gouged out U-shaped valley with frost-shattered peaks above.*

*Labels:* Horn peak · Steep headwall of cirque · Cirque · Frost-shattered peaks · Arête · Scree · Bergschrund · Tributary glacier · Firn field · Medial moraine · Crevasses · Lateral moraine · Bedrock · Subglacial moraine · U-shaped valley · Main glacier filling valley

**2 During glaciation**

## Hanging valley

A side valley ending abruptly, high above the main valley

**Tributary valleys**, which slope gently down to a larger valley below, may be sliced away at the ends by a glacier moving down the main valley. This leaves them "hanging" high above the main valley. The streams in these hanging valleys tumble down as waterfalls ▨ and cataracts ▨ to the main valley floor. In the same way, the interlocking hills or **spurs** that made the original valley curve are cut off abruptly. These are called **truncated spurs**.

*Labels:* Horn peak · Cirque with tarn · Arête · Truncated spur · Hanging valley · Striations · Roche moutonnée · U-shaped valley · Ridge of moraine · Paternoster lakes – lake chains dammed by ridges of moraine

**3 After glaciation**

**Fjord**
*Trollfjord in Norway has nearly vertical slopes that rise from the water's edge.*

## Fjord

A long, deep, sea inlet gouged out by a glacier

During the last ice age ▨, glaciers carved out deep troughs along coasts, including those of Norway and Alaska. After the ice melted, the sea level rose, flooding these troughs to form inlets often more than 3,280 ft. (1,000 m) deep. A fjord's mouth is often shallower, because this is where the glacier began to float in the sea, thereby reducing its erosive power. A small lip may also form here.

# Glacial deposition

The ice in glaciers is not clear, but is often dirty and choked with much debris. This debris falls from the mountains above, or is gouged out by the glacier from the rock below. As the glacier advances or retreats, the debris is laid down in a mass of hummocks and snaking banks.

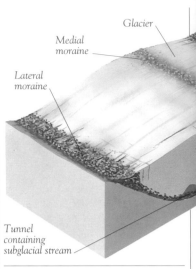

Glacier

Medial moraine

Lateral moraine

Tunnel containing subglacial stream

## Drift

Debris deposited during glaciation

Glaciers produce many kinds of debris or drift. **Glaciofluvial drift** is debris deposited by melted ice called **glacial meltwater**. **Till** is debris dropped by glaciers ■ and ice sheets ■. Some till is a mix of stones and boulders; some is like shingle ■. It may also be mixed by glacial meltwater with a fine sediment ■ (sometimes enclosing boulders) called **boulder clay**. **Lodgement till** is debris laid down beneath the moving ice. **Ablation till** is debris from the top of the glacier, dropped as the ice melts.

## Erratic

A boulder carried by moving ice to an area of a different type of rock

Glaciers may drop huge erratics, far from their place of origin, in areas of rock different from the erratics themselves. The rock type of the erratics may give clues to the path taken by the ice. They may be left on hilltops as **perched blocks**.

*Erratic movement*
*This erratic in Norber, North Yorkshire, England, has been deposited on softer rock that has been eroded to a very small base.*

## Moraine

Piles of debris left by moving ice

Moraines are piles of boulders ■, rocks, pebbles ■, and clay ■. **End** or **terminal moraines** form across the front of the moving ice. Some are just a few yards high, but the moraine in front of New Zealand's Franz Josef Glacier is 1,411 ft. (430 m) high. **Recessional moraines** form when a retreating glacier stops temporarily. **Lateral moraines** develop along the side of a glacier as debris falls from above. A **medial moraine** forms down the middle of a glacier when the lateral moraines of two converging glaciers merge. **Push moraines** are created as ice pushes its way through previously laid debris. **Washboard**, **transverse-fluted**, **ribbed**, **corrugated**, and **Rogen moraines** are all ridges laid down in front of the ice.

## Esker

A snaking ridge of sand and gravel left by glacial meltwater

Glaciofluvial drift is much finer than glacial till, and is sorted into sand ■ and gravel ■. Eskers are winding ridges of sand and gravel left by **englacial streams** of water flowing beneath the ice. **Kames** are steep-sided mounds of sand and gravel often left in crevasses ■ by meltwater running over the top of a glacier. **Sandars** or **outwash plains** are broad, flat deposits dropped by meltwater from an ice sheet.

## Drumlin

A smooth, egg-shaped hummock of glacial debris

Drumlins are mounds of till formed beneath an ice sheet. They may be over 164 ft. (50 m) high and 0.5 mile (0.8 km) long. The end facing the ice is usually the steepest and the tail is streamlined. Drumlins often occur in groups or **swarms**. Some experts believe they were deposited around rocks or balls of frozen drift. Others believe they were eroded by the ice from the underlying till.

*Streamlined drumlins*
*These drumlins in Ribblehead, Yorkshire, England, are aligned in the same way.*

## Till plain

A wide "blanket" of glacial debris

As a major ice sheet retreats, it leaves behind a vast "blanket" of till over the landscape, often up to 330 ft. (100 m) thick and smoothing over all irregularities.

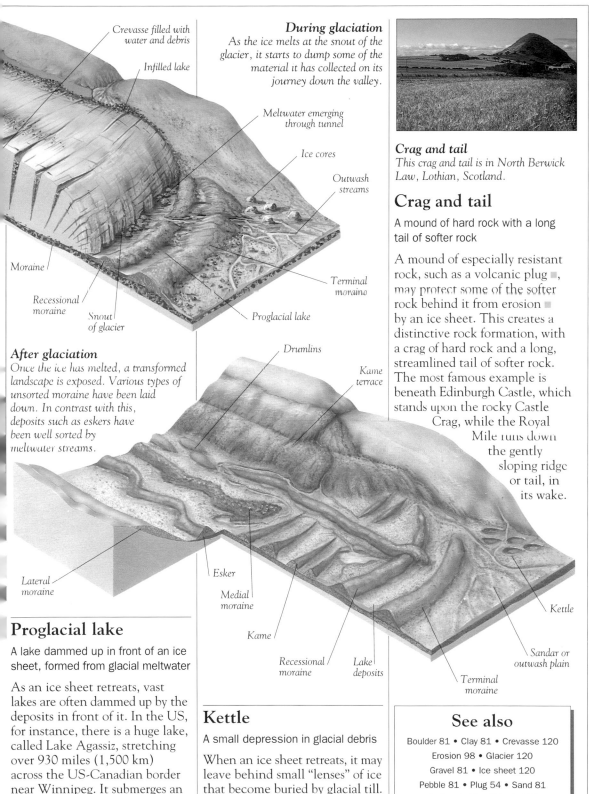

**During glaciation**
*As the ice melts at the snout of the glacier, it starts to dump some of the material it has collected on its journey down the valley.*

Crevasse filled with water and debris

Infilled lake

Meltwater emerging through tunnel

Ice cores

Outwash streams

Moraine

Recessional moraine

Snout of glacier

Terminal moraine

Proglacial lake

**After glaciation**
*Once the ice has melted, a transformed landscape is exposed. Various types of unsorted moraine have been laid down. In contrast with this, deposits such as eskers have been well sorted by meltwater streams.*

Drumlins

Kame terrace

Lateral moraine

Esker

Medial moraine

Kame

Recessional moraine

Lake deposits

Terminal moraine

Kettle

Sandar or outwash plain

*Crag and tail*
*This crag and tail is in North Berwick Law, Lothian, Scotland.*

## Crag and tail

A mound of hard rock with a long tail of softer rock

A mound of especially resistant rock, such as a volcanic plug ■, may protect some of the softer rock behind it from erosion ■ by an ice sheet. This creates a distinctive rock formation, with a crag of hard rock and a long, streamlined tail of softer rock. The most famous example is beneath Edinburgh Castle, which stands upon the rocky Castle Crag, while the Royal Mile runs down the gently sloping ridge or tail, in its wake.

## Proglacial lake

A lake dammed up in front of an ice sheet, formed from glacial meltwater

As an ice sheet retreats, vast lakes are often dammed up by the deposits in front of it. In the US, for instance, there is a huge lake, called Lake Agassiz, stretching over 930 miles (1,500 km) across the US-Canadian border near Winnipeg. It submerges an area of over 193,000 sq. miles (500,000 km²).

## Kettle

A small depression in glacial debris

When an ice sheet retreats, it may leave behind small "lenses" of ice that become buried by glacial till. When these lenses finally melt, they leave behind a small hole.

## See also

Boulder 81 • Clay 81 • Crevasse 120
Erosion 98 • Glacier 120
Gravel 81 • Ice sheet 120
Pebble 81 • Plug 54 • Sand 81
Sediment 92 • Shingle 129

# Periglacial landscapes

The bitterly cold ice ages affected the landscape far beyond the ice sheets. These "periglacial" conditions created distinctive landforms as far south as Illinois and France. Similar landforms exist today in Alaska and Siberia.

*Frozen lakes of the tundra*
*These lakes and scrub are in the tundra of the Northwest Territories of Canada.*

*Patterns of stone*
*These stone polygons, in Alaska, have formed in a dry lakebed.*

## Stone polygon

An irregular ring of stones created by cold conditions

Periglacial areas are covered with stone patterns. These are created by **frost heave**, where frost pushes stones to the surface as the ground freezes. Areas of fine sediment are also pushed up into domes. Large stones then roll to the bottom to form rings called stone polygons. On sloping ground, the polygons are elongated into **stone stripes**.

## Periglacial

Cold conditions around the perimeter of an ice sheet

The term periglacial is used to refer to the landscapes bordering ice sheets ■ during the ice ages ■. Now it refers to similar conditions that exist today. Periglacial areas include tundra ■, the barren plains of northern Canada and Siberia, and also **nunataks**, upland areas protruding above ice sheets and glaciers ■. Periglacial climates have long, cold winters where temperatures never rise above freezing and often drop to –58°F (–50°C). Short, mild summers allow the ice to melt. The land is boggy and only lichens, mosses and shrubs grow. This allows wind action ■ to help shape the land.

## Permafrost

Permanently frozen ground

In periglacial areas, only the ice in the surface layers of the ground ever melts. Below a certain level, the ground is always frozen. The distinctive landforms of periglacial regions occur because the melting of ice above the permafrost layer stirs up the ground, a process called **cryoturbation**. This twists sediments into buckled layers or **involutions**. As frozen ground contracts, cracks often form. Meltwater fills the cracks where it freezes and expands to create deep bodies of ice called **ice wedges**.

## Gelifluxion

The slow creep of melting soil

When the ice in frozen soil melts, it makes the soil so fluid that it creeps easily down slopes, creating large lobes and terraces.

## Pingo

A domed earth mound with a permanent core of ice

Pingos can be up to 160 ft. (50 m) high. The ice core of a pingo may once have been part of a shallow lake, and the earth mound formed from the lake sediments. But the ice core may be frozen groundwater ■ instead.

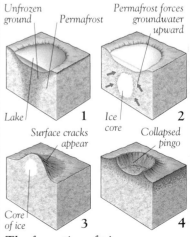

Unfrozen ground    Permafrost    Permafrost forces groundwater upward

Lake    **1**    Ice core    **2**
*Surface cracks appear*    *Collapsed pingo*

Core of ice    **3**    **4**

*The formation of pingos*
*As groundwater freezes beneath a lake, permafrost pushes it up, forming a pingo.*

### See also

# Coasts

Constant battering by waves and sea water gives coastal regions their own unique landforms. Sand shifts, beaches are built up or washed away, cliffs crumble and fall, and even big boulders are pounded to sand as waves crash against the shore.

**Sandy coast**
*This is an aerial view along the sandy coast of the Namib Desert, Namibia.*

## Coast

The boundary between land and sea

A **shore** is any boundary between land and water, whereas the coast is the boundary between the land and sea alone. The **coastline** is the line reached by the highest tides ■ each year. The **foreshore** is the band between the lowest tides and the highest tides. The **backshore** is the band beyond the highest yearly tides, reached only by severe storms ■.

## Wave

A regular undulation of the sea's surface

Wind blowing across the sea whips the water's surface into ripples. If the wind is strong enough and blows far enough over the water, the ripples build up into waves. The size of the waves depends not only on the strength of the wind but on the **fetch** – the distance wind has to build them up. In big oceans such as the Pacific and Atlantic, the fetch is so great that huge, regular, unbroken waves called **swells** develop. These can travel for thousands of miles until they meet a coast. Although waves travel far, the water in them stays in the same place, moving around in circles called **orbital paths**, like the rollers in a conveyor belt.

### The formation of waves
*Waves change form as they travel from deep water through shallow water to the shore. The circular motion of the orbital path in deep water changes to an elliptical shape in shallower water.*

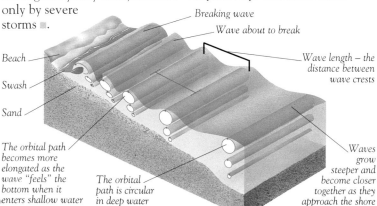

*Breaking wave*
*Wave about to break*
*Wave length – the distance between wave crests*
Beach
Swash
Sand
*The orbital path becomes more elongated as the wave "feels" the bottom when it enters shallow water*
*The orbital path is circular in deep water*
*Waves grow steeper and become closer together as they approach the shore*

## Breaker

A wave spilling over and breaking up on the shore

When waves move into shallow water, the seabed impedes the circulation of water within them, so waves get closer together and grow taller. Eventually, a wave gets so tall that the top spills over. The wave's energy is dispelled as it rushes up the beach as **swash**, then falls back as **backwash**. Both swash and backwash can carry material across the beach. If the swash is stronger, the wave is said to be **constructive**. If the backwash is stronger, the wave is said to be **destructive**.

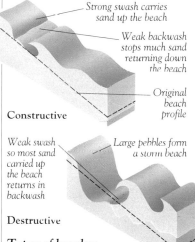

*Strong swash carries sand up the beach*
*Weak backwash stops much sand returning down the beach*
*Original beach profile*
**Constructive**

*Weak swash so most sand carried up the beach returns in backwash*
*Large pebbles form a storm beach*
**Destructive**

### Types of breaker
*Constructive breakers build up a beach; destructive ones break it down.*

## Spilling breaker

A high wave that breaks on shallow beaches

On gently sloping shores, the breakers are tall, tumbling spilling breakers. On steeper shores, they are low, smooth, **surging breakers**. In between these extremes are **plunging breakers** and **collapsing breakers**.

### See also
Storm 152 • Tide 137 • Storm beach 129

*Continued on next page* ➤

# Peninsula

A narrow neck of land projecting into the sea

Coastlines are often jagged. An area of high land jutting out into the sea is called a **headland** or **promontory**. A peninsula is a long neck of land ending in a headland. A **point** is the very tip of the headland.

# Wave refraction

The bending of waves where they hit shallows

If one part of a wave 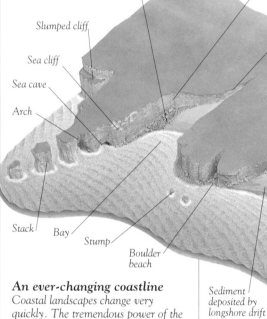 enters shallow waters before another, it is slowed down earlier, and the wave crest bends. A wave hitting a coast of headlands and bays will slow first at the headland and then curve into the bay.

# Spit

A narrow bank of sand projecting out from a bend in the coast

In places where longshore drift is strong, it can wash sand out along the coast to form a **sandbar** or spit. This often occurs across river mouths, where the current meets deeper water and it slows down, depositing the material it has been carrying. Occasionally, a spit may extend to an island, creating a sand bridge linking the island with the mainland called a **tombolo**.

Fallen rock debris

Bedding plane

Inlet

Tidal river mouth

Slumped cliff

Sea cliff

Sea cave

Arch

Mature river

Sea cliff

Headland

Stack

Bay

Stump

Boulder beach

Sediment deposited by longshore drift

Sandy spit

Mudflat

Lagoon

Estuary

Remnants of former headland

Bedding plane

***An ever-changing coastline***
*Coastal landscapes change very quickly. The tremendous power of the waves sculpts the coastline, eroding it in many places but also transporting material and depositing at other places along the coast.*

# Bay

A wide, curving indentation in the coastline

A bay is a broad coastal inlet with a headland on either side. Waves reach the headlands first, so the wave energy is concentrated there. Material is often eroded from the headlands and washed into the bay, forming a **bayhead beach**. A **cove** is a small, narrow bay, typically on a rocky coast. A **bight** is a huge bay, such as the Great Australian Bight. A **gulf** is a long, narrow bight.

# Longshore drift

A slow shifting of sand along a beach when waves strike it at an angle

When waves strike a beach at an angle, the swash of the wave carries material up the beach at the same angle. But when the water retreats in the backwash, it falls back down the beach at a right angle, pulling material with it. In this way, material is moved slowly along the beach with each successive wave. Barriers called groynes are often built out into the sea to reduce this longshore drift.

# Salt marsh

A coastal marsh formed, perhaps, behind a spit

Salt marshes begin to form where seawater is shallow and protected from the waves by, for example, a spit. Mud and fine sediments settle out of the water initially forming **mudflats**. In time, vegetation grows, stabilizing the marsh. A **lagoon** is a coastal lake cut off from the open sea behind a sandbar or coral reef, and is also the name given to the lake that forms in an atoll.

◄ *Continued from previous page*

*Battered sea cliff*
*These cliffs at Gantheaume Point,*
*Western Australia, have been eroded by*
*waves into rocky, often jagged, outcrops.*

# Sea cliff

A very steep rock face formed by
the action of waves

Waves crash on the shore with
tremendous force, especially in
storms. They wear away coastal
rocks by pounding them with
water, hurling stones at them,
and forcing air into cracks so
hard that the rocks burst apart.
On high coasts, the waves slowly
undercut the foot of the slope to
create a cliff. In well-jointed rocks,
the cliff can be sheer. Often,
waves penetrate deep into the
cliff to open up a **sea cave**, or cut
right through a headland to create
an **arch** of rock. When the arch
eventually collapses, it may leave
behind spectacular tall pillars of
rock called **stacks** which may later
be eroded into shorter **stumps**.

*The "Twelve Apostles"*
*This group of sea stacks are at Port*
*Campbell, Victoria, Australia.*

# Wave-cut platform

A level area of rock at the base of
a sea cliff

As waves wear back sea cliffs, they
carve out a broad platform of rock
at the base between the low-tide
mark and the high-tide mark. As
the tide ▧ goes out, water left in
holes in the rock forms **rock
pools**. In tropical areas, there are
platforms above the high-tide
mark; in limestone ▧ areas, there
are platforms below the high-tide
mark. Both these types of
platform are probably created by
chemical weathering ▧ rather
than by wave erosion.

*Rocky shelf*
*The wave-cut platform at Flamborough*
*Head, Yorkshire, England, is visible as*
*the shelf of rock at the base of the cliffs.*

# Beach

A sloping band of sand, shingle, or
pebbles at the sea's edge

On many coasts, the wave-cut
platform is covered by a beach
of loose, well-sorted material
such as mud, sand, and **shingle**
(rounded beach pebbles ▧).
On a steep beach, the backwash
of a wave is stronger than the
swash, so material is washed
down the beach, making the
slope gentler. On a gently
sloping beach, swash is stronger
than backwash, so material gets
washed up the beach, making it
steeper. In this way, the slope
of the beach matches the waves,
often being steeper in summer
than in winter when the waves
are bigger.

### See also

Atoll 135 • Backwash 127
Chemical weathering 100 • Coral reef 135
Gravel 81 • Groyne 177 • Limestone 94
Mouth 113 • Neap tide 137 • Pebble 81
Sand 81 • Sediment 92 • Spring tide 137
Swash 127 • Tide 137 • Wave 127

# Storm beach

A band of shingle and pebbles flung
high up on a beach by storm waves

Beaches are rarely entirely flat.
A storm beach is a ridge of gravel
and pebbles flung up above the
normal high-tide mark during a
storm. Only exceptional storm
waves ever reach it. At the limit
of swash at each high tide, there
is often a **beach-ridge** or **berm** of
shingle. Below the highest spring-
tide ▧ ridge, there is a descending
series of ridges or berms left as
the high-tide level drops steadily
toward the neap tide ▧. These
survive until they are washed
away as the high tide rises toward
the spring tide again. A **beach
cusp** is one of a series of scallop-
shaped deposits of sand or gravel ▧
scooped out along the beach
when waves strike it at an angle.

*Beach cusps*
*These well-defined beach cusps have*
*formed on Pearl Beach, New South*
*Wales, Australia.*

# Soil

Soil is the thin layer of loose material that covers much of the world's land surface, except in polar regions and most deserts. It is mostly weathered rock fragments and rotting organic matter. But the rich variety of plants and animals that live in soil help make it a dynamic, ever-changing system.

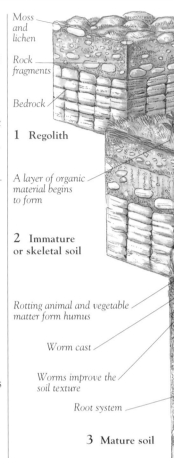

Moss and lichen

Rock fragments

Bedrock

**1  Regolith**

*A layer of organic material begins to form*

**2  Immature or skeletal soil**

*Rotting animal and vegetable matter form humus*

*Worm cast*

*Worms improve the soil texture*

*Root system*

**3  Mature soil**

## Soil

A loose mixture of small rock particles and rotting organic matter that covers the ground

Soil contains the remains of dead plants and animals, as well as fragments weathered ■ from the rock beneath. Regolith ■, in contrast, has no organic content. Tiny gaps or **pores** in the soil are filled with air, water, bacteria, algae, and fungi. These alter the soil's chemistry and speed up the decay of organic matter, making it a better environment for larger plants and burrowing animals.

Soil sample

Fine mesh

Glass funnel

Clamp

Small animals, including mites, springtails, and nematode worms

Vial

Alcohol solution to preserve the organisms

Silt and small animals

*Tullgren funnel*
*This apparatus is used to collect and identify tiny animals living in soil. When a light is placed over the soil sample, the creatures move away from the light and fall through the mesh into the vial.*

## Humus

The dark mass of rotting organic matter in soil

When plant and animal remains are attacked by microorganisms such as bacteria and fungi, they rot and form a dark brown or black mass called humus. Humus restores minerals ■ and nutrients ■ to the soil, which are important to growing plants. It also improves the soil structure, helping it to retain water. **Mull** is a humus rich in nutrients that is found in well-drained soil. Soils with a high mull content are very fertile. **Mor** is an acidic humus layer found in wet, poorly drained soils, which sometimes develops into peat. The humus **moder** has a nutrient content and acidity halfway between that of mor and mull.

## Soil organism

A living thing in the soil

Soil is home to many kinds of organism, including countless bacteria and various burrowing creatures such as ants, termites, earthworms, and rodents. More animals live in soil than in all other environments put together. The bacteria break down organic matter and help to provide plants with nutrients. Larger creatures mix up the soil. Earthworms improve the soil texture by taking soil in, passing it through their digestive tracts, and then excreting it as **worm casts**.

## Soil water

Water held in the pores of soil

Water is continually moving through most soils. This movement of water is called **soil translocation**. **Gravitational water** is the name given to water that trickles down through the soil under the influence of gravity. The water may create horizons in the soil as it washes minerals and organic matter downward. When rainwater drains away through the soil, some water is always left behind in the tiny pores. This is **capillary water**, and it is a good source of water for plants. Apart from capillary water, the remaining drops of water are unavailable to plants because they cling so tightly to the particles of soil. This is **hygroscopic water**.

## The formation of soil
*Fertile, mature soils form over many thousands of years from weathered rock fragments and the decaying remains of living organisms.*

*Grasses and small shrubs*

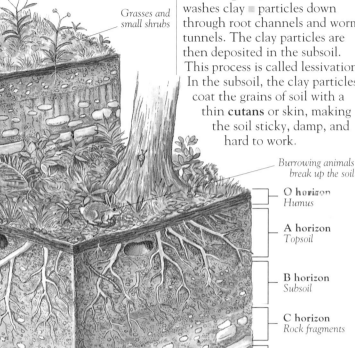

*Burrowing animals break up the soil*

O horizon
*Humus*

A horizon
*Topsoil*

B horizon
*Subsoil*

C horizon
*Rock fragments*

D horizon
*Parent rock*

## Lessivation
The washing down of soil particles through the soil

In wet regions, soil water often washes clay ■ particles down through root channels and worm tunnels. The clay particles are then deposited in the subsoil. This process is called lessivation. In the subsoil, the clay particles coat the grains of soil with a thin **cutans** or skin, making the soil sticky, damp, and hard to work.

## Soil profile
A vertical cross-section through the soil

As soil develops, distinct layers called **horizons** begin to appear. A soil profile reveals all these horizons. Each horizon has its own color, texture, and mineral or humus content. The **H·** or **O-horizon** is a thin layer of rotting organic matter that covers the soil. The **A-horizon**, also known as the **topsoil**, is the uppermost layer of soil. It is rich in minerals and humus. Beneath this layer is the **B-horizon**, or **subsoil**, which is poorer in humus but rich in minerals washed down from above. The **C-horizon** consists of unfertile weathered rock. The **D-horizon** is the unweathered parent rock beneath the soil.

## Pedogenesis
The development of soil

Soil takes thousands of years to develop. Exactly how long it takes depends on how fast the **parent rock** – the solid rock below – is weathered. Typically, the rock is first weathered to form regolith. A **skeletal soil** of coarse, sandy material with traces of organic matter slowly forms. A fully **mature soil** develops after 10,000 years or more. **Residual soils** are made from weathered parent rock. **Transported soils** such as loess ■ are made from fragments carried by wind, rivers, and ice.

## See also
Clay 132 • Desert crust 116
Loess 118 • Mineral 82 • Nutrient 161
Precipitate 94 • Regolith 105
Weathering 98

## Leaching
The washing down of dissolved minerals through the soil

Soil water may dissolve soil minerals and wash them down through the soil. This is called leaching. **Cheluviation** is when organic matter is dissolved and washed down through the soil. Leaching, cheluviation, and lessivation are together known as **eluviation**. Eluviation robs the topsoil of valuable nutrients. The dissolved minerals may then be precipitated ■, or forced out of solution, lower down in the B-horizon. This process is known as **illuviation**. Precipitated iron, for example, may form a hard layer called an **ironpan**.

## Soil salinization
The deposition of salt by evaporating soil water

Soil water can carry dissolved mineral salts upward as water evaporates at the surface, leaving the salts behind in the topsoil. In deserts, they may form a hard desert crust ■.

*River of salt*
*This hard, crusty salt layer in Death Valley, California, is the result of salinization, a process that produces barren lands with no agricultural use.*

*Continued on next page* ➤

## Soil pH

The acidity or alkalinity of the soil

The acidity or alkalinity of soil water ■ greatly affects the soil's fertility. If soil water is strongly alkaline, it cannot dissolve minerals and deliver them to plants. If it is too acidic, it will dissolve nutrients too easily and leach ■ them away before plants can absorb them. The **pH scale** measures acidity or alkalinity on a scale of 0 to 14. Low pH shows an **acid soil**; high pH shows an **alkaline soil**. **Neutral soil** has a pH of 7. Most plants grow only in soil with a pH between 4 and 10.

**Clay soil**          **Silty soil**

*Soil grain size*
*Clay soils are heavy, water-retentive, and rich in nutrients. Silty soils are reasonably moist and fertile. Sandy soils are dry, light, but relatively infertile.*

**Sandy soil**

**Acid**    **Neutral**    **Alkaline**

*Testing the pH of soil*
*A chemical solution called an indicator is added to a soil sample. The indicator changes color, showing the soil's pH.*

## Soil structure

The way soil grains clump together

Soil grains usually stick together as clumps known as **peds**. There are five main types of ped and so five main soil structures: **platelike**, **blocklike**, **crumbly** or **granular**, **prismatic** (long, many-sided columns), and **nuciform** (formless). Soil structure affects how easy the soil is to work, and its porosity ■ and permeability ■.

### See also

## Soil texture

The size and nature of soil particles

Soil texture depends on the size of the grains in the soil. Grains can be **clay** (the smallest), **sand** (the largest), or **silt** (medium-sized) – the exact size varies, depending on which system of soil classification is used. So soils are divided into **clay soils**, **silty soils**, and **sandy soils**. **Loam soils** are a fairly even mix of clay, silt, and sand. Loam soils are the best soils for plant growth.

## Soil classification

A system for dividing soil into different categories

There is a vast number of different soils in the world – one classification system recognizes at least 10,000 soils in the US alone. As a result, no one system of classifying soil has yet been adopted for international use. The most detailed is called the **Comprehensive Soil Classification System (CSCS)**, or **Seventh Approximation System**, devised by the United States Department of Agriculture. The CSCS groups soils according to certain key properties and the presence of a particular horizon ■ or a surface humus ■ layer called an **epipedon**.

## Podzol

A sandy soil with an ash gray A-horizon that develops beneath coniferous forests in cool climates

There is little organic activity in the soil of cool coniferous forests. This produces a poorly mixed soil with distinct horizons. Leaching washes iron and aluminum from the acidic A-horizon ■, leaving it colored ash gray by silica and creating a dark ironpan ■ lower down. This process is called **podzolization**. Podzols are called alfisols or spodisols in the CSCS.

Leached gray A-horizon

Ironpan

**Podzol profile**

## Chernozem

A very dark, humus-rich soil beneath midlatitude grasslands

Chernozems develop in the dry, temperate grassland regions of North America, Asia, Argentina, and southeastern Australia. They are also known as **prairie soils** and **black earth**. They have a deep A-horizon, are rich in humus, and suffer little from leaching. Chernozems are used for growing cereal crops, but they are prone to soil erosion ■. Where these grasslands are drier, **chestnut soils** develop, containing less humus. They are often used for grazing. Chestnut soils and chernozems are the equivalent of mollisols in the CSCS.

*Black, organic-rich A-horizon*

*Horizon containing illuviated carbonate or sulfate*

**Chernozem profile**

◄ *Continued from previous page*

# SOIL ORDERS (COMPREHENSIVE SOIL CLASSIFICATION SYSTEM)

| Order | Description | Location | Profile examples |
|---|---|---|---|
| Entisol | Young soils lacking horizons because of their recent development | Steep slopes & floodplains | |
| Inceptisol | Young soils with poor horizons that form the basis of paddy rice farming | Lower reaches of great tropical rivers | |
| Histosol | Wet soils made mostly of decaying plant material | Swamps & bogs in tundra | |
| Oxisol | Mature soils, well-leached, with a distinct oxic horizon | Hot, wet tropical forests | |
| Ultisol | Red soil, less leached than oxisol, with a clay-rich argillic horizon | Humid tropics & subtropics | |
| Alfisol | Soils with a clay-rich argillic and ochric epipedon | Humid midlatitudes such as the Corn Belt in the US | |
| Spodisol | Podzolized soils with strong albic and spodic horizons | Coniferous forests in northern & midlatitudes | |
| Mollisol | Fertile soils with a dark mollic epipedon | Midlatitude grasslands | |
| Aridisol | Dry soils with marked salic, calcic, and gypsic horizons | Deserts | |
| Vertisol | Dark soils with deep vertical cracks where the soil has dried out | Semiarid tropics & subtropics | |

Profile labels: *Wet surface horizon, rich in organic matter*; *Clay-rich subsoil*; **Histosol**; *Red and yellow horizon produced by iron and aluminium oxides*; **Oxisol**; *Pale surface horizon*; *Clay-rich subsoil*; **Aridisol**; *Deep cracks enable the surface layers to mix with those at depth*; **Vertisol**

# HORIZONS & EPIPEDONS

| Horizon | Description |
|---|---|
| Oxic horizon | A subsurface layer rich in iron and aluminum oxides, found in tropical and subtropical soils |
| Albic horizon | A sandy, light horizon from which clay and iron oxides have been leached |
| Spodic horizon | A dark layer below the A-horizon from which humus and iron oxides have been leached |
| Calcic horizon | A subsurface layer rich in calcium carbonate or magnesium carbonate |
| Salic horizon | A thick layer of accumulated mineral salts in desert soils |
| Gypsic horizon | A subsurface layer rich in gypsum (calcium sulfate) |
| Argillic epipedon | A layer with a high proportion of clay, usually formed beneath the A-horizon by illuviation |
| Ochric epipedon | A pale, thin surface layer lacking in organic matter |
| Mollic epipedon | A thick, dark surface layer rich in humus and important minerals such as calcium |

# The oceans

Until quite recently, the bottom of the Earth's oceans were as mysterious and unknown as the surface of Venus. Modern oceanographic surveys have now shown that the landscape of the ocean floor is as varied as that of the continents, with high mountains, vast plains, and deep valleys.

*Deep-sea channel*
*This sonar image shows a meandering channel on the seabed being buried by flows of water and sandy mud called turbidity currents (the light, rippled areas on the right-hand side).*

## Ocean

A vast, open expanse of sea water

The Earth has five great oceans – the Pacific, Atlantic, and Indian, which all merge into the Southern Ocean around Antarctica, and the small Arctic Ocean. More contained expanses of sea water are called **seas**, and include the Mediterranean, Red, and Baltic seas. Together, the seas and oceans occupy 139 million sq. miles (361 million km²), more than 70 percent of the Earth's surface area. The average depth is 12,240 ft. (3,730 m).

## Continental shelf

A gently sloping area of the seabed, between the edge of a continent and the deep ocean

The water over the continental shelf has an average depth of 430 ft. (130 m). Beyond the shelf, the seafloor plunges steeply down the **continental slope** toward the deep ocean. At the foot of the slope is the gently angled **continental rise** or **apron**, which leads to the deep ocean. The shelf, slope, and rise together comprise the **continental margin**.

### See also

Earthquake 58 • Mid-ocean ridge 50
Lagoon 128 • Oceanic crust 40
Ocean trench 48 • River valley 114
Sediment 92 • Volcanic ash 55
Volcano 52

## Submarine canyon

A deep, underwater valley sliced into the continental margin

Submarine canyons are notches in the continental slope that open out onto the deep ocean floor. The opening is usually marked by a fan-shaped pile of sediments ■ deposited by thick, churning flows of water and mud. Such flows are **turbidity currents**. They are set off by earthquakes ■ or underwater landslides, and rush down the canyons at 37 mph (60 kph) or more, carrying huge quantities of sediment. Submarine canyons may form as the continental margin is eroded by turbidity currents. Alternatively, they may be the remains of river valleys ■ cut long ago, when the area was above sea level.

## Ocean floor

The entire seabed below the low-tide mark

The term ocean floor refers to the part of the Earth's surface that is covered by seas and oceans. It is larger than the **ocean-basin floor**, which is the part of the ocean floor beyond the continental shelf. The ocean-basin floor includes continental slopes, mid-ocean ridges ■, and ocean trenches ■. Most of it is more than 6,560 ft. (2,000 m) deep.

*Submarine landscape*
*This model shows many of the ocean-bottom features that have been revealed by undersea exploration.*

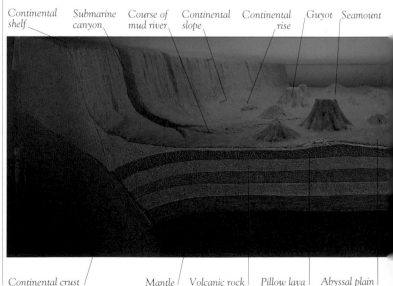

Continental shelf | Submarine canyon | Course of mud river | Continental slope | Continental rise | Guyot | Seamount

Continental crust | Mantle | Volcanic rock | Pillow lava | Abyssal plain

# THE FORMATION OF AN ATOLL

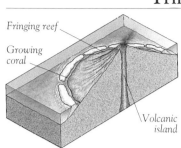

Fringing reef
Growing coral
Volcanic island

**1** *A fringing reef forms as corals grow along the shoreline of a volcanic island*

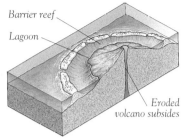

Barrier reef
Lagoon
Eroded volcano subsides

**2** *When the volcano subsides, a lagoon forms and the reef becomes a barrier reef*

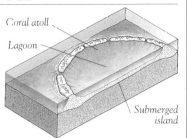

Coral atoll
Lagoon
Submerged island

**3** *The volcano is submerged, but the reef remains, topped by small, sandy islands*

## Seamount

A lone mountain on the ocean floor

The deep ocean floor, or abyssal plain, is not flat but dotted with huge mountains known as seamounts, especially in the Pacific. These mountains, which are probably volcanic in origin, are entirely submerged but may rise 3,280 ft. (1,000 m) or more from the ocean floor. In places, there are flat-topped seamounts called **guyots**. These, too, were probably volcanoes ■ but because they projected above the surface, their summits were worn down by the waves. As the ocean crust ■ moved beneath them, they were gradually submerged.

Mid-ocean ridge
Ocean trench
Rising magma
Oceanic crust

## Abyssal plain

The smooth floor of the deep ocean

The abyssal plain is up to 16,400 ft. (5,000 m) deep, and is covered with a thick slime called **ooze**. Some ooze is **biogenic** – that is, it is made from the remains of sea creatures such as protozoa and shellfish. Some ooze is **red clay**, which comes from volcanic ash ■, meteor dust, and melting icebergs.

## Abyssal zone

The ocean below 5,900 ft. (1,800 m)

The abyssal zone is the deepest, darkest area of the ocean. The **bathyal zone** is the ocean on the continental slope, too deep for light to penetrate, yet rich in animal life. The **neritic zone** is the ocean above the continental shelf. The **pelagic zone** is the open ocean beyond the continental shelf, down to a depth of about 590 ft. (180 m). The **littoral zone** is the ocean between the high and low tide marks.

## Island

An area of land surrounded by water

Islands vary from single rocks to land masses such as Greenland, which covers 0.85 million sq. miles (2.2 million km²). Large clusters of islands, such as the Greek Cyclades in the Aegean Sea, are known as **archipelagos**.

## Coral reef

An underwater ridge created by the coral polyp

Coral polyps are tiny sea creatures. They protect themselves by secreting calcium carbonate, which builds up to form hard skeletons around their soft, cylindrical bodies. Polyps stay all their lives in one place, fixed tightly to the skeletons of dead polyps. A reef builds up from the skeletons of millions of dead polyps. A reef that develops near the shore is a **fringing reef**. **Barrier reefs** are long coral ridges separated from the coast by a deep lagoon ■. The Great Barrier Reef stretches more than 1,240 miles (2,000 km) along the coast of Queensland in Australia, and is up to 124 miles (200 km) wide. A **coral atoll** is a ring-shaped island surrounding a shallow lagoon.

***Life on the reef***
*Coral reefs provide a home for a rich variety of colorful marine life.*

# Oceans on the move

The Earth's oceans are never still, but are kept in constant motion by the wind, Sun, and Moon. Winds blow up waves and drive ocean currents far across the Earth; the Sun's heat stirs the ocean waters; and the pull of the Moon's gravity tugs upon the oceans' surface twice each day.

## Seawater

The water in the Earth's oceans

Seawater is only 96.5 percent water. The rest is mostly dissolved mineral salts. The most common is sodium chloride (table salt). Other ingredients are magnesium, sulfur, calcium, and potassium. There are also traces of most other elements ■ found on land.

## Ocean thermal regime

The variation in ocean temperatures

Some parts of the ocean ■ are warmer than others. Seawater is warmest at the equator ■, where the Sun's heat is strongest. It gets steadily colder towards the poles, where parts of the Arctic Ocean are always frozen.

## Thermal stratification

The layering of ocean temperatures

Seawater gets colder with depth, because the Sun's warmth can penetrate only so far. The surface temperature of tropical oceans may reach 77°F (25°C), but 3,280 ft. (1,000 m) down the temperature falls to about 41°F (5°C). Below this depth, the temperature continues to drop, reaching as low as 34–36°F (1–2°C). Three layers within the water can be identified. On top is the thin, warm **epilimnion**, which is continually stirred up by wind and the Sun's heat. In the middle is the **thermocline**, where the temperature plummets. At the bottom is the cold, stagnant, deep water of the **hypolimnion**.

## Surface current

A mass of water flowing just below the surface of the ocean

Winds can disturb ocean waters down to a depth of about 330 ft. (100 m), setting in motion currents that may flow thousands of miles. The pattern of surface currents depends mainly on the prevailing winds ■. However, the currents do not flow in straight lines, but are pulled into curves by the Coriolis effect ■ and the shape of the ocean basins. In the subtropics, they form giant circles called **gyres**.

## Deep ocean current

A slow circulation of water far below the surface of the ocean

Differences in water temperature and salinity set deep ocean currents in motion. Cold polar waters sink gradually toward the seabed and flow at depth toward the equator. This process is called **subsidence**. Currents can also rise from the deep. This happens off the coast of Peru, where the trade winds ■ pull the warm Humboldt current away from the coast, so that cold, deep water wells up.

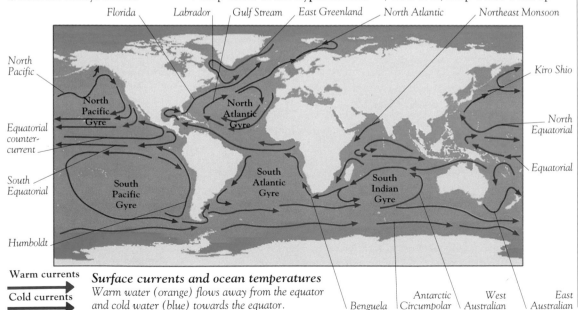

Florida · Labrador · Gulf Stream · East Greenland · North Atlantic · Northeast Monsoon · North Pacific · Kiro Shio · Equatorial countercurrent · North Equatorial · South Equatorial · Equatorial · North Pacific Gyre · North Atlantic Gyre · South Atlantic Gyre · South Indian Gyre · South Pacific Gyre · Humboldt · Benguela · Antarctic Circumpolar · West Australian · East Australian

**Warm currents**
**Cold currents**

*Surface currents and ocean temperatures*
*Warm water (orange) flows away from the equator and cold water (blue) towards the equator.*

**Fresh water**

**Salt water**

*Dense water*
*A hydrometer measures the density of a liquid. It floats higher in seawater than in freshwater, because dissolved salts increase the water's density.*

## Salinity

The amount of mineral salts dissolved in seawater

Salinity is high in the subtropics, where there is little rain to dilute seawater and high temperatures cause the water to evaporate quickly, leaving concentrated salts behind. Shallow seas in hot places have the highest salinity. The Dead Sea, for example, has a salinity of 23.8 percent. Salinity is low on the equator, where sea water is diluted by freshwater from large rivers. It is lowest of all in polar regions, where melting snow and ice dilute the water.

## Tide

A rise and fall of the oceans, occurring twice daily

Tides are caused mainly by the way gravity ▨ pulls the Earth and Moon toward each other. The pull on the Earth is strongest on the side nearest the Moon and weakest on the side farthest away from it, so the Earth is stretched into a slight oval in line with the Moon. This distortion barely affects the solid Earth, but it makes the oceans bulge up in a **high tide** either side of the Earth. As the Earth rotates, each part of the ocean rises as a high tide twice each day, and falls again twice in between as **low tide**s.

## Spring tide

An especially high or low tide

Tides are influenced by the Sun's gravity, as well as that of the Moon. When the Sun, Moon, and Earth line up, the added influence of the Sun causes especially high and low tides called spring tides. This happens twice each month, at the time of the New Moon and the Full Moon. A week after each spring tide, the Sun is at right angles to the Moon and counteracts its effect, so that the tides are neither as high nor as low. These are **neap tides**.

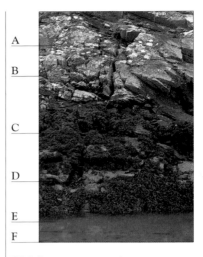

*Tidal range vegetation*
*The tidal range can be clearly seen from the vegetation growing along this Welsh shoreline. Lichens (**A**) grow above the high tide mark – the black area (**B**). Green seaweed (**C**) grows just below this mark and is only occasionally under water. Brown seaweed (**D**) is submerged most of the time. Below the low tide mark (**E**) grows red seaweed (**F**), which is permanently submerged.*

## Tidal interval

The time between two successive high tides

The Moon moves 12° around the Earth each day. This means that the interval between two tides is not 12 hours, but averages 12 hours and 25 minutes. This time varies from place to place, as does the **tidal range** – the amount by which waters rise and fall. In small enclosed seas, such as the Baltic, the tidal range can be less than 3.3 ft. (1 m). But in funnel-shaped bays off the major oceans, water piles up to create very high tides. The tidal range in Canada's Bay of Fundy is up to 69 ft. (21 m).

**High spring tide**
**(New Moon)**

**Earth**

*Tidal bulge*

*The combined pull of the Sun and the Moon causes large tides*

**Moon**

*Moon's rotation*

*How tides are formed*
*Roughly every 12 hours, the oceans on each side of the globe rise a little and then fall back. These tides are caused by the varying gravitational pull between the spinning Earth and the Moon and the Sun.*

*Earth's rotation*

*When the Sun and Moon are at right angles, their pulls counteract, causing small tides*

**Low neap tide**
**(Last quarter)**

*Tidal bulge*

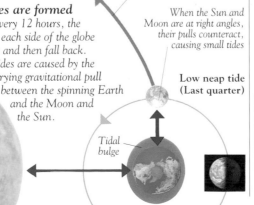

**Sun**

### See also

Coriolis effect 143 • Element 42
Equator 37 • Gravity 31
Ocean 134 • Prevailing wind 143
Trade wind 144

# The atmosphere

Wrapped around the Earth is a blanket of gases called the atmosphere. Without this very thin layer life would be impossible. It gives us air to breathe and water to drink; it keeps us warm; and it protects us from the Sun's harmful rays and from meteorites.

## Atmosphere

The thin layer of gases surrounding the Earth

The Earth's atmosphere is a colorless, odorless, tasteless "sea" of gases, water, and fine dust. It is about 430 miles (700 km) deep but has no distinct boundary, simply fading off into space as it gets thinner. It constantly loses lighter gas molecules ■ such as hydrogen and helium as they pull away from the Earth's gravity ■. The atmosphere is divided into layers according to the way the temperature changes with height.

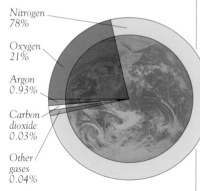

Nitrogen 78%
Oxygen 21%
Argon 0.93%
Carbon dioxide 0.03%
Other gases 0.04%

### Chemical composition of air
*Air is composed mainly of the gases nitrogen and oxygen, with small amounts of argon, carbon dioxide, and other gases.*

### See also

Climate 154 • Condensation 146
Gravity 31 • Molecule 42
Ozone hole 175 • Warm front 151

## Troposphere

The lowest layer of the atmosphere

The troposphere extends barely 7 miles (12 km) above the ground, yet it contains over 75 percent of all the atmosphere's gas (by mass) and vast quantities of water and dust. As the Sun heats the ground, it keeps this thick mixture churning, bringing us everything we call weather. The troposphere is normally warmest at ground level and cools higher up where it reaches its upper boundary, the **tropopause**. The tropopause varies in height from 11.2 miles (18 km) at the equator to 5.6 miles (9 km) at 50° N and 50° S, and 3.7 miles (6 km) at the poles.

## Stratosphere

The layer of the atmosphere above the tropopause

The stratosphere extends from the tropopause up to its upper boundary, the **stratopause**, 31 miles (50 km) above the Earth's surface. It contains 19 percent of the atmosphere's gas. There is little water vapor in this layer and it is calm compared to the troposphere. Within the stratosphere is the **ozone layer** ■, a band of ozone gas that absorbs the Sun's harmful ultraviolet rays. Air gets warmer with height in the stratosphere, rising from −76°F (−60°C) at the bottom to a maximum of about 50°F (10°C) at the stratopause.

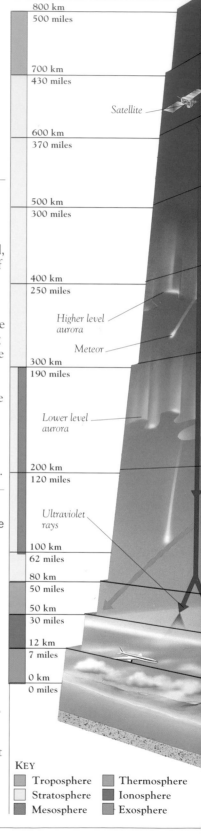

800 km
500 miles

700 km
430 miles

*Satellite*

600 km
370 miles

500 km
300 miles

400 km
250 miles

*Higher level aurora*

*Meteor*

300 km
190 miles

*Lower level aurora*

200 km
120 miles

*Ultraviolet rays*

100 km
62 miles

80 km
50 miles

50 km
30 miles

12 km
7 miles

0 km
0 miles

KEY

| | |
|---|---|
| ▨ Troposphere | ▨ Thermosphere |
| ▢ Stratosphere | ■ Ionosphere |
| ▨ Mesosphere | ▨ Exosphere |

# Mesosphere

The layer of the atmosphere above the stratopause

The gases in the mesosphere are too thin to absorb much of the Sun's heat, so temperatures drop rapidly with height, reaching –184°F (–120°C) at the **mesopause**, 50 miles (80 km) above the ground. Although the air there is thin, it is still thick enough to slow down meteorites hurtling into the atmosphere. As they slow down, they burn up, leaving fiery trails in the night sky.

*Layers of the atmosphere*
*The atmosphere is divided into five main layers plus the ionosphere. It extends over 430 miles (700 km) into the sky.*

Radio waves bounce off ionosphere layer

Mesopause

Stratopause

Ozone layer

Tropopause

Radio waves

Radio station

Weather balloon

Cirrus clouds

Cumulus clouds

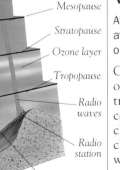

# Thermosphere

The layer of the atmosphere above the mesopause

The gases of the thermosphere are even thinner than those in the mesosphere, but they absorb ultraviolet light from the Sun, boosting temperatures to as high as 3,600°F (2,000°C) at the top.

# Ionosphere

A layer of the atmosphere above the mesopause that is full of electrically charged particles

The ionosphere is part of the thermosphere. It is made of gas particles ionized (electrically charged) by ultraviolet rays and X-rays that stream from the Sun. The ionosphere is important for communications because radio signals can be bounced around the world off this layer.

# Exosphere

The outermost layer of the atmosphere

The exosphere is the outer layer of the atmosphere, more than 430 miles (700 km) above the Earth, where gases get thinner and thinner and drift off into space.

# Weather

Atmospheric conditions at a particular place or time

Constant movement of air within the troposphere means that conditions there are always changing. Without these changes, there would be no weather. Sunshine, temperature, rainfall, wind, and cloud are all components that constitute weather. The average weather conditions over a long period of time – typically more than 30 years – is called the climate ■.

# Lapse-rate

How fast the air cools with height

Normally, air in the troposphere gets colder with height. The **environmental lapse-rate** is how much colder the air gets with height, typically 1°F (0.6°C) per 330 ft. (100 m). The **dry adiabatic lapse-rate** is how fast a parcel of warm, dry air cools as it drifts upward, typically 1.8°F (1°C) every 330 ft. (100 m). The lapse-rate for a parcel of wet air, the **saturated adiabatic lapse-rate** is lower because of the condensation ■ of water vapor and varies from 0.7–1.6°F (0.4°C–0.9°C) per 330 ft. (100 m).

# Temperature inversion

A reversal of the normal tendency of air to get colder with height

When an inversion happens, air gets warmer with height. High-level inversions occur when two fronts ■ collide and warm air is forced to undercut cold air. Low-level inversions are more localized and often happen in sheltered valleys when the ground cools rapidly on a clear night, cooling the air above it.

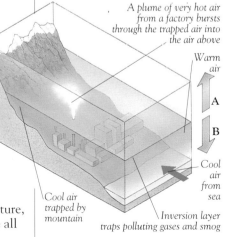

*A plume of very hot air from a factory bursts through the trapped air into the air above*

Warm air

A

B

Cool air from sea

Cool air trapped by mountain

Inversion layer traps polluting gases and smog

*Temperature inversion*
*Above the inversion (A), air rises and gets colder with height, as expected. Below the inversion (B), however, air sinks and gets warmer with height.*

# Solar energy

Half the Earth is exposed to the tremendous heat of the Sun at any one time. The Sun not only gives us warmth and light, and provides energy for plants to grow, but it also keeps the great weather system of the atmosphere in motion, by stirring up the air and evaporating moisture from oceans and lakes.

## Solar radiation

Heat, light, and other kinds of rays from the Sun

Many kinds of radiation reach the Earth from the Sun. All this radiation, including light and heat, comes in minute waves. Forty-one percent is visible in the form of light. Fifty percent is **long wave radiation**. This is made of waves too long for our eyes to see, such as **infrared waves**, although we may feel their heat. The 9 percent remaining is **short wave radiation**, such as **X-rays**, **gamma rays**, and **ultraviolet rays**. These waves cannot be seen, but they can affect the tissues of the body.

## Insolation

The amount of heat from the Sun reaching the ground

The amount of heat reaching the ground depends on the angle of the Sun, so it varies with latitude ■ and season ■. Insolation is at a maximum in the tropics ■ and during the summer months. The tropics get, on average, almost two and a half times as much heat per day as the poles. On long summer days, the poles actually get more hours of sunlight than the equator, but in winter they get almost none. Insolation is also affected by the amount of cloud cover, and by aspect ■ – the position of a place or landscape feature relative to the Sun.

## Solar energy budget

The distribution of the Sun's energy through the atmosphere

As the Sun's rays pass through the atmosphere, they lose over half their energy. Only 47 percent of the total radiation actually reaches the ground, while 19 percent is retained in the atmosphere. The rest is lost back into space.

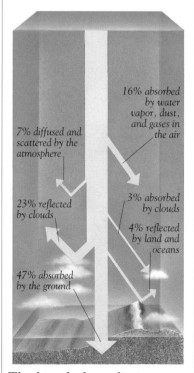

7% diffused and scattered by the atmosphere

16% absorbed by water vapor, dust, and gases in the air

23% reflected by clouds

3% absorbed by clouds

4% reflected by land and oceans

47% absorbed by the ground

**The fate of solar radiation**
*Only 47 percent of solar radiation reaches the ground. The remaining 53 percent is absorbed or reflected in various ways on its way down.*

## Greenhouse effect

The trapping of solar heat by gases in the atmosphere

Glass keeps a greenhouse warm by allowing short-wave radiation from the Sun to pass through easily, but blocking the long-wave radiation reflected back from the ground, trapping heat within the greenhouse. Water vapor, carbon dioxide, and other greenhouse gases ■ in the air act in the same way, keeping the Earth warm. As these gases increase in the air, the greenhouse effect may make the Earth warm up ■.

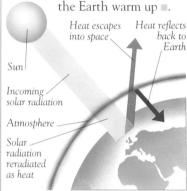

Heat escapes into space

Heat reflects back to Earth

Sun

Incoming solar radiation

Atmosphere

Solar radiation reradiated as heat

**Normal greenhouse effect**
*Certain gases in the atmosphere trap heat and keep the Earth warm.*

## Atmospheric heat transfer

The way the Sun's heat is spread through the air

The lower layers of the atmosphere are warmed mostly by long-wave radiation from the Sun, reflected from the ground. The ground heats the air slightly by **conduction** – that is, by direct contact – but this is almost negligible, because air is such a good insulator. Heat spreads up through the air by convection. **Convection** is when a parcel of air expands as it is warmed, and rises because it is less dense than the surrounding air. **Advection** is when heat spreads through the air horizontally, principally through winds ■.

## See also

Aspect 100
Environmental lapse-rate 139
Global warming 175
Greenhouse gas 175 • Latitude 37
Season 35 • Tropics 35 • Wind 142

# Latent heat

Heat taken in or given out when a substance changes its state

When water in the air changes its state it causes changes in air temperature. When water changes from liquid to gas (evaporation), heat is taken in and the surrounding air is cooled. If water changes from gas to liquid (condensation), heat is given out.

# Albedo

The capacity of a surface to reflect the Sun's energy

Some surfaces reflect the Sun's heat and warm the air better than others. Snow and ice have an albedo of 85–95 percent, and are good reflectors, so they often stay frozen even when it is warm. Forests, with an albedo of about 12 percent, absorb a lot of heat.

*Reflectivity of different surfaces*
*Different surfaces reflect the Sun's rays to vastly different degrees.*

*Map of global air temperatures*
*This map shows the wide variation in mean annual air temperatures around the world. The coldest areas are deep blue in color, and the warmest areas are deep orange.*

# Air temperature

A measure of how hot or cold the air is

Air temperature is measured either on the Celsius or Centigrade scale, where water freezes at 0°C and boils at 100°C, or the Fahrenheit scale, where water freezes at 32°F and boils at 212°F. Air temperature depends largely on insolation, but because it takes time to warm the air, the maximum temperature occurs slightly after the maximum insolation. So the warmest time of day is usually two or three o'clock in the afternoon, while the warmest days of summer are usually 30 to 40 days after the summer solstice.

# Continentality

The way continents affect temperature variations

Land surfaces heat up and cool down more quickly than large bodies of water such as oceans. This makes temperature variations in coastal areas more moderate than those far inland. The greater the continentality of a place (the farther it is from the sea), the more extreme the temperature variations will be, giving warmer summers and cooler winters.

# Isotherm

A line joining places of equal temperature

Temperature patterns around the world are plotted on isothermal maps, on which lines join points of equal temperature. But because temperature drops with height according to the environmental lapse-rate ■, the map would be distorted by low mountain temperatures. So all temperatures are reduced to sea level by adding 11°F (6°C) for every 3,280 ft. (1,000 m). The **temperature gradient** is the rate of change of temperature on isothermal maps.

5%

8%

20%

30%

45%

90%

Tar    Brown earth    Green field    Wheat field    Sandy desert    Snowy mountain

# Air pressure & wind

Air is very light, but because there is such a huge amount of air in the atmosphere, air can exert enormous pressure. But the pressure it exerts varies constantly from place to place and from time to time, and these variations create wind as air is pushed from one place to another.

## Atmospheric pressure

The force exerted by air on its surroundings

Air is pushing constantly in all directions – up, down, and sideways – with a force of over 14 lb per sq. in. (1 kg per cm²). It is sometimes said that this force or pressure is simply the weight of the air in the atmosphere ■ above. But it is really caused by the constant bombardment of billions of air molecules as they zoom about. Air pressure is greatest at sea level, where the air is the most dense and contains the most molecules, but it drops steadily with height as the air thins out.

## Isobar

A line on a map that links points of equal atmospheric pressure

Air pressure is shown on maps using isobars, and is measured in units called **millibars (mb)**. The **pressure gradient** is the rate at which air pressure changes from one place to another. When isobars are close together, there is a sharp difference in air pressure, giving a strong pressure gradient. When lines are far apart, the pressure gradient is weak.

### See also

Albedo 141 • Atmosphere 138
Circulation cell 144 • Hurricane 152
Surface current 136 • Solar radiation 140

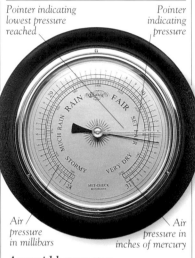

Pointer indicating lowest pressure reached

Pointer indicating pressure

Air pressure in millibars

Air pressure in inches of mercury

**Aneroid barometer**
*Low pressure indicates stormy weather and high pressure indicates dry weather.*

## Barometer

An instrument for measuring atmospheric pressure

A **mercury barometer** has a glass tube containing mercury, sealed at the top but open at the base. The mercury is held in the tube by air pushing on the open base. The height of mercury in the tube varies with pressure. At sea level, the mercury column is on average 30 in. (76 cm) high. An **aneroid barometer** is less accurate but easier to use. It has a metal box containing a partial vacuum. Changes in the surrounding air pressure make the box bigger or smaller, which moves a needle on a dial marked in millibars. Standard pressure at sea level is 1,013 mb, but varies between 800 mb and 1,050 mb.

## Cyclone

An area of low pressure

Air pressure varies constantly from place to place, and from time to time as solar radiation ■ makes the air warmer in some places than others. There are high pressure zones called **highs** or **anticyclones**, where the air is cold and under higher pressure than the surrounding air. Cyclones (also called **depressions** or **lows**) occur where the air is warm and less dense. A hurricane ■ is a storm associated with a tropical cyclone.

## Polar high

The zone of high pressure normally over the poles

Because cold air is dense, there is usually a high pressure zone over the cold poles called the polar high. There is a corresponding low pressure zone over the warm equator called the **equatorial low**. There are also **subtropical highs** 30° N and 30° S of the equator, where the air is squashed by sinking air in a circulation cell ■, and **subpolar lows** around 55° N and 55° S.

## Wind

A stream of air moving from one place to another

Air near the surface of the ground always moves from areas of high pressure to areas of low pressure. Wind is basically such a movement of air. The stronger the pressure gradient, the stronger the wind. The strength or **force** of a wind is how fast the air is moving, and is measured typically in mph or kph. The **Beaufort scale** divides wind strength into 13 forces.

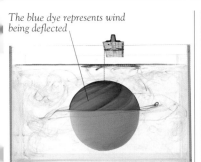

The blue dye represents wind being deflected

### Coriolis experiment

*The spinning ball in this water tank demonstrates the effect of the Earth's rotation on wind – the Coriolis effect.*

## Coriolis effect

The deflection of winds by the Earth's rotation

The Earth's rotation prevents winds from blowing straight from areas of high to low pressure. In the Northern Hemisphere winds are deflected to the right, and in the Southern Hemisphere to the left. The faster the wind blows, the stronger the effect. The Coriolis effect has a similar effect on ocean currents ■.

## THE BEAUFORT SCALE

*Background picture: birch trees being blown in a gale*

## Convergent circulation

The wind pattern blowing into a low

The Coriolis effect deflects high level winds at right angles to the pressure gradient and parallel to the isobars, creating **geostrophic winds**. Lower down, the ground reduces the deflection and winds blow at an angle across the isobars. This creates **divergent circulation** where winds spiral out of highs, and convergent circulation where they spiral into lows. In the Northern Hemisphere, winds spiral clockwise out of highs and counterclockwise into lows. In the Southern Hemisphere, the reverse is true.

## Prevailing wind

The wind that blows most often

Winds are usually described by the direction from which they are blowing. A wind blowing from southwest to northeast is called a southwesterly or a southwest wind. In most places, the wind tends to blow from one direction most of the time. This is called the prevailing wind.

### How winds are generated

*Air rises over warm areas, such as cities, creating low pressure. Air sinks over cold areas, such as the sea, producing high pressure. The extra pressure pushes air toward the low pressure zone, generating low level winds. At higher altitudes, air spreads out above low pressure areas to create high level winds.*

*Air rising over warm areas generates a return air flow at high altitude to complete the air circuit*

*Cold air sinks over forests*

*Cold air under high pressure flows to area of lower pressure*

*Warm air rises over cities*

*Corn fields have a high albedo and reflect plenty of sunshine, warming the air above and creating an area of low pressure*

*Air sinks over cool sea, creating high pressure*

*Cold air under high pressure moves to an area of lower pressure*

# Wind circulation

Wind and weather may seem chaotic, but there is a clear pattern to the prevailing winds that blow in different parts of the world. The world's winds are part of a global system of air circulation that moves warm air from the equator to the poles, and cold air the opposite way, maintaining the balance of temperatures around the world.

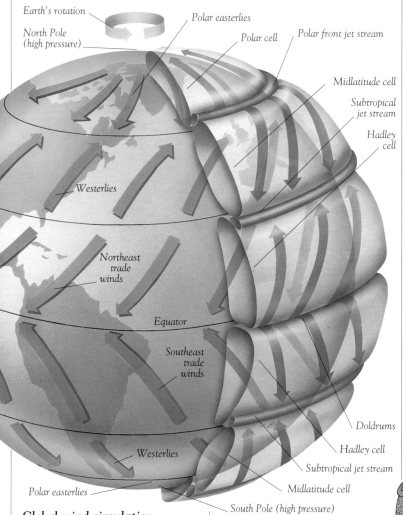

Earth's rotation

North Pole (high pressure)

Polar easterlies

Polar cell

Polar front jet stream

Midlatitude cell

Subtropical jet stream

Hadley cell

Westerlies

Northeast trade winds

Equator

Southeast trade winds

Doldrums

Hadley cell

Subtropical jet stream

Westerlies

Midlatitude cell

Polar easterlies

South Pole (high pressure)

**Global wind circulation**
*The Earth's rotation deflects the ground-level wind of each circulation cell in one direction, while the equivalent high-level wind is deflected in the opposite direction. This is called the Coriolis effect, and it creates a giant "corkscrew" of circulating winds.*

## Circulation cell
A large-scale pattern of air circulation

For every wind ■ blowing away at ground level, there is a returning wind higher up. Air tends to rise in front of the warm, ground level wind and then sink again behind it, in a circular movement called a cell. There are three major cells in each hemisphere. In the tropics, the **Hadley cell** starts as warm air rises over the equator. It blows high up toward the poles, then sinks at 30° N and 30° S, at the subtropical highs ■. Here, air flows toward the equator to complete the Hadley cell, and toward the poles to start a **midlatitude cell**. The **polar cell** involves cold, dense air flowing away from the poles.

## Global wind
One of the world's prevailing winds

The ground level part of each major circulation cell forms three belts of prevailing winds ■ on either side of the equator. In the tropics, there are dry northeasterly and southeasterly **trade winds**, with an area of low-pressure called the **doldrums** in between. In the midlatitude regions, there are warm, moist **westerly winds**, and in polar regions there are cold **polar easterlies**.

*3 Warm and cold air caught in the loops may detach to form cyclones and anticyclones*

*2 The Rossby wave becomes deeper and more pronounced*

**1** *A Rossby wave develops as a long undulation forms in the polar front jet stream*

Cold air

Warm air

### Rossby waves
*Rossby waves are giant meanders in high-altitude winds that are a major influence on weather. They are caused by the Earth's rotation, but are modified by differences in air temperature and the land below.*

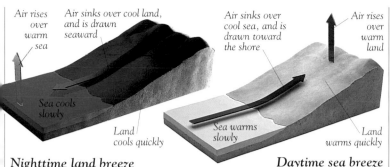

*Nighttime land breeze*
Cool air sinks over the land and moves
out to sea, creating a land breeze.

*Daytime sea breeze*
Cool air from the sea is drawn
inland, creating a sea breeze.

## See also

Climate 154 • Coriolis effect 143
Frontal storm 151 • Prevailing wind 143
Subtropical high 142 • Wind 142

## Polar front

The boundary between the
midlatitude and polar cells

Warm westerlies blowing up
from the tropics meet the cold
polar easterlies head on, along a
line called the polar front. Places
along the front are continually
subjected to frontal storms ■, set
off by the confrontation.

## Jet stream

A narrow belt of westerly winds at
high altitude

Jet streams roar around the
world at speeds up to 230 mph
(370 kph). The steadiest jet
stream is the **subtropical jet
stream**, between 20° and 30° N,
and 20° and 30° S. There is also
a **polar front jet stream** along
the polar front, an **Arctic jet
stream** and a **polar-night jet
stream**, blowing only in winter
during the long polar night.

## Rossby wave

A giant meander in the polar front
jet stream

The polar front jet stream
meanders around the world in
four to six giant waves, each
about 1,240 miles (2,000 km)
long. These Rossby waves are
caused by the Coriolis effect ■.
They have no fixed positions, but
probably snake along the polar
front, triggering frontal storms.

## Sea breeze

A local wind blowing off the sea,
especially after noon

Because the land heats up faster
than the sea, warm air rises over
the land during the day as it is
heated by the Sun. As the air
rises, it draws air in off the cool
sea and creates an onshore sea
breeze. At night, the land cools
faster than the sea, reversing the
breeze. Cool air over the land
sinks under warmer air over the
sea, setting off an offshore **land
breeze. Monsoon winds** bring
heavy rains to subtropical regions
such as Southeast Asia and
India. These massive sea breezes
blow inland off the ocean in
summer, as the interior of the
Asian continent heats up.
Monsoon winds may also be
partly caused by seasonal changes
in the subtropical jet stream.

## Föhn wind

A warm wind blowing down the lee
of a mountain range

When wind is forced up over
mountains into cool air, it loses
much of its moisture. As it blows
down the far side, it warms up
and becomes even drier, often
raising the temperature by 18°F
(10°C) in a few hours. This type
of wind is known as the **Nor-
wester** in New Zealand, the
**Samoon** in Iran, the **Berg** in
South Africa, and the **Chinook**
in the Rocky Mountains.

## Katabatic wind

A local wind blowing downhill at night

When air cools above hillslopes
at night, it often drains downhill
as a katabatic wind. In mountain
areas, converging katabatic winds
flow down the valleys at night
and create **mountain winds** where
they emerge on the lowland.
During the day, the situation
reverses as the hillslopes warm
up in the Sun, creating **anabatic
winds** up the slopes. In mountain
areas, this draws air up into the
valleys and creates **valley winds**.

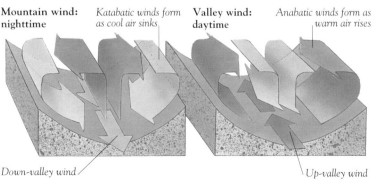

**Mountain wind:
nighttime**
*Katabatic winds form
as cool air sinks*
Down-valley wind

**Valley wind:
daytime**
*Anabatic winds form as
warm air rises*
Up-valley wind

*Katabatic and anabatic winds in mountain regions*
When mountain air cools at night, katabatic winds push air down the
valleys. As the air heats up during the day, anabatic winds draw air up the valley.

# Moisture in the air

The air is almost always moist, even when it is not raining, because it contains invisible water vapor. If the air is cooled enough, this vapor will condense into drops of liquid water, forming clouds, fog, mist, dew, and rain.

## Water cycle

The circulation of water between the Earth and the atmosphere

The Earth's water resources are constantly being recycled. Water vapor is added to the air by evaporation from seas, oceans, rivers, and lakes, and by transpiration ■ from plants. The water vapor cools and condenses into droplets of water, forming clouds. The water then falls as precipitation ■, which either soaks into the ground and is taken up by plants, or it runs off into seas, oceans, rivers, and lakes, from where it evaporates again. This process is called the water cycle or the **hydrological cycle**.

## Saturation point

The limit to the amount of water vapor that air can absorb

Air absorbs water vapor like a sponge soaks up liquid water. When the water vapor has completely filled all the spaces between the air molecules ■, the air can absorb no more vapor and is said to be **saturated**. Air expands as it gets warmer. As it does so, the spaces between the air molecules grow larger, allowing the air to absorb more water vapor. As air cools, it contracts and the air molecules pack more tightly together. This squeezes the water vapor out, forcing it to condense into droplets of liquid water. The point at which this happens is called the **dew point**.

## Humidity

The amount of water vapor in the air

**Absolute humidity** is the total moisture in grams in a given volume of air. **Specific humidity** is the vapor in grams contained in 2.2 lb. (1 kg) of air. **Relative humidity (rh)** is the moisture in the air expressed as a percentage of the maximum amount that air can hold at that temperature.

## Cloud

A dense, visible mass of water droplets or ice crystals in the air

Clouds generally form when water vapor in the air is lifted high into the sky so that it cools down and condenses.

## Condensation

The change of a gas to a liquid

Water vapor condenses into water droplets when air cools to 100 percent rh – in other words, to the dew point. For the vapor to condense, there must be tiny particles called **condensation nuclei** in the air. The vapor condenses around these minute airborne particles, such as dust and grains of sea salt. If the air is exceptionally clean, the vapor may not condense even when the air is saturated. Conversely, if the air is very dirty, the water vapor may condense before the dew point is reached.

*A never-ending process*
*Just as the Earth's rocks are constantly being recycled, so too are the Earth's water supplies. This process, called the water cycle, is vital to the existence of life on Earth.*

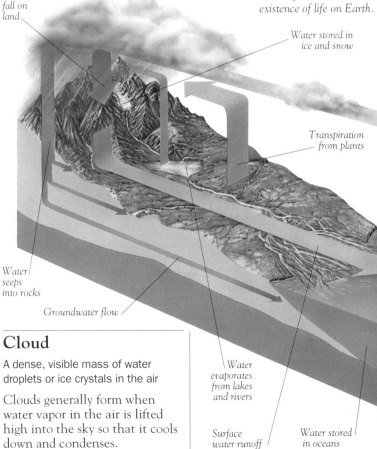

Rain and snow fall on land

Water stored in ice and snow

Transpiration from plants

Water seeps into rocks

Groundwater flow

Water evaporates from lakes and rivers

Surface water runoff

Water stored in oceans

*Advection fog*
*The Golden Gate Bridge in San Francisco disappears into thick fog. The fog forms as warm, moist air blows over cool Pacific Ocean currents.*

## Fog

Λ dense cloud of water droplets close to the ground

On cold, clear, calm nights, the ground quickly radiates the heat it absorbed during the day back into the air. As the ground cools, it may also cool the air above to its dew point, forming a dense cloud of water droplets called **radiation fog**. When warm, moist air flows over a cold surface, the water vapor in the air condenses to form **advection fog**.

*Clouds form as water condenses*

*Rain falls over oceans*

*Water evaporates from the oceans*

## Dew

Tiny drops of water that condense on the ground or other surfaces

When the ground cools at night, it may cool the air above to the dew point, so that drops of water form. These collect as dewdrops on surfaces that lose heat quickly, such as metal and blades of grass.

## Frost

A coating of ice left when moisture in the air freezes

When air cools below freezing point 32°F (0°C) the water vapor in the air may freeze without first turning to dew, covering the ground with ice crystals of white frost. **Hoar frost** is spiky needles of frost that form when damp air blows over very cold surfaces. **Fern frost** is feathery ice trails that form on cold glass when dewdrops freeze. **Rime** is a thick, shiny coating of ice. It forms when drops of liquid water in clouds and fogs stay unfrozen well below freezing point in low pressure air. As soon as these droplets touch a surface, they freeze hard. **Black ice** forms when rain falls on a cold road.

## Adiabatic cooling

The cooling that occurs when air expands

When a parcel of warm air rises through the atmosphere, it expands as the air pressure ■ drops. As it expands, the air molecules spread out, lowering the temperature at the adiabatic lapse-rate ■. A parcel of air is said to be **unstable** if it is warmer than the surrounding air and goes on rising. It is said to be **stable** if it is cooler than the surrounding air and resists upward movement.

*Hoar frost*
*When water vapor touches a very cold surface it freezes instantly, leaving spiky needles.*

*Fern frost*
*Delicate trails of ice crystal may form on windows as dewdrops cool below freezing.*

*Rime*
*Rime is a thick coating of white ice formed when moisture cools well below 32°F (0°C) before freezing.*

## See also

Adiabatic lapse-rate 139
Atmospheric pressure 142 • Molecule 42
Precipitation 149 • Transpiration 108

*Continued on next page* ➤

### Cloud column

*Cloud formations are incredibly varied, but meteorologists use only 10 main cloud categories to describe them. The ten categories are shown here at the approximate heights at which they occur.*

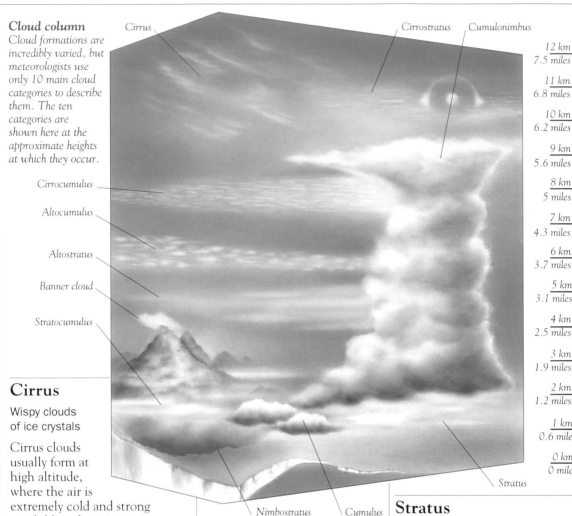

*Cirrus*  *Cirrostratus*  *Cumulonimbus*

12 km / 7.5 miles
11 km / 6.8 miles
10 km / 6.2 miles
9 km / 5.6 miles
8 km / 5 miles
7 km / 4.3 miles
6 km / 3.7 miles
5 km / 3.1 miles
4 km / 2.5 miles
3 km / 1.9 miles
2 km / 1.2 miles
1 km / 0.6 mile
0 km / 0 mile

*Cirrocumulus*
*Altocumulus*
*Altostratus*
*Banner cloud*
*Stratocumulus*
*Nimbostratus*  *Cumulus*
*Stratus*

## Cirrus

Wispy clouds of ice crystals

Cirrus clouds usually form at high altitude, where the air is extremely cold and strong winds blow them into wispy "mares' tails." Lower down, layers of puffy **cirrocumulus** form. These clouds of ice crystals have a dappled or rippled appearance.

## Contrail

A long trail of ice crystals behind a jet aircraft

The exhausts of jet aircraft emit streams of hot gases and water vapor. When these streams hit cold air, the water vapor cools and freezes, forming contrails.

### See also

Adiabatic cooling 147 • Dew point 146
Lightning 153 • Thunder 153

## Cumulus

Fluffy white clouds

Cumulus clouds pile up from a flat base as warm air rises. At the base, the air reaches the dew point ▪ as it cools adiabatically ▪. Cumulus clouds are generally short-lived. Strong updraughts in moist air may create vast **cumulonimbus** clouds that bring heavy rain, thunder ▪, and lightning ▪. These clouds may have a flat, icy top called an "anvil head," as well as a flat base. The tops of cumulus clouds may spread out sideways into a broad sheet of cloud called **stratocumulus**. **Altocumulus** are puffs or rolls of clouds at a medium height.

## Stratus

Vast, shapeless layer clouds

Stratus clouds form when a layer of air is cooled to the dew point. They often give long periods of rain. Variations are **cirrostratus**, a high-level veil of cirrus cloud, and **altostratus**, a thin, watery sheet of cloud at a medium height. **Nimbostratus** are layers of dark rain clouds close to the ground.

## Banner cloud

A cloud plume floating from the top of a mountain

Many mountains are cloud-capped, because warm, moist air is forced upward around them and cools to dew point.

◄ *Continued from previous page*

# Rain & snow

Rain and snow usually fall from clouds so thick with ice crystals and water droplets that they turn a dark, forbidding gray. Towering cumulonimbus clouds bring the heaviest downpours, but stratus clouds may give rain lasting many hours.

### See also

Cold front 150 • Condensation nuclei 146
Cumulonimbus 148 • Nimbostratus 148
Stratus 148 • Temperate climate 155

*Rain falls on the summits*

*The air warms and dries as it descends*

**Leeward side**

**Windward side**

*Moist air is forced upward by mountains*

*The rising air cools and condenses into clouds*

***Orographic rain***
*Rain falls as moist air is forced up the side of mountains. The leeward side is drier, an effect called a rain shadow.*

## Precipitation

Water drops or ice crystals falling to the ground from clouds

**Drizzle** is drops of water with a diameter of 0.008–0.02 in. (0.2–0.5 mm) that usually fall from stratus ▪ clouds. **Rain** drops falling from nimbostratus ▪ clouds are 0.04–0.08 in. (1–2 mm) across. Rain drops from cumulonimbus ▪ clouds can be 0.2 in. (5 mm) or more across. **Snow** is falling ice crystals. **Sleet** is a mixture of rain and snow, or partly melted snow. Precipitation occurs when water drops or ice crystals become so heavy that the air can no longer support them.

***Precipitation of rain***
*Rain drops form in a number of ways, including the collision of water droplets and the growth of ice crystals.*

## Supercooled water

Water below freezing point

Just as water vapor in the air only condenses around condensation nuclei ▪, liquid water only freezes if it has something to freeze onto. For this reason, clouds are often filled with drops of supercooled water well below freezing point. As supercooled drops freeze onto ice crystals, larger rain drops form.

*Strong air currents carry moisture high into the cloud*

**Cumulonimbus cloud**

*Ice crystals form*

*Small droplets of water in the cloud collide to form large drops*

*Ice crystals grow at the expense of supercooled water droplets*

*Large drops break up as they fall*

*Ice crystals form snowflakes or soft hail pellets*

**Freezing level**

*Small droplets collide again to form large droplets*

**Collision**

**Ice crystal growth**

*Snowflakes and hail pellets melt into rain drops as they fall into warm air*

## Convectional rain

Rain caused by rising warm, moist air

Rain occurs when warm air is swept up high in a cloud, so that the air cools and the water vapor in the air condenses into water droplets. Convectional rain occurs when pockets of warm, rising air form cumulonimbus clouds. **Frontal rain** occurs when air rises at warm and cold fronts ▪. **Orographic rain** occurs when air is forced up over a mountain.

## Hail

Ice pellets falling from clouds

Hailstones grow from ice crystals swept up and down by the violent air currents inside a cumulonimbus cloud. Water freezes around the crystals in layers like the skins of an onion, forming hard pellets more than 0.2 in. (5 mm) across.

## Drought

A prolonged period without rain, or of below-average rainfall

Deserts frequently have drought. In temperate ▪ zones, a drought is 15 consecutive days of less than 0.01 in. (0.25 mm) of rain.

# Air masses

A change in the wind may also herald a change in the weather. This is because each wind tends to bring with it the influence of a different air mass. An air mass is a large chunk of the atmosphere with a certain temperature and moisture content. A region's weather is determined largely by the air mass above.

*High-level cirrus clouds herald the warm front*

*Altostratus cloud*

*Advancing warm front*

*Cold air sinks under the warm air mass*

## Air mass

A vast section of the atmosphere where the air is uniformly warm or cold, wet or dry

An air mass may stretch over thousands of miles. It forms when air stays long enough over a large surface feature, such as an ocean or a plateau, to take on its humidity ■ and temperature. Far inland, one air mass may stay in place for days or even weeks. This brings stable, unchanging weather. Near the coast, a slight shift in wind ■ direction may carry in a different air mass. The most changeable, stormy ■ weather occurs along fronts, where air masses meet.

**World air masses in winter**
*In winter, the polar air masses exert the most influence on weather patterns.*

## Maritime polar

An air mass that forms over oceans toward the North or South Pole

A maritime polar air mass is cool and moist, and usually brings overcast skies, rain ■, or snow ■ along cold fronts. In summer, it brings clear, rain-washed skies and mild weather as it moves south and dries out.

## Maritime tropical

An air mass that forms over tropical and subtropical seas

A maritime tropical air mass is warm and moist, and usually brings long, steady rain showers along warm fronts. It may also cause thick blankets of advection fog ■ to form along coasts as the warm, moist air moves poleward over cooler surfaces.

## Continental tropical

An air mass that forms over subtropical deserts and plateaus

A continental tropical air mass is warm and dry, and usually brings hot, dry weather with clear skies. When this type of air mass is overhead, the weather is likely to stay fine and warm for a long time. **Equatorial air masses** are very warm, typically moist, air masses that form along the equator.

*Rising warm air*

*Strong winds and heavy rain showers may occur along the cold front*

## Continental arctic

An air mass that forms over the frozen Arctic Ocean

A continental arctic air mass forms over the Arctic Ocean, but it is described as "continental" because the ocean is frozen solid for much of the year. This air mass is very dry and icy cold, and when it lingers overhead it can bring clear skies and record low temperatures. **Continental polar air masses** form over the north of midlatitude continents. They are dry, like all other air masses, but only in winter are they really cold.

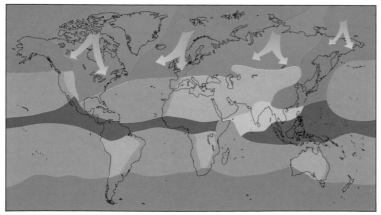

Key to air masses:
■ Continental polar    ■ Maritime tropical    ■ SW monsoon
■ Maritime polar    ■ Continental tropical    ■ Equatorial

Clouds form as the rising moist, warm air condenses

**Warm front**
*When a frontal storm passes over, a warm front arrives first, bringing steady rain.*

Rain falls from nimbostratus clouds

High-level winds blow the cloud tops into wedge shapes

Some of the moisture in the cloud-tops turns to ice

The mass of cold air dips sharply beneath the warm air

After the worst of the storm passes, light showers may linger

Advancing cold front

**Cold front**
*A cold front arrives after a warm front, bringing short, heavy showers and often thunder.*

## Warm front

**A boundary between warm and cold air masses where the warm air is advancing**

At a warm front, warm, moist air rides gradually over the cold air. This creates a long, gently sloping front that brings steady rain.

## Cold front

**A boundary between warm and cold air masses where the cold air is advancing**

Along a cold front, a mass of cold air undercuts the warm air, forcing it to rise sharply. Tall thunderclouds often develop, bringing short but heavy rain showers. As a cold front passes, the temperature drops and the clouds blow away, leaving a few fluffy cumulus ▦ clouds that bring light showers. Cold fronts usually follow a few hours after a warm front. When a cold front catches up and merges with a warm front, it forms an **occluded front** or occlusion.

## Frontal storm

**A storm associated with fronts and a depression**

The worst weather in midlatitude regions often comes from large areas of low pressure, called lows ▦ or depressions ▦, that form along a polar front ▦. In autumn, groups of depressions sweep westward. As each one moves, a kink in the center of the polar front sharpens into two "arms" – a warm and a cold front – separated by a wedge of warm air. As first the warm and then the cold front passes over, they bring stormy weather.

## EVOLVING FRONTS

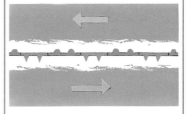

**Air masses collide**
*Cold polar and warm tropical air masses collide at the polar front.*

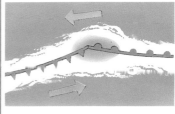

**Push and bulge**
*A depression forms where the warm air bulges into the cold air.*

**Splitting in two**
*Cold air chases warm air in a spiral. The polar front splits into two arms.*

**Occluded front**
*The cold front catches up and merges with the warm front as an occlusion.*

### See also

Advection fog 147 • Cumulus 148
Depression 142 • Humidity 146
Low 142 • Polar front 145 • Rain 149
Snow 149 • Storm 152 • Wind 142

# Storms

Every now and then, spectacular and violent storms erupt in the atmosphere, bringing torrential rain, thunder and lightning, and winds that can roar along at more than 100 mph (160 kph), spreading devastation wherever they strike.

## Storm

A violent disturbance in the weather

Colloquially, a storm is any spell of severe weather ■, but it is defined by meteorologists ■ as an event where winds ■ reach Force 10 on the Beaufort scale ■ and blow at over 55 mph (88 kph).

## Thunderstorm

A storm bringing thunder and lightning

Thunderstorms that bring torrential rain, thunder, and lightning are associated with towering cumulonimbus ■ ("thunderhead") clouds. Thunder clouds can reach up to 9–11 miles (15–18 km) into the sky, and their heads are made entirely of ice, blown out into an anvil shape. Thunder clouds are formed by strong updrafts, such as those that develop along cold fronts ■. They also form over hot ground, heated by the Sun, which is why storms often occur in mid afternoon in the tropics ■.

### See also

*Spiraling hurricane*
*Hurricanes are enormous, perhaps as wide as 500 miles (800 km). They can last for 18 hours or more. The eye of the hurricane is calm. But surrounding the eye, fierce winds blow and torrential rains fall. Spiraling bands of rain and wind may occur up to 250 miles (400 km) away.*

*Ice crystals form at the top of the clouds*

*Air billowing from the top of the storm causes the clouds to spread out*

*Spiral rain band*

*Eye wall*

*The strongest winds are found beneath the eye wall, immediately outside the eye*

*Air descends into the calm eye, leaving it free of cloud. Winds are less than 16 mph (25 kph)*

*Winds in excess of 100 mph (160 kph) occur beneath the storm*

*Warm, moist air spirals up around the eye inside the hurricane*

## Hurricane

A violent tropical storm

Hurricanes are also known as **willy-willies**, **tropical cyclones**, and **typhoons**. They develop from clusters of thunderstorms building up over warm tropical seas. Hurricanes tighten into a spiral with a calm ring of low pressure called the **eye** at the center. They then sweep westward, bringing torrential rain and winds gusting up to 220 mph (360 kph).

## Storm surge

A sudden rise in sea level linked with a storm

Storm winds can cause the sea level to rise dramatically and suddenly, causing widespread flooding ■, especially if the storm coincides with a spring tide ■. Particularly devastating storm surges are associated with hurricanes, because the very low atmospheric pressure ■ in the eye, at the center, allows the sea to rise by 16 ft. (5 m) or more.

# Lightning

A vivid flash of electricity during a thunderstorm

Inside thunder clouds, violent air currents cause soft hail pellets to collide with water droplets, thereby becoming charged with static electricity. Negatively charged particles are heavier and sink to the bottom of the cloud; positively charged particles are lighter and rise to the top, creating a difference in charge between the top and bottom of the cloud. If the charge difference builds up enough, it is discharged within the cloud, from the base to the top, as **sheet lightning** or to the ground as forked lightning. Lightning takes the easiest route to the ground, often via tall trees and buildings.

*The heat contained by the warm sea provides the energy needed to drive the whole storm*

*Negative charge*

*A flash of lightning releases the negative charge*

*The lightning is attracted to the positively charged ground, neutralizing the charge*

### Thunder and lightning
*Inside a thunder cloud there is a buildup of static electricity, with a positive charge at the top and a negative charge at the base. Lightning flashes from a negative to a positive area. The lightning heats the air around it, making it expand very fast, thereby causing a crash of thunder.*

## Forked lightning

A stroke of lightning flashing between a cloud and the ground

A fork of lightning begins with a dim flash of electricity from the base of a cloud to the ground. This is normally very fast and is in the form of 164 ft. (50 m) steps. This is the **leader stroke**. It prepares a conducting path through the air for a **return stroke**, from the ground to the cloud, a split second later. Although this is a slower stroke, it is much brighter and carries an average current of 10,000 amps.

## Thunder

A rumbling shock wave generated by lightning

When lightning surges through the air, it can instantly heat it up to over 45,000°F (25,000°C). The heated air expands so violently that it sends a huge shock wave rumbling through the air, which we hear as a thunderclap. Because sound travels much slower than light, we hear the thunder after we see the lightning – roughly 5 seconds later for every 1 mile (1.6 km) away that the storm is located.

# Tornado

A small but very intense spiraling windstorm

Tornadoes or **whirlwinds** are columns of violently spiraling air beneath thunderclouds. They roar past in minutes, bringing winds up to 250 mph (400 kph). Air pressure at the center of the column is very low. The air surrounding it rushes into this low pressure area, taking up objects in its path. Tornadoes are usually narrow, but may extend to 330 ft. (100 m) wide at the base. Over the sea, water is drawn up into a tornado, creating a **waterspout**.

### Tornado and waterspout
*The tornado (left) has "sucked" up debris. It leaves behind a narrow band of destruction. Waterspouts (right) are often gentler and last longer than tornadoes, perhaps because water is heavier than air and strong updrafts are rarer over water.*

# Climate

Some places are always much warmer, wetter, colder, or drier than others. The tropics, for example, are warmer than the Arctic. Of course, there are cool days in the tropics, just as there are warm days in the Arctic, but tropical weather is typically hot. The climate is the typical weather.

## Climate

The average weather conditions in an area for a period of 30 years or more

There are three broad climate zones: the warm tropics, the cold polar regions, and the temperate zone between. Climate involves all weather elements, not just temperature. There are various systems for classifying climates in detail, including the **Köppen system**, which defines climate zones by their vegetation, and the **Thornthwaite system**, which uses levels of evapotranspiration ■. A climate typical of a small area is a **microclimate**. Differences in the ground's albedo ■, wetness, and plant cover can make the climate vary enormously over a few yards.

## Climograph

A combination of graphs showing the climate of a place or region

To give a complete picture of a area's climate, average monthly weather conditions are plotted on the same graph, month by month for a year. Such a graph is called a climograph. Typically, climographs show average monthly temperatures, linked together as a smooth line, and average monthly rainfall, shown as a single bar for each month.

### Comparing climates

*In the climographs below, the left-hand axis shows average monthly rainfall in millimeters, and the right hand axis gives average monthly temperatures in degrees Celsius or Centigrade.*

## Tropical climate

A climate typical of the tropics

The tropics are hot. The average temperature at Manaos in Brazil, for example, is 81°F (27°C), and it rarely falls below 68°F (20°C). Some tropical places, such as deserts ■, are hot and dry; others, such as tropical rainforests ■, are hot and wet.

**Indonesian downpour**
*A van plows through torrential monsoon rains in Sumatra, Indonesia.*

## Monsoon climate

A tropical climate with distinct wet and dry seasons

Tropical regions affected by monsoon winds ■, such as India, have monsoon climates. India has a dry season from November to May, as winds blow out to sea. This is followed by a wet season lasting from June to December, as the monsoon blows inland.

## Desert climate

A climate typical of dry regions

Many deserts lie below subtropical highs ■, where the air is typically subsiding, and so is warm and dry. Cold ocean currents along the western coasts of the Sahara, Kalahari, and Atacama deserts further reduce rainfall because they cool the air. The Atacama desert, in the lee of the Andes, may go without rain for centuries. Orographic rain ■ falls on the Andes, leaving the air dry as it descends to the Atacama.

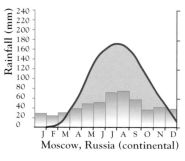

Moscow, Russia (continental)

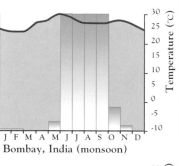

Bombay, India (monsoon)

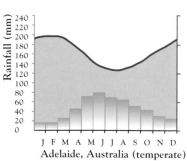

Adelaide, Australia (temperate)

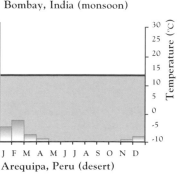

Arequipa, Peru (desert)

Key:

■ Polar

■ Tundra

□ Temperate

□ Desert & dry lands

■ Tropical

■ Mountain

**World climate zones**
*This map shows some of the world's major climate regions.*

# Polar climate

A climate typical of polar regions

The Sun is always low in the sky near the poles, and in winter it barely rises at all, giving three months of twilight. The weather is always very cold and the snow only melts in summer. Antarctic temperatures stay below –58°F (–50°C) for six months each year. **Tundra climates** are those of the cold tundra ■ regions, which have cool, brief summers and bitter winters with temperatures often below –76°F (–60°C).

# Temperate climate

A climate typical of midlatitudes

Midlatitude areas such as Japan, Europe, South Australia, and the US have warm summers and cool winters. Westerly winds bring rain all year around, and places nearer the poles may have snow in winter. A **Mediterranean climate** is a temperate climate typical of western continental areas of latitude ■ 30–40° N and 30–40° S. These areas, such as the Mediterranean, California, and South Africa, have hot, dry summers and warm, damp winters.

# Mountain climate

A climate typical of highland regions

Because air gets cooler with altitude, mountain climates are cold. They are also wetter, and windier than lowlands, but conditions vary a good deal, depending upon aspect ■. Above a certain height, called the **snow line**, there is always snow on the ground. The snow line is 16,400 ft. (5,000 m) in the tropics, 8,860 ft. (2,700 m) in the Alps, 1,970 ft. (600 m) in Greenland, and at sealevel at the poles.

# Oceanic climate

A climate typical of coastal regions

Places near the coast usually have wetter, more changeable weather than places inland. They also tend to have cooler summers and warmer winters, because the sea takes longer to heat up and cool down than the land. Warm ocean currents flowing across the Atlantic give northwest Europe particularly warm winters for its latitude. **Continental** ■ **climates**, in the interior of continents, are much drier, with colder winters and warmer summers.

# Climate change

Variations in past and future climates

Some climate changes are very dramatic, such as during the ice ages ■. More subtle changes may only be revealed by such things as variations in the size of growth rings in tree trunks. Pollution may be making climates warmer.

**Measuring climate history**
*A wide tree ring indicates a warm year during which the tree grew well.*

## See also

Albedo 141 • Aspect 100
Continentality 141 • Desert 116
Evapotranspiration 108 • Ice age 121
Latitude 37 • Monsoon wind 145
Orographic rain 149 • Subtropical high 142
Tropical rainforest 162 • Tundra 163

# Weather forecasting

Experienced observers may predict local weather from simple, natural signs. In contrast, large-scale weather forecasting relies upon giant computers and thousands of simultaneous observations of weather conditions around the world.

## Weather station

A center for monitoring weather

There are about 10,000 land-based weather stations. Some are situated on the roofs of city buildings, while others are located on remote islands or mountain tops. Weather stations collect information every three hours – called **synoptic hours** – on rainfall, temperature, wind direction and strength, and humidity. They pass on the data to the World Meteorological Organization's (WMO) network of 13 main weather centers.

## Radar meteorology

The use of radar to monitor weather

Radar ■ gives a good picture of where and how intensely rain is falling, because radar signals are reflected by any moisture in the air, including snow, hail, and rain drops.

***Rainfall on radar***
*This radar image shows intensity of rainfall in millimeters (red = 4 mm; green = 2mm; yellow = 1mm)*

***Balloon launch***
*A radiosonde balloon rises into the air, trailing a long line to which measuring instruments are attached. Radiosonde balloons are usually tracked by radar.*

## Radiosonde

A balloon for monitoring weather conditions high in the atmosphere

Hundreds of helium-filled radiosonde balloons are launched throughout the world each day at midnight and noon Greenwich Mean Time. These balloons monitor atmospheric conditions up to a height of 66,000 ft. (20,000 m). Air pressure ■, wind speed, temperature, and humidity in the upper air are all recorded automatically by instruments attached to the balloons. The data from these recordings are transmitted by radio to receiving weather stations.

## Global Telecommunications System (GTS)

A worldwide satellite network for the exchange of weather data

Weather forecasting requires an immediate and continuous supply of data. The world's weather stations are all linked by the GTS satellite network, which supplies data from balloons, radar, weather satellites, and other sources.

## Synoptic chart

A map showing weather conditions at a given time

Synoptic means "seen together." Synoptic charts are based on observations of weather conditions that are all made at the same time. If this is not possible, computers adjust the readings to compensate for time differences.

*Low-pressure circles are depressions* | *Isobars join points of equal pressure*

*Lines of spikes and bumps are occluded fronts* | *Spiked lines are cold fronts* | *Weather stations*

***Synoptic chart***
*Isobars link points of equal air pressure, and give a good indication of weather to come. The depression over the British Isles heralds wet and stormy weather.*

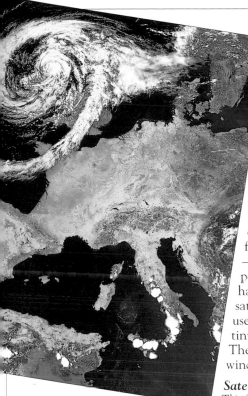

# Satellite meteorology

The monitoring of the atmosphere by satellite

Radiometers ■ on weather satellites ■ provide **visible images** of clouds, land, and sea in daylight. Infrared ■ images show air and surface temperatures and clouds by day and night. Wind speed and direction can be traced from **cloud motion winds** – that is, changes in cloud position recorded every half-hour by geostationary satellites. A **scatterometer** uses microwaves to detect tiny ripples on the sea. These show the surface wind speed and direction.

*Satellite storm*
*This false-colored satellite image shows Europe and North Africa. There is a storm system over the British Isles, but most of Europe is cloud-free.*

# Stevenson screen

A white, ventilated box for storing weather instruments

Air temperature readings must be taken in the shade, so thermometers are kept in white boxes to protect them from direct sunlight. Ventilation slats ensure that the air flows through freely.

*Sheltered instruments*
*This Stevenson screen contains thermometers and barographs, which record changes in atmospheric pressure.*

# Natural indicator

A change in nature that gives an indication of weather to come

In the days before meteorology ■, people relied on various natural signs for hints about the coming weather. Many plants and animals react to changing humidity, and so warn that rain is coming. But the sky is nature's best indicator.

Wool        Seaweed

*Natural forecasters*
*Seaweed dries and shrivels in fine weather, but swells and feels damp when rain is imminent. Wool shrinks and curls up when the air is dry, but straightens out when humidity is high and rain is on its way. Similarly, pine cones close up tight when the air is moist.*

Pine cones

*Closed in wet weather*          *Open in dry weather*

# Long-range forecast

A forecast of weather more than five days ahead

Weather forecasts are usually accurate for the next 24 hours, and reasonably accurate up to five days ahead, but beyond that they become increasingly unreliable.

## See also

Atmospheric pressure 142
Depression 142 • Infrared film 26
Meteorology 13 • Radar 27
Radiometer 26 • Weather satellite 27

# Numerical forecasting

Forecasting from grids of data

In modern weather forecasting, millions of simultaneous, or synoptic, measurements are taken of temperature, humidity, wind, and air pressure. These measurements are taken at 15 fixed heights in the atmosphere, and at evenly spaced grid points around the world. Using this data, powerful supercomputers calculate future synoptic values and so predict the weather ahead.

# Weather model

A theoretical picture of the way weather works

To make the predictions used in numerical forecasting, computers are programmed to give values based not only on recent trends, but also on weather models. These theoretical pictures show the way weather systems such as depressions ■ develop.

# Living things

The Earth may be the only planet in the Universe capable of supporting life. Inhabiting the narrow zone between the lowest layers of the atmosphere and the ocean bottoms is a rich diversity of living things. Each has its own special place in the world.

## Biosphere

The part of the Earth inhabited by living organisms

The biosphere can be thought of as the total assemblage of the Earth's plants, animals, and other living things. It is not separate from the nonliving world, because it has a complex relationship with the soil ■, rock ■, atmosphere ■, and water. For example, the oxygen in the air, on which so many creatures now depend for life, was actually created billions of years ago by tiny organisms called bacteria.

*Homemade ecosystem*
*Inside this terrarium is a sort of miniecosystem, complete with plants, animals, soil, and even its own "atmosphere."*

As plants use sunlight to make food, they take carbon dioxide from the air, and give out oxygen during photosynthesis

Water is recycled as plants first draw it from the soil and then return it to the air by transpiration

Plant roots take up nutrients such as nitrogen from the soil

## Ecosystem

An interacting collection of living organisms and their surroundings

The biosphere is made up of millions of different ecosystems contained within many biogeographical areas (known as biomes ■). All the organisms in an ecosystem interact, drawing on the same energy and nutrients ■ and continuously recycling them from one part of the system to another. The living parts of an ecosystem are described as **biotic**, while the nonliving parts are **abiotic**.

As plants "burn up" their food in respiration, they take in oxygen from the air and release carbon dioxide

## Habitat

The natural home of a living thing

The word habitat is often used to refer simply to the type of place in which a particular species of plant or animal naturally lives. The soil, for example, is the habitat of earthworms. A **community** is the collection of plants and animals within a habitat. The habitat of the community includes all the conditions that affect the way the community lives, including the climate ■, the soil type, and so on.

## Species

A group of living things that can breed together in the wild to produce fertile offspring

Biologists divide living organisms into a range of groups and subgroups, the smallest of which is called a species. What defines a species is the ability of a group of organisms to breed successfully together. Golden eagles and African elephants are examples of species. A **population** is a group of individuals of the same species within a community. Only under exceptional circumstances do different species naturally interbreed. An offspring of parents from two different species is a **hybrid**.

Earthworms feed on nutrients in the soil and improve the soil texture

Fungi, bacteria, and algae in the soil break down plant remains and release nutrients

# Flora

All the vegetation in a particular area

While the flora of an area is all the plants it contains, the **fauna** is all the animals. The range of species of flora and fauna varies from place to place. It reaches a maximum in tropical rainforests ▦, where there may be thousands of species in a tiny area.

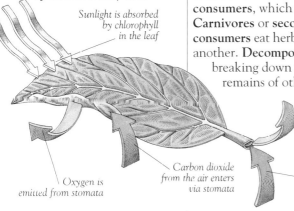

*Sunlight is absorbed by chlorophyll in the leaf*

*Glucose, a sugar, is produced and travels to all parts of the plant*

*Oxygen is emitted from stomata*

*Carbon dioxide from the air enters via stomata*

*Water collected by the roots travels to the leaf via the plant's sap*

### Making plant food
*From the raw materials of sunlight, water, and carbon dioxide, a plant makes glucose, which it uses as food. Oxygen is produced as a waste product.*

# Photosynthesis

A process that uses light energy to make food from simple chemicals

Plants make food from carbon dioxide in the air and water. To do this, they must absorb energy from the Sun by photosynthesis. This occurs mainly inside leaf cells, which contain **chlorophyll**, a substance that makes leaves green. Chlorophyll soaks up the Sun's energy and uses it to break down water in the plant's sap into hydrogen and oxygen. Carbon dioxide is absorbed from the air through pores or **stomata** on the surface of leaves. The carbon from the carbon dioxide combines with the hydrogen to make glucose sugar. When the plant uses up or "burns" this food, it leaves behind carbon dioxide and water. This process is called **respiration**.

# Autotroph

An organism that makes its own food

Organisms are either autotrophs or heterotrophs. Autotrophs or **producers**, such as green plants and algae, make their own food by photosynthesis. **Heterotrophs** – mainly animals – get their food ultimately from autotrophs. They include **herbivores** or **primary consumers**, which eat plants. **Carnivores** or **secondary consumers** eat herbivores and one another. **Decomposers** feed by breaking down the dead remains of other organisms.

# Food chain

A series of feeding links between organisms

The organisms in an ecosystem may feed off each other, which is why each plays such a vital role in the life of the ecosystem. In a salt marsh, for example, snails may feed on grass, shrews feed on the snails, and harriers feed on the shrews. The links in a food chain are often complex, so it is better to think of it as a **food web**.

# Grazing food chain

A feeding cycle involving plants, herbivores, and carnivores

Grazing food chains involve plants, the herbivores that feed on them, and the carnivores that feed on the herbivores. **Detritus food chains** usually occur in the soil and involve decomposers such as bacteria, fungi, and mites. The main stages in a food chain – producers, primary and secondary consumers, and decomposers – are called **trophic levels**.

## SIMPLE FOOD CHAIN

This sequence shows trophic levels in a simple food chain.

Sunlight

**Producers**
*Green plants such as cabbages use sunlight to make food by photosynthesis*

**Primary consumer**
*Herbivores such as small white caterpillars eat producers*

**Secondary consumers**
*Carnivores such as thrushes eat herbivores*

**Decomposers**
*Organisms such as fungi decompose dead plants, animals, and droppings, releasing minerals into the soil that may later be absorbed by producers*

## See also

*Continued on next page ➤*

## Vegetation strata

The vertical layers within a community of plants

Within most communities of plants, there are several layers or **strata**. These are, typically: the root layer; low-lying plants; taller herbs and grasses; shrubs; young seedling trees; understory trees; and, finally, taller overstory trees. Each of these plants has its own special role or **niche** – not just in the plant community, but within the ecosystem ■ as a whole. The animals of the ecosystem also have their own niches.

## Competition

The battle for resources within a habitat

As conditions in an ecosystem change, new plants and animals appear and may have to compete with one another for a particular resource. Plants may compete for light, for example. Some may overcome their rivals by growing faster and putting them in the shade. But as they do, they may provide a new area for shade-loving plants. If an animal finds its habitat fully occupied, it may **migrate** or move to another area. Plants spread by **dispersal**, such as when their seeds are blown by the wind to new places.

## Vegetation succession

The natural development sequence of a plant community

The natural vegetation of a particular place often develops through a number of stages, with plants becoming larger and more complex at each stage. This process is called vegetation or **serial succession**. In temperate forest ■ regions, for example, it begins with a simple **pioneer community** of grasses, followed by small plants that stabilize the topsoil ■ and add organic matter. Once the soil is improved, shrubs start to grow, followed by pines, and ultimately hardwood trees. A succession like this may take 200 years to proceed through all its stages.

### From grassland to oakwood
*The illustration below shows how a vegetation succession may develop in a temperate forest region – from mosses and lichens to a fully grown oakwood over the course of 200 years. In the first few years, there is a tremendous bloom of plant life, but in later years, growth and change become much slower.*

## Climax community

The final stage in a vegetation succession

It was once thought that a vegetation succession eventually produced a climax community – the most complex assemblage of plants for a particular habitat. Climax communities were thought to have stabilized and stopped changing. Most scientists now believe that such communities continue to change, because environmental conditions are also constantly changing.

## Bloom

Rapid growth early in a vegetation succession

In the early stages of a succession, plants are simple but grow rapidly, producing large quantities of vegetable matter. Later on, plants become larger and more complex, but growth slows down, and a tree can take decades to reach its full size.

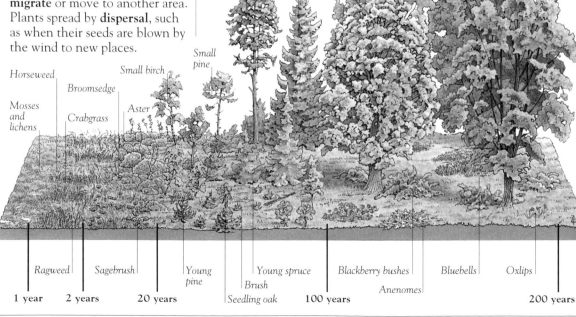

Horseweed · Mosses and lichens · Broomsedge · Crabgrass · Aster · Small birch · Small pine · Large pine · Spruce · Oak · Hickory

Ragweed · Sagebrush · Young pine · Young spruce · Brush · Seedling oak · Blackberry bushes · Anenomes · Bluebells · Oxlips

1 year · 2 years · 20 years · 100 years · 200 years

◄ Continued from previous page

# Nutrient

A chemical element needed by plants for good growth

Plants appear to need at least 18 different elements ■ in order to grow properly. **Macronutrients** are needed in large quantities. These include carbon, oxygen, nitrogen, potassium, phosphorus, calcium, sulfur, and magnesium. **Micronutrients** are needed only in small amounts, and include iron, manganese, silica, sodium, boron, chlorine, copper, cobalt, zinc, and molybdenum. Nutrients come, ultimately, either from rocks or the air. They reach plants by a variety of routes, including via soil, rainfall, and human activity. The constant transfer of nutrients between organisms and their environment is called the **nutrient cycle**, or the **biogeochemical cycle**. There is a different cycle for each nutrient.

# Carbon cycle

The transfer of carbon to and from the atmosphere

Plants and certain microorganisms take carbon dioxide from the air during photosynthesis ■. They return some to the air during respiration ■, and as they decay. Animals eating the plants breathe carbon dioxide back into the air. Some carbon is retained when plants turn into fossil fuels ■. The oceans have a separate cycle. Carbon dioxide dissolves in seawater: some evaporates back into the air, but some is taken up by the shells of sea creatures. After they die, the carbon is locked in sediments for millions of years.

*Green plants give out carbon dioxide during respiration*

*Green plants take in carbon dioxide from the air during photosynthesis*

*Animals breathe out carbon dioxide*

*Animal dung contains carbon*

*Animals take in carbon as they eat plants*

*Dead plants and animals decay in the soil*

*Decomposers such as fungi and bacteria give out carbon dioxide as they feed on organic remains*

**Recycling carbon**
*All living things contain the element carbon. This carbon ultimately comes from, and returns to, the atmosphere.*

# Nitrogen cycle

The transfer of nitrogen between organisms and their environment

Plants cannot obtain nitrogen directly from the air. Instead, bacteria in the soil (often on fungi and algae) absorb nitrogen in a process called **nitrogen fixation**. Some plants take up nitrogen from bacteria called **symbiotic nitrogen fixers**, which live on their roots. Most plants obtain it in the form of compounds called **nitrates**. These are produced by other bacteria that feed on the nitrogen fixers, in a process called **nitrification**. Plants turn nitrates into more complex compounds. These return to the soil and are reduced to nitrates again when plants die. Bacteria then release the nitrogen back into the air, in a process called **denitrification**.

*Denitrifying bacteria break down nitrates and release nitrogen back into the air*

*The atmosphere is mostly nitrogen gas*

*Rain contains nitrogen in the form of weak nitric acid*

*Roots take up nitrates*

*Some plants take up nitrogen from bacteria living on their roots*

*Nitrifying bacteria in the soil convert nitrogen compounds into nitrates*

*Manure and decaying plant and animal remains release nitrogen compounds into the soil*

**Recycling nitrogen**
*This simplified nitrogen cycle does not include nitrogen introduced into the soil by artificial fertilizers used in farming.*

# Phosphorus cycle

The transfer of phosphorus between organisms and their environment

Phosphorus enters the soil when certain rock minerals, such as apatite and clay minerals ■, are weathered. Plants get most of their phosphate from soluble phosphorus dissolved in soil water ■. The phosphorus is returned to the soil in animal wastes, especially manure. In the **potassium cycle**, plants obtain potassium from rock minerals such as feldspars ■ and micas ■ dissolved in soil water. It returns to the soil in manure, and when plant and animal remains decay.

## See also

# World biomes

The natural world is rich and varied, with many groups of plants and animals adapted to specific environments. These biomes, or "biogeographical areas," vary from deserts to tropical rainforests. In each biome there may be different ecosystems.

*African savanna*
*A herd of African elephants graze in the Samburu National Reserve, Kenya.*

## Vegetation region

A large area of the world with a similar range of plants

It is possible to identify major areas of the Earth with similar vegetation. The **physiognomic approach** classifies vegetation by its appearance or **physiognomy** – in other words, its color, how dense and lush it is, and so on. This scheme divides continents into **formations**, which are groups of plant communities with a similar physiognomy. Formations may be divided into **associations**, which are groups of similar plants dominated by one or two species.

## Biome

A large collection of plants and animals adapted to survive within their geographical zone

A region's soil ■ and animal life are closely related to its vegetation. This, in turn, is linked to the climate ■ and the nature of the environment. Such a system is called a biome. Extreme conditions, such as high altitude in **mountain** ■ **biomes** or flooding in waterlogged **wetlands**, may create different ecosystems ■ within the same biome. Human activity can modify biomes. For example, **scrubland** is land that has been extensively grazed. Oceans can be described as biomes containing **marine ecosystems**, including the open ocean, littoral (shallow) and benthic (bottom) regions, rocky and sandy shores, estuaries, and tidal marshes.

## Tropical rainforest

Dense forest in tropical areas of high rainfall

Tropical ■ rainforests cover 17 percent of the Earth's land area. With average temperatures of more than 70°F (21°C) and annual rainfall exceeding 79 in. (2,000 mm), the dense, lush vegetation is home to 40 percent of all plant and animal species. There may be 40 different tree species in a single acre.

**Tropical rainforest layering**

*Emergents*

*Canopy*

*Understory*
*Ground layer*

## Rainforest layering

The vegetation layers in a tropical rainforest

In the gloom just above the ground-level vegetation is the **understory**, where young trees, small conical trees, and shrubs grow. Tall, straight trees form a dense, unbroken **canopy** of leaves and branches 100–165 ft. (30–50 m) above the ground. Isolated trees called **emergents**, 200 ft. (60 m) or more tall, tower above the canopy.

## Savanna

Extensive grassland in the tropics

Savanna covers 20 percent of the Earth's land surface, and is usually dominated by sedges and grasses. But savanna can vary from treeless grassland to open forests of trees and shrubs with grass beneath. These areas usually have distinct wet and dry seasons. Rainfall is from 20–79 in. (500–2,000 mm) per year; temperatures rarely drop below 68°F (20°C).

## Desert biome

The plants, animals, and soil of very dry regions

Arid and semiarid lands cover more than 30 percent of the Earth's land surface. Very little of this area is actually barren – most is scattered with grass and scrub. Moving in from the edge of a desert ■, woody plants become more gnarled and spreading, leaves get fewer and more spiny, and bushes are usually evergreen. There is a great diversity of specially adapted animal life, especially insects.

*Desert vegetation*
*Cacti abound in this view of the Baja desert in California.*

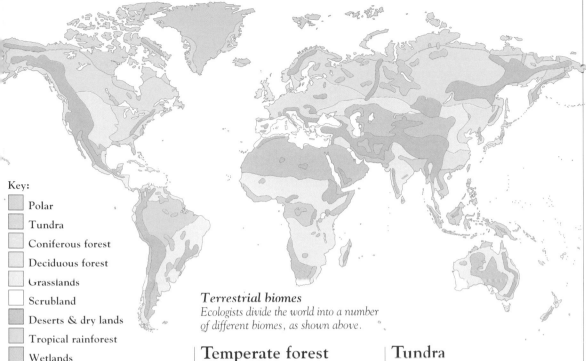

**Key:**

- Polar
- Tundra
- Coniferous forest
- Deciduous forest
- Grasslands
- Scrubland
- Deserts & dry lands
- Tropical rainforest
- Wetlands
- Mountains

*Terrestrial biomes*
*Ecologists divide the world into a number of different biomes, as shown above.*

## Temperate grassland

The grasslands of midlatitudes

There are three major areas of temperate ▪ grassland: the **steppes** of Russia, the **prairies** of the interior of the US, and the **pampas** of Uruguay. These were once vast natural grasslands, but much has now been intensively cultivated and grazed, especially the American prairie. This can have devastating effects, for these grasslands are very prone to soil erosion ▪. Only the dry, almost desert fringes remain totally wild.

## Temperate forest

The woodlands of midlatitudes

In the cold north of Asia and North America are **boreal forests** or **taiga**. These coniferous forests of pine, spruce, larch, and fir have an understory of willow and alder. Near the tropics are **broad-leaved evergreen forests** of oak, magnolia, holly, and sabal palm. In between are **temperate deciduous forests** of oak, beech, and hickory, with an understory of birch, hazel, and sycamore. Dry Mediterranean climates ▪ have patches of **sclerophyllus forest**, made up of hard-leaved trees that retain water well.

## Tundra

Cold, treeless regions that lie mostly inside the Arctic Circle

The bitterly cold tundra regions of Siberia, Scandinavia, Canada, and Alaska have temperatures of less than 14°F (−10°C ) for 6–10 months of the year. Extreme cold in these periglacial ▪ landscapes usually restricts vegetation to mosses, lichens, sedges, and rushes. But during the brief summer a huge variety of small flowers and deciduous dwarf shrubs, such as alder and birch, bursts into bloom. In polar ▪ regions, it is so cold that no plants and only a few specially adapted creatures can survive.

### See also

Climate 154 • Desert 116
Desert climate 154 • Ecosystem 158
Mediterranean climate 155
Mountain climate 155
Periglacial 126 • Polar climate 155
Soil 130 • Soil erosion 176
Temperate climate 155
Tropical climate 154

*Texas prairie*
*A profusion of wildflowers covers this prairie in Texas.*

*Temperate woodland*
*A carpet of leaves covers the floor of a beech wood in Berkshire, England.*

# Agricultural ecosystems

In the temperate world, there is barely a landscape that does not somewhere bear the imprint of human activity. Forests have been cleared for farmland, grasslands have been cultivated, and wetlands have been drained. The new ecosystems that develop show considerable differences to natural systems.

***The effects of agriculture***
*In many parts of North America, agriculture has changed the varied tall-grass prairies (left) into a monotonous landscape of wheat fields (above).*

## Agricultural ecosystem

An ecosystem maintained by farmers

Farming can radically alter natural ecosystems ■ by reducing the number of species in an area. For example, a diverse forest, which contains many species, may be cleared to make way for a single crop species, although a few other species may find a niche ■ as well. Species are also lost if the food chain ■ is broken. Because farming tends to interrupt nutrient cycles ■, soils ■ become depleted, and to maintain crop yields the soil must be enriched by natural and artificial substances called **fertilizers**.

## Cereal cropping

The cultivation of grain

Cereal crops such as wheat, rice, corn, oats, rye, and barley are the world's most important sources of food. Cereals are all types of grass, and the edible grain is their seeds – the leaves and stalks are left to rot or fed as **silage** to livestock. To grow grain, the land is plowed, harrowed, and rototilled to break up the soil and remove other plants. The soil is also crushed by machines when the crop is harvested. Pesticides are used to keep out unwanted plants and animals, and fertilizers are added to maintain high yields.

## Pesticide

A chemical used to kill pests such as weeds and insects

The use of pesticides – herbicides, insecticides, and fungicides – has increased dramatically in the last 40 years. They are now beginning to accumulate in runoff ■ water and in the soil in high amounts. Insecticides, particularly, have a long **half-life** – the time taken for their concentration in the soil to be halved. Pesticides may also kill off beneficial soil organisms as well as pests.

## Herbicide

A chemical used to kill weeds

Herbicides may be chemicals that kill all plants, or they may be more specific, killing only certain types of plant. They are usually applied as liquid sprays.

## Insecticide

A chemical used to kill insects

The first insecticides were plant extracts, such as pyrethrum and nicotine. But in the 1950s, farmers began to use synthetic insecticides such as DDT. Some countries banned DDT when it was found to linger in the food chain in dangerous amounts, pushing some birds close to extinction. Farmers now use carbamates and organophosphates, that are more toxic but have a shorter half-life.

## Fungicide

A chemical used to kill fungi

Plants may be ruined by diseases caused by fungi such as mildew, rust, and blight. Early fungicides such as mercury chloride and copper sulfate were applied to leaves. These have now been replaced largely by synthetic liquids that are sprayed on the seeds or on the soil and taken up through the roots.

# Zero-tillage

A farming technique designed to reduce soil damage

Intensive agriculture damages the soil, so some farmers practice zero-tillage. Seed is sown into undisturbed soil, and insects and weeds are limited with pesticides.

# Fallow

Land left uncropped to recover fertility

Soil fertility is reduced by heavy crop farming. In the past, the soil was allowed to recover by lying fallow, or unused, for a few years. But in the industrialized world, as pressure on land increased in the 18th century, fallows were cut and then eradicated. Many farmers now practice **crop rotation**, where the main crop is periodically replaced with **break crops**. Today, many farms are **monocultures**, growing one crop without a break for many years, and relying on artificial fertilizers to sustain yields.

***Returning to nature***
*A variety of plants recolonize the land once it is left to return to its natural state.*

***A clearing in the forest***
*This clearing has been made by people practicing shifting cultivation in the equatorial rainforest in Kenya. A small village has grown up toward the back of the clearing.*

# Shifting cultivation

A tropical farming system with very long fallow periods

Tropical soil is easily exhausted, so in many tropical areas farmers practice shifting cultivation. This involves clearing an area of land and growing crops for just a few years, before moving on to find fresh soil. Once abandoned, the land is allowed 30 years or more to regain its fertility.

# Slash-and-burn

A farming system based on the repeated clearing of forest land by fire

Many early farming systems probably involved slash-and-burn. Trees are cut down, the land is cleared of most of the trunks, and the remaining vegetation is burned. The exposed land is cultivated for a few years. The ash formed from burning may act as a natural fertilizer. When yields decline and wild plants start to grow, the plot is abandoned in favor of a new site, allowing the old plot to recover. But as populations grow, each plot is allowed less and less time to recover. The ecosystem may then decline and more fertilizers will have to be added to maintain yields.

# Desertification

The change of fertile land into a dry wasteland

Desertification is the slow expansion of the world's deserts ■, as rains fail in desert margins and the land is heavily farmed. It is also the change of fertile land in areas of low rainfall into barren wasteland as the vegetation cover is stripped by over-grazing, cultivation, and firewood collection, allowing the soil to dry out completely.

***Over-grazed land***
*These goats have contributed to the over-grazing of the land in Bogoria, Kenya.*

# Green Revolution

The rise in grain harvest with modern farming methods

In the 1950s, farmers in the industrialized world began to grow fast-growing, high-yield varieties of wheat, rice, and corn that gave bumper harvests two or three times a year. When these were adopted in the developing world, harvests were so boosted that it was called a "Green Revolution." Asian grain yields doubled between 1971 and 1976. Such high outputs need high inputs of pesticides, machinery, fertilizers, and much irrigation ■. The use of nitrogen fertilizer has risen tenfold since the Green Revolution.

## See also

Desert 116 • Ecosystem 158
Food chain 159 • Irrigation 172
Niche 160 • Nutrient cycle 161
Runoff 108 • Soil 130

# Gems & metals

The Earth's rocks and minerals hold many useful resources. Some mineral crystals can be cut and polished to make beautiful gemstones. Metals are also found in rocks and minerals. They are valued because they can be used to make a huge variety of objects, from huge ships to tiny electrical parts.

Smoky quartz

Chalcedony

Carnelian

Jasper

Onyx

Geode lined with amethysts

## Gemstone

*A mineral prized for its beauty, rarity, or durability*

Some gemstones or **gems** occur as transparent or opaque crystals. The crystals grow from minerals dissolved in hot water seeping through volcanic rocks ■. Not all gems are crystals, and some form from organic material. A **geode** is a round rock-hollow that is lined with crystals. Geodes are found in rocks that form around bubbles of gas in hot magma ■.

## Precious stone

*A rare and valuable gemstone*

Precious gems are rare because the conditions needed to form them – the right temperature, pressure, mix of elements, and so on – are also rare. **Diamonds** form under extreme pressures in narrow igneous intrusions ■ called **pipes**, which harden into the rock **kimberlite**. **Aquamarine**, green **emeralds**, and clear **beryls** form as granite ■ intrusions cool and solidify, or as rock is metamorphosed (changed) by intense pressure and heat. The mineral **corundum** forms in basaltic ■ igneous rocks and some metamorphic rocks ■. Traces of chromium turn corundum to red **rubies**, traces of titanium and iron turn it to blue, green, and yellow **sapphire**. **Opal** is a multicolored stone that forms slowly around hot springs or in sedimentary rocks ■.

## Semiprecious stone

*A commonly occurring gem*

Semiprecious stones form in igneous, sedimentary, and metamorphic rock. **Quartz** is one of the most common of all gemstones. It occurs in many different forms, including rock crystal, rose quartz, and amethyst. **Amethyst** gets its purple color from impurities of titanium and iron. The best amethysts come from geodes in volcanic rock in India, Uruguay, and Brazil. **Chalcedony** is a gemstone made from crystals of silicon dioxide. It is found as nodules in lava ■ cavities in various forms – from blood-red **carnelian** and rusty **jasper**, to brown-striped **onyx**.

## Artificial gem

*A gem made in a laboratory*

Natural gems sometimes contain imperfections, but synthetic gems can be made flawless. It is possible, for example, to make high-quality sapphires and rubies by melting powdered aluminum oxide in a flame. As the resulting drops of liquid cool, they build up to form a single crystal called a **boule**.

Diamond

Beryl

Ruby

Emerald

**A parade of precious stones**
*A selection of gems is shown attached to the rocks in which they formed. The crystals will be cut and polished for use in jewelry.*

Blue sapphire

Amber

Jet

## Organic gem

A gem formed from
living or dead organisms

Organic gems include jet, amber,
pearl, and coral ■. **Jet** is a fine-
grained, black rock formed from
fossilized wood, in a similar way
to coal ■. **Amber** is the fossilized
resin, or sap, of trees. **Pearls** are
tiny pellets of calcium carbonate
that form inside the shells of
some shellfish, such as oysters.

## Metal

A shiny element that is usually
hard and strong

All metals except mercury are
solid at room temperature, 68°F
(20°C), and conduct heat and
electricity well. But it is their
hardness and strength – and the
ease with which hot metals can
be shaped – that makes them so
useful. Metals can be "improved"
by mixing them to form **alloys**.
If iron is mixed with tin, for
example, it forms the alloy
**steel**, which is stronger than
iron alone.

## Ore

A rock or mineral containing metal
that can be profitably extracted

The metallic element iron is
found in the ore **hematite**, while
lead is found in **galena**, mercury
in **cinnabar**, and copper in
**chalcopyrite**. After the ore is
extracted, the pure metal must
be separated from the ore by
industrial processes.

Chalcopyrite    Cinnabar

## Igneous ore

An ore formed in volcanic rock

The magma that wells up from the
Earth's interior is rich in metallic
minerals. Metals such as zinc,
iron, copper, and nickel combine
readily with sulfur. They build up
in hot sulfurous liquids deep in
magma chambers, eventually
crystallizing out of the liquid.
The nickel and copper deposits at
Sudbury, Canada, were formed in
this way. Metals that join readily
with silicates ■ dissolve in the
silicate-rich hot water produced
as magma begins to cool. When
magma cools to form granite, for
example, metals such as beryllium,
potassium, uranium, lithium, and
tin crystallize in cracks in the rock.
**Porphyry deposits** are tiny veins
of copper, molybdenum, and
gold that form when hot fluid
is forced at high pressure into
cracks in basaltic rock.

## Sedimentary ore

An ore formed in sedimentary rock

As rocks are broken down by
weathering ■, they may leave a
metal-rich residue. In the tropics,
the aluminum ore **bauxite** forms
as feldspar ■ rocks are weathered.
These residues may be washed
into the sea and collect on the
seabed. In this way, rich layers of
copper formed in Zambia's
"Copper Belt" region, as did lead
and zinc in Broken
Hill, Australia.

Bauxite

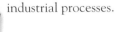

Hematite

Galena

## Precious metal

A rare and highly valued metal

Gold, silver, and platinum are
often used in jewelry. Their
durability, beauty, and rarity
make them very expensive. **Base
metals** are common and fairly
inexpensive. They include copper,
iron, lead, zinc, and tin, and are
used to make articles for everyday
use. Base metals are generally
tougher than precious metals.

Gold veins in quartz

Silver          Platinum

## Placer deposit

A deposit of weathered material that
contains valuable or useful minerals

Rivers may wash weathered rock
into concentrated deposits of
sand and gravel. These often
contain metals such as gold, tin,
and platinum, and also diamonds.
Placer deposits occur below
rapids or waterfalls, in lakes and
pools along the river's course, on
floodplains ■, and at deltas ■.

# Fossil fuels

Most of the energy we use comes from fuels that occur naturally in the ground, as a solid (coal), a liquid (oil), or a gas (natural gas). These fuels were made from plants and animals that lived millions of years ago.

## Fossil fuel

A fuel that is formed from the buried remains of living organisms

Coal, oil, and natural gas formed over millions of years. The buried remains of animals and plants were changed by intense pressure and heat into substances that can be burned to provide energy.

*Marine organisms die and are buried beneath the seabed*

*Oil and natural gas form in porous sedimentary rock*

1

2

## Natural gas

A fossil fuel gas

Natural gas forms in a similar way to oil, and is found trapped in underground reservoirs. It is the most clean-burning of all fossil ■ fuels, and can be piped directly from the ground for use in the home. It is mostly methane, but sometimes contains helium, which has many industrial uses.

3

### See also

Carboniferous Period 73 • Fossil 70
Lithification 92 • Porosity 107

## Oil

A dark liquid fossil fuel

Oil, or **petroleum**, is formed from tiny plants and animals that lived in warm seas. As these organisms died and decayed, they were slowly buried beneath the seabed. When the seabed sediments were lithified ■ into porous ■ rock, the remains of the organisms turned gradually to oil. Oil is drawn from the ground as black **crude oil**, and has to be "refined" to separate out fuels such as gasoline and diesel.

*Oil and gas migrate upward*

*Nonporous rock*

4

*Trapped oil and gas*

*Fault*

### Oil and gas
*When plant and animal remains (1) were compressed below the seabed (2), oil and gas formed. Pressure forced the oil and gas up through the porous rock (3). When they met a layer of nonporous rock they became trapped in underground pockets (4), or reservoirs.*

## Coal

A solid fossil fuel

Coal is made from the remains of plants that grew in huge, warm swamps in the Carboniferous period ■. When the plants died, they fell into the swamps and were buried deep in mud, forming a compact layer of rotting vegetation called **peat**. Over millions of years, the weight of the overlying mud squeezed the peat solid. Finally, heat and pressure turned it to coal.

1

2

3

4

5

### How coal formed
*Millions of years ago, plant remains (1) were buried and compressed into peat (2). As they became buried ever deeper, heat and pressure changed the peat first to lignite (3), then to bituminous coal (4), and lastly to anthracite (5).*

## Coal rank

The quality or grade of coal

Coal rank depends on how deep the coal is buried. Generally, the deeper the coal is buried, the more carbon and the less water it contains, so the better it burns. **Lignite**, or **brown coal**, is the lowest rank of coal. It is often found so near the surface that it can be dug from a shallow strip. **Bituminous coal** contains more carbon and burns better. The highest rank is **anthracite**, which has the greatest carbon content.

# Bulk materials

The Earth's rocks and sediments yield huge quantities of useful materials. Most cities are built almost entirely of these "bulk" materials – roads of gravel, buildings of clay bricks, stone pavements, glass windows made of sand, and much more.

## See also

Chemical weathering 100 • Clay 93
Evaporite 95 • Feldspar 83
Granite 90 • Ice age 121
Ice sheet 121 • Lime 94 • Mineral 82
Oxide 83 • Sulphate 83

## Kaolinite

A clay mineral used for pottery and paper making

Kaolinite

Clay ■ that contains the mineral kaolinite is known as **kaolin**. Kaolin forms as the feldspar ■ in certain types of granite ■ is broken down by chemical weathering ■. Kaolin is also called **China clay**, because it was first used for making pottery in Kiangsi province in China. Kaolinite is one of four main clay minerals ■. The others are **montmorillonite**, **illite**, and **vermiculite**. Illite is used for making bricks. Montmorillonite is used for cleaning wool and for lubricating oil drills. Vermiculite is used as an insulator. Clays can be molded when wet, then fired in a kiln or furnace until hard.

## Gravel pit

A place where loose deposits of small stones are extracted

At the end of the last ice age ■, huge rivers on the margins of ice sheets ■ washed sand and gravel into large deposits. These are dug up in gravel pits and **sand pits**. Both sand and gravel are used in building. If sand is heated with soda (sodium oxide ■) and lime ■ (calcium oxide) it forms glass.

## Cement

A building material made by heating crushed limestone and clay

Cement is mixed with sand and water for building. When the resulting paste dries, it holds bricks and other materials firmly together. Cement, sand, gravel, and water form **concrete**, a fluid material that can be molded or cast into shape before it sets hard.

## Pigment

A substance that gives a color

In prehistoric times, people mixed clays, chalks, and soils to give rich brown colors. Since then, many different rocks and minerals have been used as pigments. For example, **azurite** gives a deep blue, **malachite** a brilliant green, **orpiment** a deep yellow, **cinnabar** a deep vermillion red, and **lapis lazuli** ultramarine.

*Azurite*

*Powdered azurite*

### Ancient blue
*Azurite, a copper compound, was a popular blue pigment in ancient times.*

*Azurite blue paint*

## Potash

A potassium rich mineral used as a fertilizer

Where inland seas evaporate in warm climates, they become very salty. They may eventually dry up altogether, leaving evaporites ■. These often include the mineral potash, which is the basis of all potassium fertilizers. Evaporites also include calcium sulfate ■, from which plaster of paris is made, and sodium chloride, or common salt. Huge quantities of salt are found where prehistoric seas evaporated and were then buried. This underground **rock salt** is extracted from below the surface either by mining or by pumping down water to make a salt solution – brine – which can then be piped back to the surface.

**Construction materials**
*In most countries, the major building materials are derived from the Earth's rocks and minerals.*

Clay bricks

Glass windows

Clay roof tiles

Cement

Concrete blocks

Sand and gravel

# Locating resources

The Earth's crust contains an enormous wealth of mineral resources – from fossil fuels such as oil, coal, and natural gas to a wide variety of metal ores. However, these resources are rarely easy to find, so a range of increasingly sophisticated detecting techniques have been developed.

## Geological prospecting

The search for resources in the Earth's crust

Useful resources are normally concentrated where particular conditions have turned ordinary minerals into valuable materials. Geological prospecting targets areas where such concentrations are likely to occur. Typically, these target areas are found by remote sensing ■. Satellite pictures, for example, may reveal large-scale rock structures likely to contain mineral deposits. When a target area has been located, prospectors survey the area with other techniques.

*North Sea oil rig*
*Once fossil fuel and mineral deposits have been located, they must be pumped out by oil rigs, or dug out from mines and quarries.*

*Geochemical testing*
*These ocean-bottom rock samples will be geochemically tested for chemicals that may help locate oil deposits.*

## Geochemical prospecting

Hunting for resources with the aid of chemistry

Geochemical tests are carried out on rock and soil samples in order to find evidence of chemicals that may indicate the presence of an ore ■ deposit nearby. These chemicals can then be traced back to their source to pinpoint the location of the ore deposit.

*Magnetic detection*
*Different rocks produce local variations in the Earth's magnetic field. These variations give very distinctive readings on a magnetometer.*

Ores just below the surface

Deeply buried ores

Country rock

## Geophysical prospecting

Hunting for resources with the aid of physics

**Geophysical surveys** locate resources by measuring a variety of physical properties, including electrical conductivity, gravity, magnetism, radiation, moisture content, and the reflection of seismic waves ■. Geophysical measurements are also used for the more general mapping of underground geological features.

## Magnetic survey

A geophysical survey that measures variations in the Earth's magnetic field

Certain metal ores, such as iron ore, cause variations in the geomagnetic field ■. These variations, called **anomalies**, can be measured at the surface by an instrument called a **magnetometer**. A surveyor then analyzes the results and eliminates the regional magnetism that originates from country rock ■. Any remaining anomalies may come from buried ores.

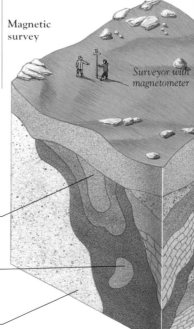

Magnetic survey

*Surveyor with magnetometer*

## Gravimetric survey

A geophysical survey that measures differences in rock density

Differences in the density of rocks beneath the Earth's surface can be detected with an instrument called a **gravimeter**. This basically consists of a weight on a coiled spring, which is held above the survey area. The greater the density of the rock, the stronger is its gravitational pull and the more the spring is stretched. Oil ■ prospectors look for low-density areas, such as salt domes, which are often associated with oil deposits.

### Geophysical surveys

*The four main types of geophysical survey are shown below. The equipment and techniques may vary according to the size and depth of the area being surveyed. Such surveys tell geologists about the make-up of the Earth's crust, and help to locate valuable resources.*

## Electrical survey

A geophysical survey that measures variations in electrical activity in the ground

Deposits of certain electrically conducting ores can be detected by electrical surveys. Pulses of high-voltage electricity are sent out from electrodes inserted into the rock. These pulses generate an electric current in the ore deposit, which can be picked up by sensitive receiving equipment on the surface. Electric currents can also be generated in the ore by radio waves sent out either from aircraft or from nuclear submarines.

**See also**

Country rock 56 • Geomagnetic field 44
Oil 168 • Ore 167 • Remote sensing 26
Seismic wave 58 • Seismograph 59

## Seismic survey

A geophysical survey that measures the reflection of seismic waves

A seismic survey involves setting off seismic waves, often with explosives. The rock layers below reflect the waves back to the surface. Seismographs ■ or instruments called **geophones** detect the reflected waves. The return time shows the depth, type, and shape of the rock layers.

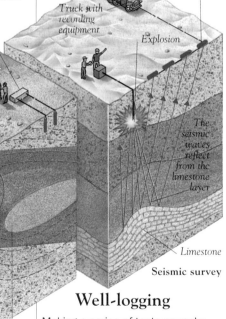

*A powerful transmitter stimulates the rock strata with pulses of high-voltage electricity*

*A sensitive receiver measures the current produced by the ore deposit*

Geophones

Truck with recording equipment

Explosion

*The seismic waves reflect from the limestone layer*

Limestone

**Seismic survey**

*Normal reading* *High reading* *Low reading*

*Ore deposit*

*Electrical field produced by the ore deposit*

*Fault line*

*Basin of low-density sediments*

*Electric current produced by transmitter*

*Up-faulted block of metamorphic basement rock* **Gravimetric survey**

**Electrical survey**

## Well-logging

Making a series of tests on rocks using a drilled borehole

Once a likely mineral-bearing feature has been located under the ground, prospectors try to examine it by drilling a borehole. They then lower instruments into the borehole to carry out a series of tests on the physical properties of the rock, such as its moisture content and radioactivity.

# Water resources

Water is essential for life. The human body consists of 75 percent water, and cannot survive for more than a few days without it. Huge amounts of water are needed for agriculture and industry. Without an abundant and reliable water supply, modern society could not function.

## Hydrosphere

All the Earth's water

Almost 75 percent of the Earth's surface is covered by water, including oceans, seas, rivers, lakes, and so on. Although there are over 326 million cu. miles (1.33 billion km³) of water on the Earth, little of this water is easy to use. More than 97 percent is saltwater in the oceans ■. Less than 3 percent is freshwater. This includes 2.24 percent frozen within glaciers ■, and about 0.6 percent hidden as groundwater ■. Less than 0.01 percent is in lakes, and less than 0.001 percent is in rivers ■ where it is easy to use.

### See also

Aquifer 109 • Artesian well 109
Catchment area 109
Evapotranspiration 108 • Glacier 120
Groundwater 108 • Infiltration 107
Ocean 134 • River 110 • Runoff 108
Water pollution 175 • Water table 108

*Algerian oasis*
*This oasis in Taghit, Algeria, breaks up the barren landscape of the desert.*

## Water resource

A usable source of water

Most of our water falls as rain, before it runs into lakes and rivers or infiltrates ■ into the ground. Because rain water runs away quickly, groundwater is extracted from aquifers ■, and artificial lakes or **reservoirs** are built to store surface water. In deserts, a moist area called an **oasis** occurs if the water table ■ reaches the surface, or if water is brought to the surface through an artesian well ■.

## Water consumption

The water used by humans

Industrial societies use huge amounts of water. In Europe, this averages about 800 gal. (3,000 liters) per person each day for all uses. Consumption elsewhere is lower. People in Africa consume just over 0.5 gal. (2 liters) a day.

## Industrial water use

The way in which industry uses water

It takes 660 gal. (2,500 liters) to make 2.2 lb. (1 kg) of steel. In the US steel mills alone use more than five times as much water as all of New York City. A single paper mill uses enough water for a town of 50,000 people.

## Agricultural water use

The way in which farming uses water

Agriculture in developed countries uses water in vast quantities. It is believed to require 2,600 gal. (10,000 liters) of water to produce every 2.2 lb. (1 kg) of food we eat. To make 2.2 lb. (1 kg) of bread, more than 300 gal. (1,200 liters) of water are needed to grow the wheat, and to produce 2.2 lb. (1 kg) of beef, it takes 6,600 gal. (25,000 liters) of water to provide food and water for the cattle.

## Irrigation

The artificial delivery of water to crops and pasture

The balance between rainfall and evapotranspiration ■ is rarely so perfect as to give maximum crop yield. To boost yields, many farmers irrigate their land. Recently, the area of land under irrigation in the world has risen sharply, especially in Asia. Almost 20 pecent of the world's cropland is now irrigated, and 33 percent of the world's food is grown on irrigated land.

*Irrigating the land by hand*
*These Bangladeshi farmers are irrigating their paddy fields by hand.*

## Water resources

*The supply, treatment, storage, and use of water involves many different processes.*

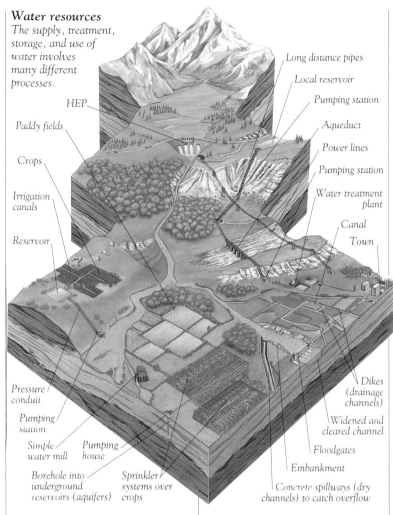

HEP

Paddy fields

Crops

Irrigation canals

Reservoir

Long distance pipes

Local reservoir

Pumping station

Aqueduct

Power lines

Pumping station

Water treatment plant

Canal

Town

Pressure conduit

Pumping station

Simple water mill

Pumping house

Borehole into underground reservoirs (aquifers)

Sprinkler systems over crops

Dikes (drainage channels)

Widened and cleared channel

Floodgates

Embankment

Concrete spillways (dry channels) to catch overflow

## Water power

Power from running water

People have long used running water in water mills to drive machines directly. But during the 20th century, water has been used more to produce **hydroelectric power (HEP)**. HEP is electricity generated by turbines that are driven by falling running water. Almost 20 percent of the world's power is now HEP. For the water to have enough speed and pressure to turn the turbines, it must have a sufficient "head." **Head** is the distance the water falls. Because of this, many HEP stations are situated below barriers or **dams** that collect water and build up a good head.

## Flood management

Measures to control flooding

The danger of river floods can be reduced in many ways. A river may be confined or its waters redirected. Raised banks called **artificial levees** or **embankments** increase a river's capacity to carry water. Straightening and clearing channels and increasing the gradient allows the water to flow faster. Dams may be built, along with **spillways** to catch overflow, and **bypass channels** that redirect the water. **Flood barriers** may be built across river mouths. Their floodgates close if an extra high tide threatens. Trees may also be planted in the river's catchment area ▪ to reduce runoff ▪.

## Water supply

The delivery of water to where it is needed

Water to supply large cities comes from three main sources: reservoirs in upland areas with high rainfall; rivers and lakes (via a reservoir that guards against pollution ▪ and maintains the supply when water levels are low); and from aquifers underground. It is delivered via a network of pipes and aqueducts. **Water treatment** is the cleaning of water to make it safe for domestic use. Old treatment systems allow dirt to settle out in a reservoir, then filter it through sand. Modern fast filters use a variety of chemical treatments.

## Aqueduct

A channel built to carry water over a long distance

The Romans built many aqueducts to supply their cities with water. Today, major cities such as Los Angeles and New York, US, have extensive aqueduct links to areas of high rainfall. Where terrain permits, they are built to a gradient of at least 1 in 6,000, so the water runs downhill. In a **pressure conduit**, water can move uphill under pressure – either from a siphon or a pump. To cope with the pressure, the conduits are built from welded steel or reinforced concrete, or bored through solid rock.

**Flood barrier**
*The Thames flood barrier was built to prevent London, England, from flooding.*

# Pollution

As human consumption of energy and other resources spirals upward, the Earth becomes more polluted. Car exhausts and power stations belch fumes into the air, farming poisons soils and rivers with pesticides, tankers spill oil into fragile marine habitats – these are just a few of the ways in which our environment is contaminated.

*Air attack*
*Urban air pollution and acid rain have eroded the face of this statue.*

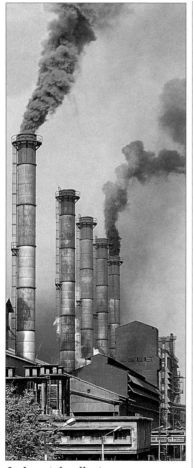

*Industrial pollution*
*Factories, such as this steel plant in India, are a major souce of air pollution.*

### See also

Compound 42 • Condensation nuclei 146
Fossil fuel 168 • Greenhouse effectt 140
Stratosphere 138 • Volcano 52

## Air pollution

The contamination of the air by toxic gases and dirt particles

Most air pollution comes from car exhausts, incinerators, factories, power stations, and the burning of fossil fuels ■ in homes. But pesticides sprayed onto crops and dust raised by farming and mining can also pollute the air. Erupting volcanoes ■ may throw up clouds of volcanic dust and ash, and thus add natural pollutants to the air.

## Primary pollutant

A contaminating substance emitted into the air

Besides solid primary pollutants such as soot and ash, there are many gaseous ones. **Sulfur dioxide** and **nitrogen dioxide** are gases produced when materials are burned in factories, power stations, and waste incinerators. **Hydrocarbons** are chemical compounds ■ that include fuels such as oil, gasoline, and natural gas. When these fuels are burned in vehicles, petrochemical plants, and refineries, some is always left unburned and escapes into the air. **Carbon monoxide** is a gas emitted by vehicles, factories, and metal smelters. **Secondary pollutants** form when primary pollutants mix in the air. **Ozone** is a secondary polluting gas that forms when sunlight causes hydrocarbons to react with oxides of nitrogen.

## Urban air pollution

The contamination of the air in cities

Air pollution is a major problem in many cities, affecting human health, buildings, animals, and plants. Breathing air in Mexico City is said to be as harmful as smoking 40 cigarettes a day. Each year, the factories of Benxi, China, emit 3,072 million cu. ft. (87 million m³) of polluting gases and 235,000 tons (213,000 tonnes) of smoke and dust, making Benxi invisible from space satellites.

*Smog-bound*
*The city of Los Angeles still has severe photochemical smogs, despite the compulsory fitting of catalytic converters to car exhausts.*

## Smog

A dense, discolored fog thick with pollutants

Heavy urban air pollution can encourage choking smogs to form, because the polluting particles act as condensation nuclei ■. There were notorious smogs in London, England, until the burning of coal was banned in 1956. Now cities such as São Paulo, Brazil, and Bangkok, Thailand, suffer from bad smogs. A **photochemical smog** is a haze created when car exhaust gases react in sunlight to form ozone.

# Acid rain

Rain containing dilute acids

All rain is slightly acidic, but damaging acid rain is created when sunlight makes sulfur dioxide and nitrogen dioxide combine with oxygen and moisture in the air. This makes dilute sulfuric and nitric acid. Normal rain has a pH of 6.5; acid rain has a pH of less than 4.5 and often as low as 2.5. Acid rain damages buildings and trees, and kills fish in freshwater lakes.

# Water pollution

The contamination of the water supply by pollutants

Rivers are polluted by industrial waste, sewage, and agricultural chemicals. There are now very few rivers in the world which are entirely free from pollution. Out of 78 monitored rivers in China, 54 are seriously polluted with untreated sewage and industrial waste. In Europe, river water concentrations of nitrates and phosphates from chemical fertilizers have risen sharply. River pollutants eventually flow into the sea, where they do further damage to marine life.

*Effluent flow*
*Large amounts of contaminated water from industrial processes are discharged, via the sewage system, into rivers.*

# Effluent

A flow of sewage, liquid industrial waste, or solutions of agricultural chemicals into the environment

Radioactive or toxic effluents pose an obvious threat to the environment. But a hot effluent can also disrupt the ecology of a cooler environment such as a river. Effluents that absorb oxygen readily may suffocate aquatic plant and animal life.

# Global warming

The warming of the atmosphere due to pollution

There is a danger that rising levels of polluting gases in the air may increase the greenhouse effect ■ so much that the world starts to warm up. These gases, known as **greenhouse gases**, include carbon dioxide released by burning fossil fuels, ozone, methane from animals, and chlorofluorocarbons. Some scientists believe that if levels of these gases continue to rise at current rates, the world could be as much as 7°F (4°C) warmer by the middle of the next century. This would melt much of the polar ice caps and cause devastating floods.

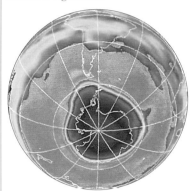

*Hole in the sky*
*The violet and pink areas of this satellite map show the depletion of the ozone layer over Antarctica in springtime.*

# Ozone hole

A gap in the atmosphere's protective layer of ozone

**Chlorofluorocarbons (CFCs)** are gases used in aerosol sprays, refrigerators, cleaning products, and to blow foam plastics for fast-food packages. CFCs are thought to attack the layer of ozone in the stratosphere ■ which protects us from some of the Sun's harmful rays. The holes in the ozone layer that appear over the poles every spring seem to get bigger and last longer each year.

*Pesticide pollutants*
*Pesticides sprayed on crops may be washed by rain into rivers and streams, where they contaminate plant and animal life.*

# Changing the land

In many parts of the world, there is barely a inch of the landscape that has not been altered in some way by human activity. Forests are felled for farmland, roads and railways cut through the countryside, and vast areas of land are covered by the concrete and brick of cities.

## Deforestation

The clearing of forest and woodland

Forest clearance has been going on since the earliest days of civilization. Already, 50 percent of the world's tropical rainforests ■ and 75 percent of its temperate forests ■ have been destroyed. Many temperate forests were cleared long ago. Europe, for example, had lost 80 percent of its forests by the end of the 14th century. Today, about 49 million acres (20 million hectares) of tropical rainforests are being destroyed each year. The felled trees are often used for lumber. Cleared rainforests make good grazing for cattle for a few years, but it takes centuries for them to regrow – if, indeed, they ever do.

***Soil erosion due to deforestation***
*The removal of the trees in Madagascar has caused severe soil erosion.*

## Soil erosion

The rapid wearing away of soil

When land is cleared of vegetation for farming, it loses its soil easily, especially in arid or semiarid regions. Every year 12–17 million acres (5–7 million hectares) of farmland are lost through soil erosion. Soil is washed away in three main ways. **Gully erosion** is when soil is washed away down deep channels cut into hillsides by rain, as in the Badlands of the US. **Sheet erosion** occurs when soil is washed downhill by thin sheets of surface water or sheetwash ■. **Rain-drop erosion** is when the soil is washed away by the impact of large rain drops. Wind ■ can also blow away dry soil, especially in deforested areas where it blows over the ground unhindered. The creation of the "dust bowl" in the American Midwest in the 1930s was caused by the removal of the grassland, and the subsequent intensive farming. The topsoil was later blown away by the wind.

***Rainforest removal***
*These trees in Java, Indonesia, are being felled for lumber. Rainforest destruction may upset the global balance of carbon dioxide and oxygen in the atmosphere.*

## Afforestation

The planting of forests in previously clear areas

In the developed world, with the exception of the US, more trees are planted than are cut down. Large financial incentives are offered to ensure that this balance remains. But many of the trees planted are fast-growing conifers used for lumber and paper, rather than the native hardwood trees.

***Tree planting by hand***
*Young trees are being planted along a line of earth mounds or "diguettes" in Burkina Faso, West Africa.*

*Hillside terraces*
*These paddy terraces in Ubud, Bali,*
*Indonesia, have been made to maximize*
*the use of available fertile land.*
*Streams are diverted so that water*
*collects in the stepped fields. The*
*multitude of small fields then supports*
*intensive rice growing.*

## Land reclamation

The process of bringing land into use or restoring it to its former condition

Land reclamation means two different things. Firstly it means "reclaiming" land from nature – by draining waterlogged areas to create new land, some of which may be suitable for farming, and also irrigating ■ arid areas. Secondly, it means restoring polluted land and land blighted by industry and mining to its natural state. It may also involve the construction of **terraces** to prevent soil erosion. The land that is removed is used to build retaining walls for the terraces. Terracing also makes the most efficient use of the fertile land available by increasing the amount of surface area that can be farmed. Terracing is practiced in much of Asia.

## Coastal protection

The defense of coastlines against erosion by the sea

**Groynes** are fences built on beaches at right angles to the sea, to stop sand being washed away by longshore drift ■. Other sea defenses include breakwaters and sea walls. **Breakwaters** are long barriers of large boulders or concrete projecting out into the sea. They protect harbors and coasts by breaking up waves and reducing their destructive power. **Sea walls** are stone walls built along the coast to stop waves washing away soft coastal material, and to prevent damage to buildings close to the sea.

*Coastal defenses*
*These sea defenses at Barton-on-Sea,*
*Hampshire, England, are being*
*renewed and built up again.*

## Urbanization

The rapid spread of cities

The number of people living in cities is increasing rapidly, especially in the developing world. In 1940, only 1 person in 100 lived in a big city. By 1980, the number had increased to 10 in 100. Now it may be as high as 20 in 100. By the end of the century, 26 million people will live in Mexico City and 24 million in São Paulo, Brazil. Cities often take over valuable agricultural land. Between 1980 and the year 2000, the urbanized area of the developing world will more than double from 30,890 sq. miles (80,000 km²) to 65,650 sq. miles (170,000 km²).

## Waste management

The disposal of unwanted material

Waste disposal is a major problem. All industries produce waste. Mining, for example, creates huge dumps of debris, chemical factories produce polluting effluent ■, and nuclear power ■ stations produce dangerous radioactive waste. The quantity of domestic garbage is also rising. Most waste is either dumped, buried, or burned.

## Landfill

The disposal of domestic garbage in large holes in the ground

Burning garbage in incinerators can pollute the air, so many countries bury their garbage in pits. In **controlled pits**, garbage is layered between rubble or soil to reduce the generation of heat as the waste decomposes. In the US, 82 percent of all urban garbage goes to controlled garbage dumps. Due to a shortage of suitable land, existing holes such as quarries and clay pits may be used instead.

*Filling a landfill site*
*This bulldozer is shoveling garbage into*
*a landfill site in Tucson, Arizona.*

### See also

Effluent 175 • Irrigation 172
Longshore drift 128 • Nuclear energy 178
Sheetwash 108 • Temperate forest 163
Tropical rainforest 162 • Wind action 118

# Earth management

Humans dominate the Earth in a way that no species has ever done before, and our demands are beginning to place a tremendous strain on the planet's limited resources. Scientists are now asking what can be done to develop a more sustainable way of life before it is too late.

***Harnessing the Sun's energy***
*These solar panels in California use photoelectric cells to generate electricity from sunlight.*

## DAILY ENERGY USE

| Country | Energy per person in kilojoules (kJ) |
|---------|--------------------------------------|
| US | 34 million kJ |
| UK | 17.5 million kJ |
| Australia | 16.5 million kJ |
| Chile | 4 million kJ |
| China | 2.5 million kJ |
| India | 0.6 million kJ |
| Ethiopia | 0.1 million kJ |

NB The values above represent all sources of energy, including food, electricity, gas, and gasoline.

*Background picture: city traffic at night*

## Global energy use

The amount of energy used worldwide

The human race uses over 100 times more energy per year than it did in 1806, and consumption is still rising. In 1992, energy consumption was the equivalent of 1.54 tons (1.4 tonnes) of oil for every person on the Earth. But the industrialized world, with less than a quarter of the world's population, consumes more than 70 percent of the world's energy. The average North American, for example, consumes about 340 times as much energy as the average Ethiopian.

## See also

Air pollution 174 • Atom 42
Fossil fuel 168 • Greenhouse effect 140
Hydroelectric power 173

## Renewable energy

A source of energy that does not use up the Earth's finite resources and is easily replenished

Barely 5 percent of the world's energy comes from renewable sources, such as running water, waves, tides, wind, and sunlight. Fossil fuels ▪ provide about 90 percent of our energy. In 1990, 38.6 percent came from oil, 27.2 percent from coal, and 21.6 percent from natural gas. Fossil fuels take millions of years to form and are broken down in the process of providing energy, so they are **nonrenewable** sources. At present consumption rates, all the coal and oil will be used up in 60 years and the natural gas in 220 years. **Nuclear energy**, produced by splitting atoms ▪, is nonrenewable, but uses less resources than fossil fuels.

## Recycling

The reuse of waste material

Environmental damage caused by extracting resources and problems with waste disposal have spurred efforts to recycle waste. Items such as glass bottles can be cleaned and reused directly; others are recycled so that the materials they contain, such as plastic, metal, and paper, can be used to make new items. But recycled goods are often of poor quality, and recycling can be costly in energy terms. A better solution may be to concentrate on reducing energy consumption.

## Alternative energy

Energy from sources other than fossil fuels and nuclear power

Fossil fuels are irreplaceable and cause pollution ▪, so there is a move to develop renewable, cleaner energy sources. The main alternatives are wind, solar, wave, tidal, geothermal, and hydroelectric power (HEP) ▪. Of these, only HEP as yet supplies more than a tiny fraction of our energy needs. **Wind power** uses giant, wind-driven turbines to generate electricity. **Solar power** converts sunlight to electricity using photoelectric cells in solar panels. **Wave power** generates electricity with floating booms that are rocked by the waves. **Tidal power** uses the falling sea tide to generate power in a similar way to HEP. **Geothermal power** draws heat from the Earth's hot interior to turn turbines that generate electricity.

***Wind farm***
*This cluster of huge, 400 kW turbines in Cornwall, England, uses the power of the wind to generate electricity.*

# Planning controls

Legal restrictions on the kind of land development permitted

Few industrialized countries now allow development of the land to proceed completely uncontrolled. Most have planning controls to ensure that the land is used in a certain way. Planning permission is usually needed before mining, quarrying, drilling, and sometimes even test drilling, can begin in a rural area.

*Antarctic wilderness*
*These nesting Gentoo penguins on Cuverville Island, Antarctica, inhabit one of the Earth's last great, unspoiled wildernesses. There are moves to establish international laws to restrict economic exploitation of the continent's mineral and fossil fuel reserves.*

## Protected area

An area of land protected by law from the worst effects of economic exploitation

About 5 percent of the Earth's land surface is now protected in the form of nature reserves, national parks, special sites, and wildlife sanctuaries. The first national park – Yellowstone in Wyoming – was set up in 1872, but most protected areas are quite recent. These vary from vast, natural wildernesses, such as Greenland National Park, which covers more than 1.73 billion acres (700 million hectares), to tiny coral islands.

## Fishery protection

Restrictions on commerical fishing

Fish catches rose from 22 million tons (20 million tonnes) in 1905 to almost 110 million tons (100 million tonnes) by 1990. There is now a real danger that some fish populations will never recover and will go on declining.
**Exclusive Economic Zones (EEZs)** were set up to prevent over-fishing. They extend 200 miles (320 km) from the coast of every seaboard nation. EEZs give each nation total control of the fishing rights in its own zone, but the economic need to maintain fishing industries has prevented EEZs from being wholly effective in preventing over-fishing.

*Fished to extinction?*
*The populations of the most heavily fished species – herring, cod, mackerel, redfish, and jack – may never recover.*

## Gaia theory

The idea that the Earth is a single, living organism

**James Lovelock** (born 1919) proposed the Gaia theory in 1979. This theory states that the Earth and all the life upon it are linked together as if they were a single living thing. He suggested that, just like any organism, the Earth is both self-regulating and self-organizing. It automatically adjusts to changes in the environment to maintain the right conditions for life. In this way, it ensures that there is enough oxygen for animals and carbon dioxide for plants, and that the atmosphere and oceans stay at the right temperature through the greenhouse effect ■.

# Earth science pioneers

**Jean Louis Agassiz**
Swiss-American naturalist (1807–73)
Proposed the idea of an ice age during which North America and Europe were covered by huge ice sheets.

**George Biddell Airy**
English geophysicist (1801–92)
Proposed that mountains float at different depths in the Earth's mantle according to their height.

**Edward Appleton**
British physicist (1892–1965)
Discovered layers in the ionosphere that reflect radio waves.

**Aristarchus of Samos**
Greek astronomer (c.320–250 BC)
Perhaps the first to suggest that the Earth moved around the Sun.

**Aristotle**
Greek philosopher (384–322 BC)
Advocated science based on observation. Demonstrated that the Earth is spherical.

**Avicenna**
Arabian philosopher (980–1037)
Wrote influential works on minerals, earthquakes, the erosion of valleys, and the deposition of sediments.

**Francis Beaufort**
British hydrographer (1774–1857)
Devised the Beaufort scale to describe wind strength.

**Hugo Benioff** (See page 49)

**Vilhelm Bjerknes**
Norwegian meteorologist (1862–1951)
Proposed the idea of air masses and fronts.

**Pierre Bouguer**
French physicist (1698–1758)
Led an expedition to the Andes to establish the Earth's shape, and noted anomalies in the Earth's gravity.

**Norman Levi Bowen**
American petrologist (1887–1956)
Showed how minerals form in igneous rocks as they cool.

**William Buckland**
English geologist (1784–1856)
Pioneered historical geology and the concept of glaciation in England.

**Thomas Burnet**
English philosopher (1635–1715)
Proposed that the Earth had a solid shell and a watery interior. He also suggested that mountains were created by flood waters that gushed up from the interior.

**Jean de Charpentier**
Swiss mining engineer (1786–1855)
Pioneered the idea of ice ages in Switzerland.

**William Daniel Conybeare**
English geologist (1787–1857)
Pioneer in stratigraphy.

**Nicolas Copernicus** (See page 33)

**Gaspard Coriolis**
French physicist (1792–1843)
Showed how things moving on the Earth's surface can be deflected by the Earth's rotation – the Coriolis effect.

**Georges Cuvier**
French zoologist (1769–1832)
Founded paleontology and the classification of fossil creatures.

**Reginald Daly**
American geologist (1871–1957)
Suggested that submarine canyons are carved out by turbidity currents.

**James Dwight Dana**
American geologist (1813–95)
Proposed the idea of geosynclines, and the now discredited idea that the Earth is shrinking.

**Charles Darwin**
English naturalist (1809–82)
With his fellow English naturalist **Alfred Russel Wallace** (1823–1913), Darwin developed the theory of the evolution of life through the natural selection of species.

**William Morris Davis**
American geologist (1850–1934)
Established geomorphology (the study of landforms). Developed Hooke's idea of a cycle of landscape erosion.

**Clarence Edward Dutton**
American army geologist (1841–1912)
Early expert on seismology; introduced the word isostasy.

**Eratosthenes** (See page 39)

**Maurice Ewing**
American geophysicist (1906–74)
Discovered that the ocean floor is made of very young volcanic rocks.

**Jean Fernel**
French scientist (1497–1558)
Calculated the Earth's circumference to within 0.1 percent accuracy.

**Benjamin Franklin**
American statesman & scientist (1706–90)
Proved lightning's electrical nature. Discovered ocean surface currents.

**Archibald Geikie**
Scottish geologist (1835–1924)
Studied erosion by ice and rivers, and tried to calculate the age of the Earth from rates of denudation.

**Grove Karl Gilbert** (See page 65)

**William Gilbert**
English physician (1540–1603)
Established the nature of the Earth's magnetic field.

**Jean Étienne Guettard**
French geologist (1715–86)
Made the first mineralogical maps of France and North America.

**Beno Gutenberg**
German seismologist (1899–1960)
Established the size of the Earth's core and the depth of the asthenosphere.

**George Hadley**
English meteorologist (1685–1768)
Explained how the tropical trade winds are generated by a circulation of air from the equator to the poles.

**James Hall**
American geologist (1811–98)
Developed the idea of geosynclines.

**Edmond Halley**
English astronomer (1656–1742)
Showed that winds are created by differences in air pressure.

**Harry Hammond Hess**
American geophysicist (1906–69)
Proposed the idea of seafloor spreading, and discovered guyots.

**Hipparchus of Rhodes**
Greek astronomer & geographer (c.170–c.125 BC)
Improved methods of calculating latitude and longitude.

**Arthur Holmes**
British geologist (1890–1965)
Developed the idea of convection currents within the Earth's mantle.

**Robert Hooke**
English physicist (1635–1703)
Suggested that landscapes are shaped by successive cycles of erosion.

**Edwin Hubble** (See page 30)

**Friedrich von Humboldt**
Prussian scientist (1769–1859)
Studied volcanoes, climate, ocean currents, and mountain ranges.

**James Hutton**
Scottish geologist (1726–97)
Suggested that landscapes are shaped slowly by gentle processes. Showed the significance of unconformities.

**Philip Kuenen**
Dutch geologist (1902–72)
Pioneered work on sedimentation. Expert on marine geology.

**Jean Lamarck**
French naturalist (1744–1829)
Proposed that species evolve by inheriting characteristics acquired during an individual's lifetime.

**Inge Lehmann**
Danish geophysicist (1888–1992)
Proposed that the Earth has a solid inner core.

**Xavier Le Pichon**
French marine geologist (born 1937)
Developed Hess's idea of seafloor spreading. Calculated the geometry of plate movements on a sphere.

**Willard Frank Libby** (See page 77)

**James Lovelock** (See page 179)

**Charles Lyell** (See page 74)

**Robert Mallet**
Irish engineer (1810–81)
Studied and mapped earthquakes.

**Motonori Matuyama**
Japanese geologist (1884–1958)
Showed that the Earth's magnetic field reverses periodically.

**Matthew Maury**
American oceanographer (1806–73)
Made the first map of the North Atlantic ocean bed.

**Guiseppe Mercalli**
Italian scientist (1815–1914)
Developed the Mercalli scale to describe earthquake intensity.

**Gerardus Mercator** (See page 39)

**John Michell**
English philosopher (1724–93)
Discovered the role of the epicenter and of seismic waves in earthquakes.

**Milutin Milankovich**
Yugoslavian physicist (1879–1958)
Proposed that the Earth's climate goes through cycles of change because of changes in the Earth's orbit around the Sun.

**John Milne**
British mine engineer (1850–1913)
Developed the first accurate seismograph.

**Andrija Mohorovicic**
Croatian seismologist (1857–1936)
Discovered the boundary between the Earth's crust and the mantle beneath – now called the Mohorovicic discontinuity.

**Friedrich Mohs** (See page 84)

**Marie Morisawa**
American hydrologist (born 1936)
Researched river meanders.

**Roderick Impey Murchison**
British geologist (1857–1936)
Pioneered fossil-based stratigraphy.

**Albrecht Penck & Walther Penck**
German geologists (Albrecht 1858–1945; Walther 1888–1923)
Father and son who studied the evolution of landforms.

**Ptolemy**
Egyptian-Greek astronomer (c.90–170)
Wrote the summaries of Greek astronomy, geography, and optics which formed the basis of Western knowledge for 1,300 years.

**Pythagoras**
Greek philosopher (c.560–c.500 BC)
One of the first to accept that the world is spherical.

**Charles Richter**
American geophysicist (1900–85)
Devised the Richter scale to describe the magnitude or size of earthquakes.

**Carl-Gustaf Rossby**
Swedish-American meteorologist (1898–1957)
Discovered jet streams and global (Rossby) waves in the upper air that drive weather systems.

**Horace Saussure**
Swiss naturalist (1740–99)
Studied metamorphism in the Alps.

**Adam Sedgwick**
British geologist (1785–1873)
Defined bedding planes (boundaries between sedimentary rock layers).

**William Smith** (See page 72)

**Nicolas Steno**
Dutch anatomist & geologist (1638–86)
Pioneered the study of fossils and crystals. Established the principle of superposition used in stratigraphy.

**Eduard Suess**
Austrian geologist (1831–1914)
Suggested the past existence of a great southern continent, later called Gondwanaland.

**Marie Tharp**
American oceanographer (born 1920)
Discovered mid-ocean ridges.

**Evangelista Torricelli**
Italian physicist (1608–47)
Discovered atmospheric pressure and invented the mercury barometer.

**Jacobus van't Hoff**
Dutch chemist (1852–1911)
Pioneered work on sedimentation and the theory of salt deposition.

**Felix Vening-Meinesz**
Dutch geophysicist (1887–1966)
Early advocate of continental drift, aided by his innovative study of anomalies in the Earth's gravity.

**Kiyoo Wadati** (See page 49)

**Alfred Lothar Wegener** (See page 47)

**Abraham Gottlob Werner**
German mining geologist (1750–1817)
Pioneer of mineral classification.

**John Tuzo Wilson**
Canadian geophysicist (born 1908)
Devised the term "plate" for the pieces of the Earth's crust. Proposed the idea of transform faults, and "hot-spot" volcanoes for Pacific islands.

# Index

The index gives the page number of every entry and subentry in this book. For a subentry, the main entry under which it appears is given in brackets ( ). Tables, table entries, and boxed features are shown by the italic word *table*.

# Acknowledgments

## PICTURE CREDITS
t=top, c=center, b=bottom, r=right, l=left, a=above

Aerofilms Ltd: 22tc, 24tc
The Ancient Art & Architecture Collection: 39tr
Peter Appel: 78cr
U.C.-Berkeley, California: Jules Le Baron 78tr
British Petroleum: 170b
Courtesy of the Archives, California Institute of Technology: 49c
Chief Constable of Cheshire: 76tr
John Cleare/Mountain Camera: 122c
Bruce Coleman Ltd: Mr. Jules Cowan 12bl, 93tl, 117t; C.B. & D.W. Frith 12br; Norman Myers 36bra; C.B. Frith 48c; Dr. Frieder Sauer 66br, 67tl; John Murray 67tc; Charlie Ott 89bl, 131br; Erwin & Peggy Bauer 98b, cover; Stephen Bond 101t; Jen & Des Bartlett 109cl; Jeff Foott 116tr; Steven Kaufman 116b; John Fennell 117cl; Stephen J. Krasemann 120–121tr, 155b; Gerald Cubitt 127cl, 176bl; Jan Taylor 129t; Fritz Prenzel 129bc; Kim Taylor 137tr; Alain Compost 176–177t; Konrad Wothe 176c; Geoff Dore 177c; Mark Boulton 178–179b
Comstock: Georg Gerster 118t
Steven J. Cooling: 10bl, 16cl, 17cl, 20tl, 62–63b, 70tl, 90b, 98tr, 99tc, 99cl, 99br, 105br, 107l, 108tr, 109cr, 112b, 113b, 122br, 124bl, 129bl, 141bc, 141br, 170t
Crown copyright: 26b, 156bl
Ecoscene: Sally Morgan 18cl; Andrew Brown 164clb; Gryniewicz 165t; Meech 165cr
ELE International Ltd: 17t, 18tc, 19cl
Mary Evans Picture Library: 47tr
G.S.F. Picture Library: 14l, 96bc
Robert Harding Picture Library:169b; Geoff Renner 52tr; Krafft/Explorer: 55tl
Michael Holford: 97tl
Holt Studios: Nigel Cattlin 165bl
Christopher D. Howson: 35cr, 106t, 141bl
Hulton Deutsch: 33tr
The Hutchison Library: Tuck Goh 141bcr
The Image Bank: Fong Siu Nang 102t; Harald Sund 164cl; Larry Dale Gordon 147br, 179r; A.T. Willett 177br; Jake Rajs 178l
Images Colour Library: 13bc, 57r, 153tr
Landform Slides: 100r, 125tr, 129c
FLPA: S. McCutcheon 11bl; Silvestris 143tr; G. Nystrand 147cr
Mats Wibe Lund: 51t
P.J. May: 153bc
Microscopix Photo Library: Andrew Syred 69cr
Dr D.J. Mitchell: 17br, 18br
NASA: 138b
The Natural History Museum, London: 10cr; Geological Society 72tr
NHPA: Bryan & Cherry Alexander 126cl; B. Jones & M. Shimlock 135br; E.A. Janes 147tr
National Maritime Museum, London: 37br
National Rivers Authority: 173b
Nature Photographers Ltd: Paul Sterry 162t, 162b; Frank V. Blackburn 163br
Institute of Oceanographic Sciences Deacon Laboratory 134t
OSF: Charles Palek/Animals Animals 10tr; Tui De Roy 86b; G.I. Bernard 159c; C.M. Perrins 163bl; Colin Monteath 179t
Panos Pictures: Chris Stowers 154r; Ron Giling 172br; Fram Petit 174l; Jeremy Hartley 176br
Pictor International: 19t
P & O: 39b
Planet Earth Pictures: Robert Hessler 51cr; R. Chesher 153br
Rex Features Ltd: 157b; Butler/Bauer 58–59t; Donatello Brogioni/Agenzia Contrasto 174tr
Science Photo Library: David Weintraub 2br, 55br, cover; Dr. Rudolph Schild 5c, 31cr; Joe Pasieka 5t, 16tr; NASA 7cl, 33b, 51bc, 175cr; D.A. Peel 11tr; ESA/PLI 12–13t; Stephen J. Krasemann 19cr; Restec, Japan 26tr; Geospace 27cr; US Naval Observatory 30–31t, cover; Royal Observatory, Edinburgh 31bc; George East 36br; Jack Finch 44–45b; Peter Menzel 54l; David Parker 60–61b; John Reader 78c; Alfred Pasieka 96bl; European Space Agency 157tl
Scripps Institution of Oceanography, University of California, San Diego: 11cl
Frank Spooner Pictures: Lovgren Torbjorn/ Gamma 156c; Zimberoff/Liaison 174cr
Tony Stone Images: 64–65t, 119tc, 178t
Oliver Benn 94–95t; Arnulf Husmo 123tr; Robert Everts 172tl; David Woodfall 175t; Bruce Hands 175b
Telegraph Colour Library: Space Frontiers 110l
U.S. Geological Survey: 65tr
Tony Waltham: 48tr, 56l, 124br, 126tr
Woods Hole Oceanographic Institution: Rod Catanach 10br
Zefa: 13br, 35br, 88t, 147tl; Horst Zeidl 82–83c; Mehlig 101b

## ARTWORK CREDITS
Illustrators:
Roy Flookes: 34–35t, 36t, 80bc, 80–81t, 138–139c, 140bc, 140rc, 148, 149b
Andrew Green: 14b, 15tl, 15bl, 58bl, 58br, 59bl, 72l, 73tl, 75tr, 130–131t
Nick Hall: 56–57b, 103r, 104–105
Christopher Howson: 106cl, 138cl, 153tr
John Hutchinson: 20tr, 20br, 21tr, 21br, 76–77b, 84tc, 89r, 91tl, 94c, 95b, 96c, 96b, 109rc, 110rc, 111tl,r, 119r, 136bl, 139br, 141b, 145bl, 151r,tc, 168rc
Janos Marffy: 8–9c
Colin Rose: 30bl, 32–33, 40bc, 41tc, 42c, 49c, 50c
Colin Salmon: 11tl, 16b, 25t,c,b, 26bl, 27bc, 36bc, 37tc, 42bl, 43bc, 44cl, 45tr, 46br, 50bl, 53b, 60bl, 62tl, 63t, 63br, 79tr, 79rc, 79rb, 107bl, 107c, 107r, 108b, 120tl, 126br, 128c, 134t
Mike Saunders: 70bc, 72–73b, 92b, 100l, 112tr, 113tr, 114bl, 115tr, 121bl, 123t, 123c, 123b, 125t, 125c, 127cr, 127bl, 132cr, 132br, 133tl, 144cl, 144br, 146–147b, 161t, 161b, 168bl
Patrizio Sempori: 76bl
Raymond Turvey: 66–67, 170–171b, 173
Peter Visscher: 160b
John Woodcock: 159c, tc

## MODEL CREDITS
Dave Donkin: 1, 2tl, 2b, 14bl, 34–35t, 34bl, 36t, 38l, 47, 61r, 64c, 80–81t, 102–103b, 114–115, 128, 134–135b, 137b, 143b, 144t, 149t, 152c, 150–151t,c,
Alison Donovan: 23t
Christopher Howson: 64b, 106, 136t, 158
Edward Lawrence Associates: 52–53c